T0358597

information systems
The Connection of People and Resources for Innovation

A Textbook

information systems

The Connection of People and Resources for Innovation

A Textbook

Cheng Hsu
Rensselaer Polytechnic Institute, USA

 World Scientific

NEW JERSEY · LONDON · SINGAPORE · BEIJING · SHANGHAI · HONG KONG · TAIPEI · CHENNAI

Published by

World Scientific Publishing Co. Pte. Ltd.

5 Toh Tuck Link, Singapore 596224

USA office: 27 Warren Street, Suite 401-402, Hackensack, NJ 07601

UK office: 57 Shelton Street, Covent Garden, London WC2H 9HE

British Library Cataloguing-in-Publication Data
A catalogue record for this book is available from the British Library.

INFORMATION SYSTEMS
The Connection of People and Resources for Innovation — A Textbook

ISBN 978-981-4383-51-6

In-house Editor: Yvonne Tan

Typeset by Stallion Press
Email: enquiries@stallionpress.com

Printed in Singapore by World Scientific Printers.

Dedicated to
Susan and Diana

Preface

This book is written for serious students of Information Systems (IS). The author intends to provide a concise textbook on system analysis and database design that covers a range of deep knowledge integrated from the field. However, the author also strives to develop new thinking on the science and practice of IS for a knowledge economy. In particular, we ask: what does the "connected world" mean, and how can we design IS in such a world? An answer is developed by *combining the emerging network science and service science with classic IS results*.

One would say, why bother? Indeed, IS design is a mature field. The literature is full of commercially available techniques and tools for IS strategic planning and industry-proven models of structured system analysis. As for databases, an enormous body of knowledge has been accumulated over past decades. It is just that a great deal of change has taken place in the world since the pioneering works of, e.g., Davis and Olson (1974/1981). For example, the age of corporate mainframe computers has given way to one of person-centered digital connections and computing. We are witnessing the convergence of social networking and business; customers and providers; and physical world and cyberspace. The time may have come for the field to take another fresh look into "the concepts, structure, and development" of IS as its pioneers did.

The author is always fascinated by how quickly we the people innovate on the Internet, such as finding new ways to network and promote our causes. It is also marvelous to see obscure entrepreneurs inventing new business designs and thereby surpassing long-established conglomerates in market valuation. However, what fascinates the author most, from an academic perspective, is the pivotal role that IS plays in all these innovations — connecting people and resources to make them happen. The flipside of the coin is that the field does not seem to have been credited fully either by the science community or by the general public. When such progress as e-commerce first came about, people credited it to Information Technology (IT) and asked about the intellectual nature of such IT-induced revolution, in the face of the by-then already matured discipline of IS. The author was amazed, and dismayed, by the obvious lack of recognition for IS.

In hindsight, the field should have done a better job on incorporating IT into IS, to show that IS brings about serendipity; IS spawns innovation; and IS enables this knowledge economy. Then, the field should explain why the key to understanding the future is to understand the future IS. Instead of building this big picture, many IS textbooks virtually reduced the science of IS to mere anecdotes of IT, and treated students as casual readers. This book is an attempt propelled by these lessons to move forward, and focuses on designing IS for innovation.

The intellectual roots of innovation may be found in the seminal works by economist Joseph A. Schumpeter, who described capitalism as the perennial gales of creative destruction and attributed economic growth to innovations (*Capitalism, Socialism, and Democracy*, 1942). One can safely argue that the stories of e-commerce and information revolution are testaments to Schumpeter's thesis. However, the author further argues that these stories are actually stories of IS: innovation by IS and IS innovation. An e-commerce site is an IS; a social networking site is an IS; and the Web itself is an IS, too. An enterprise inventory system is an IS; a global supply chain where the participants are digitally connected with each other is an IS; and all these IS form systems of IS on the basis of societal cyber-infrastructure. Furthermore, information systems never die, they just reincarnate in the world of systems of IS. When the world is increasingly connected, the world becomes a system of IS, as well. Where is IS design science heading in such a world?

This book suggests a simple theme: the perennial gales of creative destruction in the 21st century will see IS renovating the networking of people and resources to bestow new values on the digitally connected society. That is, it starts with *a connectionist definition of IS: the networking of IS Elements (people, processes, information resources, computing platform, and communications infrastructure) in the connected world for value creation.* Then, in accordance, it builds the IS design science on the analysis of IS elements; networking for value creation; and the analytic properties of the connected world.

This definition reflects the profound progress in the IS field since the pioneers' time. It establishes that the immediate scope of an IS can be the world, a domain, an enterprise, a person's life, or just a particular job. Information systems bring about innovation by enabling new value propositions, new connections, and new IS elements; and hence they should be designed as such. The new thinking of IS in this book is embodied in the principles for strategic planning, which are based on the core concept of human value networks (Chapters 1–3). These principles are linked to the standard results of structured system analysis and database design in the field (Chapters 4–7).

The first chapter develops the basic concepts that support the connectionist definition of IS, and calibrates them on the empirical evidence in the field. It identifies the economic concept of transaction cost and the engineering concept of cycle time to be the underpinnings of the basic values of IS, and shows that an IS is a human value network from the perspective of service science. On this basis, it explains the evolution of IS. Finally, it presents the new concepts of sustainable IS and societal cyber-infrastructure to show how the notion of systems of IS gives a unique perspective to the connected world. The foundation for a new design science of IS, the networked design, is laid.

Chapter 2 establishes the relationship between network science and information systems and thereby develops generic strategies of innovation by IS. After reviewing the basic discoveries of network science such as the scale-free propensities and the small world phenomena, it analyzes e-commerce business designs to show that their novelty is really due to new thinking in human value networking. A hyper-networking model is then presented to capture the analytic nature of the human value networks. This analysis leads to a set of strategies for developing IS visions; i.e., IS strategic planning.

Chapter 3 is devoted to IS engineering (master plans): providing guidelines and roadmaps for determining the overall architecture of IS and the scope of IS elements. This chapter uses a design scenario of hyper-networking alumni and their alma mater to lead the discussion. Design methodologies, along with industrial examples, are provided for the digitization of IS elements; information integration within an enterprise, and collaboration across an extended enterprise. It also analyzes how societal cyber-infrastructure can add value to IS. This chapter concludes with certain IS design principles for service enterprises, further solidifying the networked design.

The above three chapters represent the new theory of IS that this book presents. The next four chapters synthesize standard IS design results in the literature. The particular presentation of these materials in this book reflects the author's many years of experience in teaching them to students at all levels and applying them to real-world projects. Some analysis and guidelines in these chapters are unique contributions of this book.

Chapter 4 is concerned with process modeling, or structured system analysis for determining the specific IS elements required according to the IS master plan. This book elects to focus on an original method, the data flow diagram (DFD), since it captures the essence of process modeling and encompasses the basic logic of many other methods. This method is fully illustrated with modeling guidelines and examples to help the reader apply it for actual work.

Chapter 5 presents a succinct and yet practical review of architectural designs on the whole range of databases, from PC systems to Internet systems. The concept of systems of IS is substantiated in this chapter by the review. A baseline database model is first built on the classic three-schema design, whose ensuing extensions explain the evolution of information integration from standalone enterprises to extended enterprises. As such, the prototypical distributed environments of data warehouses, federated databases, and custom designs are presented in a uniform treatment, to ready the reader for further exploration into the emerging challenges of massive numbers of independent databases on the Internet. Some experimental but lab-proven design ideas are also introduced for connecting global information resources.

Chapter 6 deepens the coverage of database design from the level of architectures in Chapter 5 to the level of data modeling and data normalization. It reviews the paradigms of relation, Entity-Relation-Attribute (ERA), and Object-Orientation (O-O), from the perspective of their common driving force: the need to consolidate enterprise data resources in the presence of differential user requirements for them. This chapter covers data normalization to the level of Boyce–Codd normal form, and includes the unified modeling language (UML) in data modeling. A particular experimental design of Chapter 5 is further developed here.

Chapter 7 presents the de facto standard database language in the world today — the ANSI SQL (Structured Query Language) — and shows how it may be extended to support global query of Internet databases, in a systems-of-IS manner. This chapter starts with relational algebra and calculus, and moves progressively to the data definitional part and the data manipulation part of SQL. It also reviews some prototypical design ideas (e.g., XQUERY and Metadatabase) for extending SQL to achieve global query of multiple databases on the Internet.

Chapter 8 brings this book from the SQL level of details back to the level of IS strategic planning. It focuses on IS innovation by convergence of physical environment and cyberspace. A real-world case (the I-87 Northway Corridor in New York State, USA) is analyzed here to show how the concept of hyper-networking people and resources can generate IS visions to help renovate a regional economy. This chapter concentrates the analysis of innovation on highway administration, personal safety, tourism, intelligent network flows, and global logistics. It represents a substantiation of the basic IS principles developed in the first three chapters.

The conclusion of this book is provided in Chapter 9. Several student projects from the author's past classes which have applied the materials in this book to real-world IS problems are presented first. This chapter then moves to contemplate on the role of IS in continuing innovation in a knowledge economy. It interprets the notion of hyper-networking people and resources via IS in terms of microeconomics, especially production functions, to show the significance of IS in a knowledge economy.

Most chapters have incorporated exercises in their discussion to help illustrate the abstract concepts that they develop. These exercises are joined with many classroom examples and industrial cases which are developed by the author based on his past teaching and research. In addition, Chapter 5 reconstructs the classic three-schema design and the federated schema design from the literature; and Chapters 6 and 7 also include a few tables inspired by some examples in Atre (1980) and Date (2004). These original sources have been credited in the appropriate places. The author wishes to acknowledge generally all the textbooks that he has consulted for teaching, which are too numerous to mention individually here (see Bibliography).

On this note, the author wishes to thank his many colleagues and former students, whose participation in his career has made this book possible. The TSER and Metadatabase work has contributed significantly to Chapters 5–7. Although proper credit and citations to the work have been included where appropriate, the author still wishes to express his inexhaustible gratitude to all his former advisees and research associates. Special thanks are due to Drs. Laurie Rattner Schatzberg, M'hamed Bouziane, Lester Yee, Waiman Cheung, Gilbert Babin, Yi-Cheng Tao, Jangha Cho, Somendra Pant, Veera Boonjing, David Levermore, Hsiang-Rui Kung, Mike Ming-Chuan Wu, Mark Dausch, and Jeffery Morris; and Mr. Alvaro Perry, Mr. Otto Schaefer, Mr. Myung-Jun Jung, Mr. Jinsong Mao, and Mr. Parag M. Dixit. It is indeed the author's fortune to have had the chance of working with these outstanding talents. This book has also incorporated results that the author published in co-authored papers with other colleagues. In addition to the citations given in the text, the author wishes to expressly recognize Dr. James Spohrer of IBM for work on the concept of DCS; Dr. Victor Wai-Kin Chan for work on the mathematical properties of hyper-networking; and Dr. William (Al) Wallace for work on verifying the Northway Corridor messages. Both Victor and Al are close colleagues at Rensselaer. Furthermore, the author wishes to thank his professors during the formative years of his career: Professors Wilpen Gorr, William Cooper, and Prabuddha De; who enlightened him on information, systems, and information systems. Numerous other colleagues, students, and friends have participated in the author's experience of teaching and research, which went into this book. Some are recognized in Section 9.1 of Chapter 9, but most would remain to be thanked only in the author's private thoughts due to the limitation of space here. Finally, the author happily recognizes his daughter, Diana, for helping to proofread the manuscript.

The field of Information Systems has come of age. The author's academic career has also come of age. This book presents a tribute to both.

Contents

Chapter 1

Information Systems: The Science and Practice of Connecting People and Resources to Create Value

The whole Web is an information system. The individual Web sites are information systems. The digital applications in offices, factories, and universities are information systems. The smartphones with apps are information systems, too. Less tangibly, a supply chain is an information system. The organization of any enterprise is also an information system; and so is the market mechanism of the economy. Information systems have enabled agile manufacturing, e-commerce, and social networking over the past few decades; and they promise to continue spawning innovations in our knowledge economy. So, what is the design science of Information System (IS) for the 21st century? This book synthesizes proven results from the field with contemporary research and presents a reference point from this *innovation* perspective: IS seeks to *network* five types of Information System Elements — people (users), process (application software/analytics), information resources (data repositories of data and knowledge), computing (digital devices), and communications infrastructure (networks) — for value creation in the *connected* world. Its scope could be global, or for a domain, for an enterprise, for a person's life, or just for a particular job. This chapter develops a cohesive set of information system principles, which constitute a basic *connectionist theory of information systems*. The basic values of IS, recent history of IS evolution, and the collective life of systems of IS in the connected world are studied.

1.1 The Connectionist Definition of Information System

The term "information system" has become a part of our daily lingo. It first appeared in the academic lexicon during 1970–1980s, when computer applications became commonplace in the economy and society. The significance was that people recognized that computers were playing a much larger role than computation per se. These two words, information and system, separately had a very long history in human languages before they were bonded into one. In fact, the separate journeys of these two words and their evolution into one may have heralded the progress of modern civilization. We do not intend to define these two words away from each other, other than acknowledging that many theories have existed for decades in the attempt to explain what is information (see, e.g., Shannon and Weaver, 1949; and von Neumann, 1956) and what is system (see, e.g., Charnes and Cooper, 1961). We just use them according to the common sense. However, we do ask, what is "information system (IS)"? Clearly, the answer must be more than just a "system of information".

Here, competing definitions exist (see, e.g., the many IS textbooks), each of which exerts profound ramifications on the theory, design, and performance of information systems in actuality. Instead of providing a critical review of the field, which does not serve the cause of this book, we humbly accept all definitions that make sense in the myriad practices of the field. Yes, inventory systems, online banking systems, Google, Facebook, and all the specimens that someone calls information systems are indeed information systems. We just ask how to capture the *unique* nature of IS in our *connected* world, so as to foster its growth into the future.

Yes, the premium is on the understanding of the word *connected*. An information system is connected, of course, as everyone agrees; but is it also always connected to other information systems in the world in some way? Should this nature of connection be deliberately recognized, analyzed, and fostered in the design of IS? For example, if an IS never dies, but just reincarnates, because some of its elements (including analytics and data resources) may last indefinitely, then should the design science of IS consider sustainability? If the IS supports enterprises in a "flat world", then should the design be flat, too? If the Web is pervasive, then should the design take advantage of this pervasiveness? If the IS represents an innovation for the economy, then should the design foster the innovation of business designs, enterprising, and inter-person collaboration in return, to help sustain the economy's eternal pursuit of better and more value creation?

If the IS connects, then exactly what does it connect, what for, what to sustain or expand if the IS grows, and how? Where do IS visions come from, and how does one recognize the inherent logic of the planning, analysis, design, development, and control of the connecting IS? The long journey of developing an answer starts with recognizing the common and basic Information System Elements from all application domains — i.e., identifying the core value propositions for all IS applications and postulating a connectionist theory of IS from them. This book embraces the service science worldview (Hsu, 2009) as the starting point: scaling IS up to support the (host enterprise in the) global economy; down to facilitate individuals' tasks (as a knowledge worker or just a person); and transformationally to enable new business designs and mode of production. This chapter then calibrates the theory on the history of IS since 1970–1980s, and reviews its continuing evolution. The following is a short list of the *basic Information System Elements* that this book recognizes:

- **People:** the user of IS. In the automated version of IS, users could be machines such as robots, software agents, and application systems. This element may include dedicated security, interface, and embedded tools for interaction with each other as well as with other IS elements. Although users tend to be proprietarily defined, they can also be open such as in the case of a Web site. They include both the customers and knowledge workers of the host enterprise as well as IS professionals.
- **Process:** the enterprise processes (e.g., workflows, applications, and analytics) and IS controls, including functions and online tools that facilitate these processes. Examples range from the automated processing of pro forma data for routine jobs such as

operations control, personalized marketing (e.g., product recommendations), and key performance indicators, all the way to ad hoc analyses for new product/innovation approval and custom connection of people and their required resources under security control. This IS element enacts on the rest of the elements and turns the IS into actions for its mission.

- **Information Resources:** the sharable data, knowledge (rules, heuristics, cases, etc.) and other information resources. They also include repositories of digital representation of persons, processes, and other physical production factors, and the standards and protocols that define them (e.g., ontology and embedded intelligence, business component models, and Modelbase). Software programs in and of themselves are a form of information resources, too, when they are not running, and in the sense that they can be accumulated, shared, and reused like other resources do.

- **Computing:** the digital platform (hardware) on which the IS executes. This category includes computer of any class, personal digital devices such as cell phone, and any other physical information technology (IT) components that constitute the computing capacity of the IS. The tasks of the platform encompass the processing and storage of processes and information resources, connection of persons to the infrastructure, and connection of this computing capacity to the shared external facilities that provide utilities of computing to the IS.

- **Communications Infrastructure:** the (digital) platform for connection within and without the IS. It includes networks of any scale, telecommunications (wired or wireless), and (built-in) protocols and network management systems that connect computing elements and administer the infrastructure. Typically, a significant IS nowadays deploys and employs the Internet and other public cyber-infrastructure as well as proprietary enterprise cyber-infrastructure to connect the IS elements. Often, third party vendors also provide (parts of) the infrastructure.

The last four classes of IS elements may also be collectively referred to as simply the *IS resources*. The classes of processes and information resources include the usual representation data about physical resources such as raw materials, buildings, and civil infrastructure. However, since physical resources could also be augmented by digital devices (e.g., sensors and computing chips — see Chapter 8), this book broadly incorporates such "digitization" of the physical resources in the scope of IS. Therefore, we say that *an IS connects people and resources*.

We note that an IS enterprise may not be able to, or at least not need to, proprietarily own every IS element that it uses. Rather, they may deploy and employ open source technology and/or public cyber-infrastructure resources to fulfill their needs. This approach may actually be preferred if the IS requires openness and scalability to operate across multiple organizations.

The connectionist view recognizes that an enterprise possesses rich IS elements, of course. However, it trains the vision on the fact that society possesses an enormous repository of these IS elements, too, from which any IS can potentially draw for its use. That is, all the IS elements from all information systems, private or public, have the potential, and indeed the promise, to become assets capable of being used by any other IS anywhere, new or existing. The question is only to make the connection: what, why, and how. Proprietary rights and controls are the common constraints to connection between information systems of different ownership, while the (lack of) openness and scalability of IS elements involved often are the inhibitors to the connection of information systems of the same ownership. The concern for cyber-security presents one more deterrence to pursuing systems of IS — the more connected, the more exposed. Overcoming such barriers is a predicate to innovation by IS. Indeed, deliberate effort here promises to lead to powerful new business value propositions and scientific progress in the IS field. Without making any value assertion, we point out that this connectionist definition of IS is amenable to the ideal of "one for all and all for one" in a connected world.

EXERCISES

1. Please analyze what are the IS elements for the whole Web?
2. Suggest what may be the possible IS elements for Google, Amazon.com, and Netflix.

3. Pick an information system from your organization, or any organization that you know, and specify its IS elements as definitively as you can (e.g., a student information system).
4. Define an IS by connecting Facebook, Twitter, Google, and some other IS on the Web: first state what are the IS elements and what is the purpose of the IS (the value of the connection); and then recognize the particular IS elements from these systems that you need to connect for your IS.
5. Search the Internet to find some open source technologies that you may use to make the connection envisioned/required in (4) above. Hint: visit apache.org, php.net, mysql.com, omg.org, oasis.org, alice.org, and locate some sources (by Google-search?) for VBA applications, SQL-based database triggers (in, e.g., PL/SQL), and Web services (mobile objects).
6. Discuss some possible new business designs (paradigm shifting changes) on the Internet, along the general idea of making the Web a more cohesive IS to support personal and organizational life cycle tasks (e.g., one-stop buying, selling, and managing).

One can go as deeply as one wishes to do the above six exercises. Here, we offer some basic ideas. Looking at the Web as a whole, this IS is rich in information, but sporadic in transactions and lacking in cohesive decision support. Its security and integrity control are ad hoc at best, but its user interface and infrastructure are sustainably open and scalable. In particular, the Web IS includes the following well-known elements:

- People: everyone that has access to the Internet, with the common user interface being the homepages (or, the HTTP protocols).
- Process: mainly search engines, functions at Web access providers (proprietary and public domain protocols), and all application software at individual Web sites.
- Information Resources: all the contents of individual Web sites (or, all the homepages, documents available at Web sites, and open source software and technologies).

- Computing: all the hardware at the disposal of all users and individual Web sites.
- Infrastructure: the Internet (protocols and hardware) and the proprietary networks at the individual Web sites and user sites.

Google obviously has specific and proprietary IS elements, such as the (soft agents) processes for acquiring Web contents from the globe, their onsite repositories of Web contents, and the arrays of computing and communications technologies. However, their proprietary IS elements are deliberately integrated with the public domain practices and systems. In general this observation applies to all other Internet enterprises including Netflix, Amazon.com, Facebook, and Twitter, too. Processes for online products (e.g., calendars and geographical directions at Google), social networking (e.g., "following" at Facebook and Twitter), and promotion of products (e.g., clustering of customers and products for online recommendations at Netflix and Amazon.com) are of course the hallmarks of these powerful Web information systems. Their information resources are largely obvious: (digitized) books, movies, and members' homepages. However, the customer information they acquired, including the digital trails of the member activities at their sites, may represent the most innovative part of the strategic advantages that these Internet enterprises enjoy over their traditional counterparts (if any).

In fact, the Internet has prompted many open source communities as generic IS elements that any enterprise can use to develop its proprietary IS, as well as providers of solutions using such open source technology. The famous PHP-Apache-MySQL alliance is one visible example, and the popular Wikipedia is another. One can readily develop complex enterprise IS from these open source technologies and solutions, with or without common proprietary software. An entire software industry has been founded on doing this. Numerous open source technologies and solutions are available from the Web and industry giants such as IBM have embraced them to complement proprietary technology and solution providers. The so-called Web services, SaaS (software as a service), and consortia of consulting firms (e.g., OASIS.org) are well-known examples. Although the line separating non-profit from for-profit is thin in the field, one could safely argue that new open source contributors are emerging and joining forces throughout the Internet in a spirit of something other than making a buck. On the other hand, hackers represent the dark and often destructive side of the same coin of this individuality on the Internet. We would rather look positively and call the spirit of open sources "one for all and all for one".

The sixth exercise, concerning new business designs on the Internet, begs a review of the short but nonetheless unprecedentedly explosive history of e-commerce since the late 1990s. This book devotes the next chapter to this review. Here, we simply comment that many new business designs can fall under a generic umbrella of connections provider: to assemble IS elements and facilitate their (on-demand) connections for performing (customized) life cycle tasks. The notion of cloud computing actually describes an important aspect of this connection: providing computing as an IS element to connect to other IS elements for value creation applications. If one borrows the proprietary branding due to Apple, then the providers of connections may be branded as iIS, iWeb, and the like, following iPod, iPhone, iPad, and iCloud. In fact, one can see clearly that all the (unwieldy) app stores of smart phones are really ad hoc connection providers, and the smart phone concept begs to connect to PC and TV to become a personal controller for the person's entire information world.

An intriguing perspective is for one to sit back and imagine, either as a person going about his/her private life, or as a professional undertaking some job assignments, or both: how s/he may wish to use the future Web as her/his personal IS working in sync with the proprietary systems at work. This is the best way to contemplate the sixth exercise suggested above. We submit that IS has seen scaling up from individual functions and applications such as inventory control to enterprise-wide such as enterprise resources planning, and now to extended enterprises such as the IBM notion of Globally Integrated Enterprises and Smarter Planet. This evolution clearly reflects on the extension and expansion of connections of IS elements, and even the inter-connection of different information systems, in the pursuit of ever inter-connected value propositions in the connected world.

The path may just lead IS to such a point of iWeb. The technology has also been opened up from purely proprietary to public domain. Thus, a next step in the form of *cyber-infrastructure-enabled, Web-embedding, and person-centered IS* may not be so outlandish but in fact quite natural and even inevitable. This concept of IS does not exclude the traditional form of proprietary, function-oriented IS, but rather extends and expands it for the global economy. In this inclusive and evolutionary sense, we embrace it as the full scope of the connection for IS.

Thus, we provide the following *connectionist definition of IS* as consummation to the above discussion:

Information Systems *is the networking of IS Elements (people, processes, information resources, computing platform, and communications infrastructure) for value creation in the connected world. Its immediate scope can be the world, a domain, an enterprise, a person's life, or just a particular job. Information systems bring about innovation by enabling new value propositions, new connections, and new IS elements.*

A *corollary* is the innovative nature of such connections in IS: the connections enable new value propositions among persons, facilitated by new access to (new) resources (non-person elements). A second *corollary* is concerned with the design of IS: an IS should be cyber-infrastructure-enabled, Web-embedded, and person-centered, to maximize the benefits of connections.

Next, we turn to the phrase "value creation".

1.2 The Basic Values of Information System: Reduction of Transaction Cost and Cycle Time

The field has been struggling to find the most accurate ways to measure the performance of an IS and assess its value (e.g., payoffs and return on investment) ever since the IS profession formed. We are content in this book to establish the basic, generic values that an IS is expressly poised to produce: the *reduction of transaction costs and cycle times*. Please note that one may develop IS to create particular values such as providing decision information to certain management processes, or pursue particular value propositions such as enabling specific innovative information products to sell to customers. The IS value in these cases may be broad and even abstract, unlike the values in straightforward automation or computerization, which often take the form of labor saving. However, it is these forms of value that innovative IS aims to create for all kinds of users. The point is that both levels of value, and indeed all forms of value that IS creates, are reducible to the same fact of reducing transaction costs and cycle time.

Just consider a simple example: searching for someone on the Web. If doing so without the Web is hard because it is difficult to get to identify the various sources of information and even more difficult to gain access to and comb through the sources, then the basic value of the Web as an IS is its savings on reducing the transaction cost and cycle time that made the search without the Web hard. Thus, in general, if the IS makes it easier or possible to obtain certain information or achieve some higher degree of precision of information and thereby facilitates or enables the job, then the root cause of the value to the job is the reduction of transaction cost and cycle time associated with obtaining such information without the IS. Labor savings in straightforward IS applications, such as automation, are traceable to the same reductions, too.

Incidentally, these generic values offer a way to uniformly measure the returns from intangible benefits as well as tangible ones. When both values are accounted for and included into the usual methods of valuation such as return on investment (ROI), then firms may be able to more accurately measure the contributions of their IS investment. The so-called "productivity paradox" of late 1990s and early 2000s is an illustration of the need for this kind of uniform measures. The economy back then did not register much productivity gains from the astronomical investment on information technology (IT), at a time when the whole society was witnessing an IT-driving transformation of the economy. The gap between the evidence and the perception of IT contributions was puzzling. Obviously, the way of "registration" has serious flaws in it. Later, researchers were able to dispute the assertions from other data and measures.

We wish to point out here that transaction cost and cycle time are not the same thing: the former is primarily operation-based, while the latter is primarily process-based. One may reduce the cycle time of a job by reducing its transactions involved, such as answering a query or performing a search; but one may also reduce the cycle time by increasing the transactions. An example is concurrent processing of a sequential job, as in office workflows. An IS that supports concurrent processing typically can reduce the cycle time at the expense of increased processing due to control or other coordination and monitoring.

EXERCISES

1. In many places, soft drinks are sold with a deposit on the bottle (say, a nickel or 5 cents), which can be redeemed at designated places when the bottles are returned. Then, why in those places may bottles still litter the ground or fill trash cans, while few nickels receive the same treatment — i.e., why is it that people might throw away bottles but not nickels?

2. How would one measure the value of an IS to a professional who can use the IS to get information which otherwise, without the IS, would require making a number of phone calls or other forms of research to obtain?

3. What is the (inherent) transaction cost associated with buying or selling a house?

4. If a project requires 1,000 man-hours to complete, then what is the minimum labor that the project requires to complete it in one hour?

5. Office workflows typically involve a series of tasks, and some common examples are found in job interviews and business proposal review. Suggest some general IS design principles to make the IS an enabler for turning a sequential workflow into concurrent and thereby reducing its overall cycle time. (Hint: think connection.)

6. How can you measure the value of cycle time reduction?

7. If one (e.g., the Nobel Laureate in Economic Science, Herbert A. Simon) considers a human organization to be an "information processor" for facilitating data handling, information exchange,

and decision making among all the stakeholders to discharge their common missions, then the organization is a transactions processor, too. Can this view be generalized to explain economics?

8.   What role may IS play in the transaction cost view of economics?

Some of the answers are plainly obvious. Considering the first question: Turning a nickel into currency that one can spend right away, anyway, requires zero transaction cost, while doing this to a bottle involves considerable *transaction cost* (taking it to the right place for exchange, handling it to get credit, and making the credit an unrestricted currency). In other words, transaction costs, albeit abstract compared to traditional price tags, are every bit as tangible and for real as the traditional cost: it means people losing real money in this case.

The second question shows that transaction cost is often translated, or valuated, into time whose monetary value, in turn, is measurable by wages and the like. How much time did the professional in question usually spend on acquiring the information that the IS provided, and how much money is this amount of time worth to the company? Equally measurable, directly, is the monetary worth of the "red tape" involved in any transactions: how much is one willing to pay for someone else to do it for him/her? All the buyers and sellers pay to all the brokers and agents involved reflect on the minimum cash equivalent of the transaction cost of the house sale process (plus that the buyers and sellers pay for themselves).

Clearly, one thousand men working simultaneously is the minimum requirement for finishing a 1,000 man-hour job in one hour, since more men may be needed to coordinate among all simultaneous tasks. The (unique) role of IS in this enterprise, therefore, is equally clearly to be the facilitation of this concurrent processing: making this possible through the connection of persons to (information) resources required in the coordination and execution of the simultaneous tasking. This is simply the connectionist definition of IS. A common database shared by all persons (generalists or specialists) to support their respective tasks makes the connection, and hence will spell out the design principles for the enabling IS. We shall come back to this point in great details in later chapters.

The value of *cycle time* reduction manifests itself in the same way as transaction cost reduction does, of course. However, it also arises from quality of service and quantity of production (productivity); both of which determine the competitiveness of an enterprise. It is worthwhile to note that the quality to customers may translate into avoidance of lost sales (e.g., customers balking due to long wait) as well as attracting additional customers. Although not all such measures are readily available to an enterprise, they nonetheless are not infeasible to quantify, either. We submit that even conservative implementation of some measures for the reduction of transaction cost and cycle time due to the deployment and employment of an IS promises to greatly enhance the accuracy of the ROI and other traditional methods.

The last two questions actually represent the high-end vision of the connectionist definition of IS in a connected world. The short answer to the seventh question is yes, as found in the concept of *organizational transaction cost* — see Williamson (1985). This school of thought, continuing in a sense the so-called Carnegie-Mellon School of Barnard, Simon, March, and Cyert, theorizes that firms came into being as an optimization of organizational transaction cost for economic enterprises. In this worldview, on the one hand, societal institutions including laws represent some mechanism of regulation of common transactions costs for all; and, on the other hand, an organization is an embodiment of processes that transact (producing, exchanging, and transforming) on information to accomplish the organization's goals. The interesting point is that this abstract concept of organizational information processing is "visualized" in and by IS; i.e., an IS is not only a tool for societal or organizational information processing, but also a realization of the organization. Therefore, the IS contributions to the enterprise processes are contributions to the organization as an information processor, and ultimately contributions to the (micro)-economy to which the firms are the foundations.

The big picture here is the simple fact that transaction cost is a scalable concept connecting the whole economy together from the minute level of redeeming a bottle to the level of economic value chain optimization and societal welfare. Just imagine how much more difficult it would make our daily lives if the society is lawless — i.e., how much more transaction cost at all levels it would cause us at every turn of going about life. Therefore, transaction costs do reflect the efficiency, effectiveness, and welfare for persons, organizations, and the society. In this picture, IS deals directly with transaction costs at all levels as the scope of its connection of IS elements scaling up or down across persons and organizations. Therefore, the ultimate characterization of the IS contributions to the economy is by evaluating its contributions to (damping the transaction costs in) the microeconomic production functions; and furthermore by recognizing its role in technological innovation (e.g., new capacity, efficiency, and value chains) and how the innovation uplifts the overall economic performance. This book does not develop this line of analysis, but is content with the long accomplishments of this line of thought starting from, e.g., Joseph Schumpeter (1945), whose work is the theoretical foundation to our new results in Chapter 9. For convenience, at the enterprise level, we measure the IS contributions to organization transaction cost in terms of the reduction to the total transaction cost and cycle time; which in turn are a function of the individual processes' transaction costs and cycle times.

If transaction cost is activity-based, and hence generic to any economic enterprise, then cycle time is evidently process-based and more amenable to system design — i.e., it is concerned with the engineering question of how to connect activities. Enterprise cycle times such as the time to market for new product development and the throughput (service or physical output) of a system are subject of intensive studies in engineering and management. Common design principles include simplification (removing transactions), integration (removing non-value-added connections), and concurrency (removing idleness). Examples include agile manufacturing, concurrent (simultaneous) engineering, and supply chain integration. All these enterprises rely heavily on innovative IS designs, which in turn rely on innovating the way IS elements are connected: simplifying them, integrating them, and sharing and reconfiguring them. The design of connections also determines the relationship between transaction cost and cycle time. If a cycle consists only of sequential processes, then the cycle time is proportional to the sum of the transaction costs in these processes. Otherwise, when concurrent processes are involved, the total cycle time could be more a function of how these processes are connected than a function of the sum of the individual transaction costs.

We recap the above discussion into a *valuation theory for IS*: Transaction cost and cycle time can be applied to measure the quality and productivity for any personal, organizational, and the societal IS. The value of the Web as an IS, for instance, can be substantiated as the sum of the values of all contributions that the IS makes to the tasks by all people. One of these tasks is college applications. The difference between the total expenditures on college applications (e.g., the application fees, sales of all college data books, and personal inquiries and trips) before and after the Internet indicates a lower bound of the fungible value of the Web on this task. The values of the reductions in transaction cost and cycle time for all other tasks due to the Web can be assessed case by case in a similar way. Generally speaking, the so-called "red tape" is precisely transaction cost, and the amount at which one is willing to pay to facilitate/remove it is its valuation according to one's utility function. The tax breaks offered to attract a direct foreign investment is an example. The value of a proposed global database query system to an organization is, according to this theory, minimally calculable by compiling the time its employees spend on the phone and meetings that the new IS could save. The point is that the value is measurable, and the measures of reductions in transaction cost and cycle time are feasible. This valuation method is applicable to both *a priori* planning and *post priori* auditing.

The phrase "value creation" in the IS definition is generic, of course. It refers to any value proposition that the stakeholders of the IS determine to be suitable, such as enabling supply chain integration, renovating procurement processes, and enabling particular e-commerce applications. The valuation of such contributions may be self-evident, in and of the functions provided themselves. If so, then nothing more is needed. However, we submit that underlying all these particular value propositions are the generic value of reductions of transaction costs and cycle times for the missions. They promise to supplement the direct valuation; and more importantly, when direct valuation is difficult to come by, they provide the measures of intangible value needed. Therefore, we present the following generic elaboration for the generic phrase of value creation:

The Value Principle of Information Systems: *An IS creates and connects IS elements to reduce the transaction costs and cycle times of the enterprise that it supports, at the personal, organizational, and societal levels.*

A *corollary* is that the IS is itself designed to minimize its own internal transaction costs and cycle times. That is, the valuation applies to the design of the IS, as well. Another *corollary* is the recognition of the following generic design principles needed for IS to minimize transaction costs and cycle times: digitization of IS elements, simplification or integration of transactions, and connections for concurrent access to resources and execution of tasks. These three design principles will be elaborated later in Chapter 3.

At this point, we review the notion of a "connected world" next.

1.3 The Connected World: Human Value Networks Using Systems of Information Systems

The world is connected, as everyone says. So, we travel, work, and socialize in a world where most parts of it are not isolated from any other parts. Some even say that the world is "flat" as a global village. However, how to understand this connectivity? The world will not change regardless of how we see it, but our understanding of it will; and this change in understanding can lead to profound new results that affect our work and lives, and may even ultimately benefit the world that we pass to our heirs. To enact on the connections of the world and seek new results, we need to go beyond semantic acclamations. Again, the particular perspective here is IS.

The most obvious evidence of a connected world is arguably cyberspace — the wired and wireless networking of persons, organizations, and habitats at the global scale. Added on top of the physical space and networked via human or machine interactions by land, sea, and air, this cyberspace presents a connected world. The connectionist definition of IS strives to extend further. We ask, is it not true that products are connections of parts? Are organizations connections of persons, enterprises of processes, and processes of activities? Are social networks connections of persons, just like nations, families, and religions? Are economies connections of systems, and systems of systems, such as firms, factories, and, yes, information systems? In a unifying way, can we simply say that a society, or an economy, is made of *human networks* that operate on resources of value creation to discharge common missions? Here, networks and connections, and networking and connecting, are used interchangeably to highlight the notion of networking.

To highlight the notion of networking is to make way for this assertion: the emerging network science helps establish the much needed basic understanding of what is a connected world, in which IS belong. Network science came from disparate studies of biology (e.g., diseases and insect colonies), engineering (e.g., artificial habitats and systems), and sociology (e.g., social networking and group behaviors) that synthesized on certain common scientific methods and analytic findings. For many, the driving force of this new field is really the new phenomena of social networking using cyberspace. For instance, the traditional connections of humans in a society are well-known to sociology, but the cyberspace connections of humans are not — the latter are not only overwhelmingly versatile and numerous in quantity compared to the connections before the Internet, but they also promise to change the social norms and constraints. That is, "social networks" is not just an observation of facts (a noun), but is susceptible to change and design (a verb). This ability to change, to design, to evolve rapidly, makes the network-scientific study of social networking a must for, e.g., fighting terrorists, monitoring cyber-security, and promoting all sorts of ideas and commodities on the Internet.

We establish the essence of the network-scientific understanding of the connected world here, with more salient details elaborated in Chapter 2. Our connected world has yielded unlimited possibilities for human connections. Cyberspace has vastly opened up the relatively stable genres of traditional connections for new expansions: mass-customization design, or turning manufacturing into service (personalized products, agile processes, and extended enterprises); collaborations at work (company intranet) or professional promotion (open source communities on the Internet); and congregation (mobility among habitats and acquaintances networks). However, the greatest potential comes from serendipity: chance interactions among humans for any value propositions and collaborative value creation at personal, organizational, or societal levels. The ideal IS supports this connected world every step along the way, and draws from the connected world the IS elements that it comprises. It even immerses its connection in the connection of cyberspace. An IS should facilitate serendipity via the IS elements within the scope commissioned. The connectionist definition of IS actually envisions an IS to be a part of many systems of information systems pertaining to this connected world.

We further elaborate on this basic view here. To be precise, we define a connected world to predicate on cyberspace and other physical means of making interactions among humans, with the driving forces for designing and making connections being value propositions, or value creation. For simplicity, we also refer to this view of the connected world as the *human value networks*. The connected world is an all-encompassing human value network of human value networks, each of which may be facilitated by IS in the pursuit of their particular values. As discussed above, this view guides the design of IS (see Chapter 3), and hence has direct implications on how we behave in the connected world and reap benefits for all.

EXERCISES

1. What is openness and scalability of an IS following the connectionist definition?
2. How does openness and scalability define systems of information systems?
3. What should be some of the design principles for IS in the connected world?

4. What are the Pareto distribution and the so-called 80–20 law of operations management (e.g., inventory control, bill-of-materials, and office tasks)?

5. What is the decay power law? How does it describe the Pareto distribution?

6. What do you expect to see if you plot the size of cities (the Y-axis) against the number of such sized cities (the X-axis)? Would the pattern change in the following cases if you substitute other appropriate measures of size for the population measure in this case: the distribution of incomes for persons; number of times individual articles being cited by others; memberships at social networking sites (or destination e-commerce sites)...

7. What is six degrees of separation? What is the small world proposition?

8. How do social connections between congregations (e.g., habitats and nations) differ from those within them? What are "long connections" and outlier connections?

The first three questions are rather self-evident: Both openness and scalability are applicable to any connections of an IS. They prescribe how the IS elements within an IS should be connected in order to make the IS connectible with others, and they also prescribe how systems of IS could be "clustered" from connecting individual IS. For example, a system of five information systems may be developed from connecting just the persons, just the information resources, or just the infrastructure; but they could also connect all five IS elements across the systems horizontally and then vertically. For the resulting system of systems to be open and scalable, these connections must be, too; and the more open and scalable the connections of the individual systems are, the easier their connection into a whole system will be.

That is, the openness and scalability of connections incidentally represent some of the basic requirements for the design and construction of IS elements if they need to be connected flexibly across information systems. Clearly, an IS does not have to be open and scalable, and many existing systems are completely proprietary or even "hard-wired". However, when one seeks to promote value propositions with the help of IS in a connected world, then making both the IS and the IS elements open and scalable becomes advantageous. It follows that an IS of IS must feature open and scalable connections within and across. Therefore, as a design principle, an IS with this vision should employ and deploy open source technology for making the IS elements and their connections, to the maximum extent possible.

The rest of the questions explore the intellectual nature of the connected world. The approach embraced here is to focus on human value networking: how humans network themselves; how humans connect "things"; and how these connection laws may guide IS design. We start with empirical evidence exhibited in previous practices.

The Pareto distribution and 80–20 law are common in virtually all operations. The classic example is inventory control: a few items account for the lion's share of value while a large quantity of items amount to small percentage of the value. Therefore, the control should focus on these few high-valued items, such as gold nuggets, and leave the "majority", say bolts and nuts, alone. The distributions of office tasks as measured by labor required or value-added show similar patterns, too. Thus, it has been a common practice of management in any time and space for the manager to concentrate on the 20% of tasks that account for 80% of the value.

These patterns are generalized into the so-called decay power law of probability, or the negative exponential distribution (see Section 2.1 of Chapter 2). Taking the distribution of city sizes as an example, very few cities have mega populations while a lot of cities have a very small population. When the data are normalized into percentages and smoothly plotted on a (X,Y) plain, they will show a curve where the left end shows the maximum size as marked on the Y-axis corresponding to a very small percentage on the X-axis. At the other end of the curve one sees the maximum percentage on the X-axis corresponding to a very small size on Y (see Figure 2.1). The same class of decay power law holds for income distribution, citations, and popularity of e-commerce sites. A common property to all these cases is a propensity to *preference by choice* when humans congregate. Of course, as in the case of habitat and income, one could debate that to what extent such preferences are bounded by factors that one cannot control, or subject to design and modification. At the least, IS design could benefit from understanding these connection laws as some generic built-in usage patterns to guide the connections of IS elements.

Opposite to choices, ***natural binding*** by blood, resources, and other mechanisms or constraints of making a living also drive human networking. Thus, many congregations are arguably formed naturally or inherited, rather than by free will. Managerial and mandated organizations are one example, and tribes and religious sects are another. One could argue that the choices that are based on fixed attributes actually reflect some bindings, as well. Examples include professional associations, interest groups, and even self-regulated open communities on the Internet. A country, in the largest sense, is a habitat of natural binding, too. The reason that one wants to distinguish binding from choice is to recognize another basic class of human networks — the small world — and reap its promises for IS design, too. No scientific rule states that the small world phenomena occur only to human congregations formed by natural binding; but we suspect that this is the case. At the least, we feel very comfortable to expect human networks that follow this class of connection laws (binding) to exhibit the small world properties. The commonly accepted definition of small world phenomena is a congregation that shows the so-called six-degree separation law.

A degree of separation is an intermediary required to connect two persons. Parents and their children are of zero degree separation because they know each other directly, without having to rely on any others to make the connection for them. Friends are of zero degree separation between them, too. However, the friend's friends will be one degree separation from the person in question. The friend's friends' friends are of two degree separation, and so on. Therefore, a small world congregation, be it physical or logical, is one where no member is separated from any other members by more than six degrees. It was hypothesized that the United States is a small world. Some have suggested that the whole world is one. The burden of proof may be unbearable in large cases. However, we can discuss some provable implications.

An interesting observation of bounded congregations, or small world human networks, is their recursive structures. That is, a small world may consist of a few densely clustered subnets linked by only a few connections between them — or "long connections" between clusters. Needless to say, these clusters may show similar structures when one looks closely at their internal distributions of connections. By the same token, small worlds may cluster into super-small worlds by long connections with one another. This observation conforms to our common sense about human habitats. For instance, a country is densely connected from the within, but only sparsely connected from the without, between a few nodes scattered in the respective countries. Thus, one could even consider this topology, i.e., densely connected lumps with long connections between them, to be a signature or working definition of a small world congregation. It is worthwhile to stress that long connections represent outliers and exceptions, and they make the small worlds connected. Christopher Columbus, for example, was an outlier who provided the long connection to the New World. The beauty is that outliers and exceptions can be cultivated, designed, and managed, out of natural binding. International exchange programs (students, scholars, leaders, etc.) between countries are a ready illustration for creating long connections.

We submit that these long connections may hold some of the most original innovations for IS design, since they are unobvious to the point of being counter-intuitive. In short: outliers count, and facilitating exceptions may lead to the most cost-effective applications of IS. If the decay power law teaches one to concentrate the IS software functions on connecting the most valuable IS elements within and across the organization, then the long connections law reveals the necessity to explore the promises of certain classes of low usage for linking up lumps of applications. Data exchanges and "tunnels" of repositories come in as some ready examples.

There are many other (possible) types of connection laws, each of which may define some particular genre of networks. The most fundamental and prototypical one is the so-called random graph, where a node connects to other nodes by an equal chance. Many networks may be driven by collective desires that researchers call them as centrality (to facilitate the average distance between nodes in the network). At the other extreme from random graphs are totally regulated networks such as the inter-state highway system and other artificial physical connections. They may manifest themselves in mission-specific connection laws for IS.

In general, network science uses mathematical models, especially the graph theory, to capture the analytic properties of any human networks and to complement the traditional knowledge of social and economic sciences. Many of the peering results were published in *Nature, Science,* and other leading journals of natural sciences, in particular applied physics. While leaving these results for Chapter 2 to review, the above discussion highlighted their essentials. The basic point is that the human networking models are scalable to represent any human congregation from persons, organizations, and societies; and hence uniquely suited to provide the context of connections for IS. More specifically, if an IS is a part of many systems of information systems in the connected world, then all the persons of this IS join with the other people of such systems of IS and constitute a "consortium" of human value networks. They could potentially tap into all IS elements of these systems of IS to enable the value creations sought. Both the individual IS and the IS for the whole of them are bound to exhibit certain connection laws in these value networks, stemming from the basic properties revealed by network science. The IS, furthermore, is also a tool for the management of such connection laws and the design of new ones to optimize the value creation for all stakeholders.

At this point, the notion of Web-centered and person-centered IS in the IS definition of Section 1.1 should have become self-evident. The term "Web-centered" delineates the Web as both a tool for making connections and the scope for possibly connecting the IS with other IS in a manner of systems-of-IS. People are the ultimate users and stakeholders of the IS, hence their networking for value creation ultimately drives the design of IS. The term "person-centered" reminds the designers that the IS must be flexible for the individuals to use, and be strategic for the users to collaborate in developing and pursuing value propositions.

The Networking Principle of Information Systems: *An IS maximizes its value by being an enabler to the global human value networks. It networks with other IS as all their users (the people) do, and uses networked IS elements to facilitate value creations from this networking.*

The first *corollary* of this principle is to design openness and scalability into the connections of IS elements, and maybe into the construction of the IS elements themselves. The second *corollary* is the recognition of these generic connection laws for networking: preference in usage (focusing on the distribution of value-added), long connections by usage (focusing on the tunneling effects of exchange in IS elements), and other generic and mission-specific connection laws such as centrality (focusing on spreading out the density of connections in the network, or the average distance between nodes). The third *corollary* is concerned with the implementation of the above generic IS design principles: maximize the benefits of open source technology and societal cyber-structure and pursue as possible Web-centered and person-centered connections of IS elements.

The connectionist definition of IS is now fully explained. The next section applies this definition to trace the evolution of the field of IS since its origination in the 1980s.

1.4 The Evolution of Information Systems

Does the connectionist definition of IS explain the evolution of IS practices in the professional field since its scholarly conception? Do we see empirical evidence of such notions as systems of information systems? We continue the above discussion and put IS to action: how this connection technology enabled the recent innovations of business design in, particularly, manufacturing; and how it evolved along with the innovations.

The history of information systems is arguably as old as human civilization itself; or at the least, as old as when the first written language appeared on earth. Question: Why did humans invent symbols? Answer: To record information. However, the academic articulation for information systems as a separate subject of scientific study and education emerged only around the 1970s (see, e.g., Davis and Olson, 1974). Practically speaking, the field of IS emerged as a solution to the limitations of the computer applications before it: number crunching. The basic argument was that information is much more than data processing, and a system that generates management information (e.g., sales, accounting, and inventory analysis) is much different from an electronic brain that does scientific calculation. Thus, the new field was branded Management Information System (MIS), with its contrast, the old days computing, labeled Electronic Data Processing (EDP). This concept blended computers with mainstream management, but it also prompted traditional organizational behavior scholars to refer to it as the computer-based IS, as a qualification of an organization being an information processor.

However, with the rapid explosion of information technology (IT) and the pervasive application of IT, the field soon realized that the power of IT (even just for business) was not restricted to management. The term MIS, rather than broadening the appeal of IT in general, actually relegated it to a special segment of promises. Thus, theorists and practitioners now customarily drop M and refer to the field simply as IS: Information Systems; i.e., the application of IT in all aspects of enterprises and extended enterprises, from management to production and logistics in all sectors of the economy and the society. The connectionist definition of IS follows this broad interpretation but further specifies its unique intellectual nature to assist design.

From the perspective of this connectionist definition, we may classify EDP as a specific connection of the following IS elements: EDP professionals (e.g., computer technicians, data entry clerks, and method engineers and EDP managers), data crunching software, data resources, mainframe computer, and remote terminals. In a similar way, MIS is a connection of managers, MIS professionals, managerial report-generating software and data crunching software, mainframe, mini, and personal computers, and local area networks. Some variations of MIS, including Decision Support Systems (DSS, see, e.g., Alter, 1980) and Expert Systems (ES, see, e.g., Nilsson, 1980), can be classified this way, too. There, DSS features analytics and group collaboration software to facilitate decision makers' jobs, while

ES seeks to automate certain classes of professional judgments (including internal medicine) by embodying decision rules and knowledge representations. Both require versatile databases. Neither recognized the role of openness and scalability for their IS elements and connections, nor made them a requirement.

Then, sea changes came in 1980–1990 due to new enterprise IT, which enabled numerous new models of enterprise engineering in, especially, the manufacturing sector of the economy. The routine management applications of IS were completely aligned with manufacturing functions, by such models as enterprise resources planning (ERP, e.g., the SAP system). As a result, extended enterprises became a norm for IS applications. The notion of open and scalable connections started to make sense as enterprises discovered the value of broadening the small set of regular suppliers to semi-regular supplier pools (e.g., certified suppliers) and networking with them. A second wave came in the form of the Internet in 1990–2000. Globally scaled networking for customers and companies entered the realm of enterprising and business design. Since 2000, including this decade, the field is wide open for new innovative business designs to thrust in all directions as long as the progress of IS/IT can support them. The connectionist definition of IS uniquely sheds light on this evolution of IS design.

What happened since 1980 can be summarized in three topics: agile manufacturing, e-commerce, and social networking. How does the IS definition describe them?

EXERCISES

1. What are functional IS, such as sales, payrolls, and accounting in the administration sector of a company; and process planning, production scheduling, and shop floor control in a factory? What makes them "islands of automation"?

2. Why is a database system an open and scalable way to connect standalone application files and software, while structurally integrating them?

3. What are computer-aided design (CAD), computer-aided manufacturing (CAM), manufacturing execution system (MES),

computer-integrated manufacturing (CIM), concurrent engineering (CE, or simultaneous engineering), agile manufacturing (AE), and mass customization?

4. What are the differences between ERP, product data management (PDM), and product life cycle management (PLCM)?

5. How does supply chain integration compare to supply chain management, on the one hand, and e-engineering on the other?

6. What characterizes e-business, on-demand business, and globally integrated enterprises?

7. Is there any concrete technical characterization of systems of information systems?

Of the three topics — agile manufacturing, e-commerce, and social networking — this book will discuss the last two in Chapter 2 in greater detail. Here, let the focus be on agile manufacturing. More precisely, let the focus be the evolution of agile manufacturing and its repercussions on IS. For convenience of discussion, we recognize these six main divisions of a manufacturing enterprise: administration, product design and production planning, (execution of) production, supply chain, demand chain, and customer services. Each of these divisions consists of its own functional areas and operational processes, with the administration also including the enterprise level management and control. Collectively, they encompass the entire enterprise.

A functional IS dedicates itself to a particular function(s) in a particular division. The scope of the IS elements and connections define the dedication. These information systems are islands of automation simply because they are mutually exclusive with no online connections in between: any given IS element in any of these IS islands cannot inter-operate with any other in another island. Thus, a sales manager who wants to determine a "rock bottom" price for a product, for example, does not have access to the information about the sale product in the accounting IS, nor to the information in the production IS. This notion of islands of automation equally describes the separation of one enterprise in a supply chain from another, of course. The central concept is straightforward: if one needs an integrated wholly view of certain IS elements across a scope, then one needs proper connections of such elements throughout the scope. They become islands of automation when the required connections do not exist.

A database, such as Oracle, DB2, and PostgreSQL, is an integration of data resources (see Chapter 5 for the whole concept and design of databases). It features a conceptual schema to provide semantic (logic) integration for the whole spectrum of its applications, and implements the integration into storage structures using generic access methods (the internal schema). It derives (groups of) external views from the conceptual schema, each of which is fine-tuned for the data input and output designs of some particular applications (or application families) that it supports. The provisions of a full-fledged database system typically include tools to run assortment of programming languages, as well as some generic native programming facilities (e.g., ANSI SQL). The internal schema allows a database to be transported from one hardware platform to another and minimizes the transaction costs for doing so. The external views and programming facilities together supports foreign application software developed elsewhere outside the database environment to run on the data resources integrated in the database, without much need to modify the software — or, again, with minimum transaction costs.

When the external applications are some functional IS in and of their own right, or, if one connects certain functional information systems by virtue of connecting their information resources, then the database technology offers a relatively open and scalable way to construct the connections and the resulting integrated information resources. The openness is achieved because the design methods for developing all three schemas are generic, and hence applicable, to a great many classes of information resources in a great many information systems. The scalability comes from the extensiveness and changeability of the database technology itself, delivered through, e.g., the relational system and SQL programming environment. With this integration, the original application programs can continue to run for their original IS users and all others when needed, with minimal transaction costs. Thus, connecting functional IS via an integrated database is a ready example of open and scalable construction of IS elements and connections. The three-schema model of databases is itself scalable to the integration and inter-operation of databases within and across enterprises, on the Web or not (see Chapter 5).

The third question is concerned with the connection of the product design and production planning division with the production division. A CAD system is an IS that connects design engineers to drawing and engineering analysis software, and thereby enables them to produce digital product data and designs for the ensuing product development tasks (e.g., process planning). The system often uses proprietary computing hardware and networking infrastructure. A CAM, on the other hand, connects machinery (and operators) to the dedicated machining controls software, hardware, and infrastructure. Cluster such CAMs and enrich them by connecting to automated shop floor control data acquisition and feeding, and an MES results. Extending the MES to include connections (or integration) to production scheduling IS, inventory control IS, and all other functional ISs of the production division will provide the minimum CIM. Connecting it with CADs, process planning IS, and select functional ISs in the administration sector progressively will expand the CIM towards covering the entire manufacturing enterprise. Connecting CADs across the product design and production planning division and overlapping the design process with the manufacturing process (e.g., team up design engineers with manufacturing engineers) will give rise to CE. Technically speaking, there have been many different designs of the above models, each of which typically come from some particular way of making the connections in the particular models.

Agile manufacturing is as much a business design as a technology. Unlike the other models discussed above, AE expressly calls for the involvement of customers in the model as a driver for the chained reactions through all six divisions. In a sense, we can consider AE an implementation for the ideal of mass customization: Make the manufacturing system agile so as to be able to respond to customers' on-demand orders. Clearly, this is a high-end vision that requires a high-end IS to support it. We stop our discussion here by simply stating that the ideal IS for AE must be a system of systems, whose design is still unfolding today.

An ERP is usually a tight integration of select IS islands in administration, production, and those for inter-operation with the supply chain. Vendors often provide total solutions for the integration as a standalone ERP IS running on its proprietarily designed IS elements. The model of PDM tends to be implemented by inter-operating the information resources that contain product data from IS in any divisions required. For instance, the product data captured in customer services IS (failures on parts, functions, etc.) will be connected to the product data of CIM, by virtue of some unifying data models. The individual systems so connected in this case will continue to operate autonomously.

The model of PLCM is even looser, connected often by the enterprise's internal cyber-infrastructure and some common user interface to switch in between the member systems of the PLCM confederation. In this sense, one may say that the PLCM is embedded in the enterprise cyber-infrastructure, whose appearance is the collected presentation of all component ISs. This loose connection is more a result of practicality than by any logical design. Conceptually speaking, the PLCM encompasses the entire manufacturing enterprise since the life cycle of a product starts with customer demand (marketing) and business strategizing, and moves through all other sectors. To tightly connect all the IS elements involved across software technology and vendors would present a major challenge to the field. The practices of PLCM IS in the field clearly illustrate the notion of systems of IS.

Supply chain management is comparable to PLCM, except that the scope now is the entire extended enterprise of the chain. It remains mainly a managerial practice depending directly on IS support. However, under this loose umbrella, the notion of supply chain integration tends to imply some technical integration of supply chain tasks beyond savvy management by humans. A famous example is the CFAR project (King, 1996): the connection of Wal-Mart's procurement IS with Warner-Lambert's order processing IS and ERP, by dedicated application software (processes) over the Internet (infrastructure). Albeit dated, this practice still represents a top-notch vision and a high bar in the attempt to tightly integrate retailer IS with supplier IS across the supply chain. This integration has reportedly reduced at least the cycle time of inventory (e.g., Listerine) replenishment for Wal-Mart. The connectionist definition of IS views the supply chain IS as a system of systems. Indeed, when the supply chain is considered an extended enterprise in and of itself, then all the enterprise IS models discussed above may be applied to this extended enterprise, as well. The e-engineering model is precisely the application of the CE model to the extended enterprise of supply chain as a whole. The e-engineering IS will be an IS of the prime's IS and the suppliers' IS where the product design information resources and design engineers are connected in some way.

Answering the sixth question requires a new concept: the demand chain, or the customers and the customers' customers, and so forth. Demand chain and supply chain could be mirror images, of course, except that customers are commonly people while suppliers are companies. All three models, e-business, on-demand business, and globally integrated enterprises, are based on demand chains and feature the (direct) collaboration among people either as the customer or as the knowledge worker for common value creation. Clearly, in all the above models, the easiness of making the connections depends squarely on the openness and scalability of all the IS and the IS elements concerned. The fundamental values of these innovations in business design are reduction of transaction costs and cycle times in the execution of all functions throughout the value chains, such as the time to market for new products.

The seventh question highlights a fundamental aspect of IS: the connections could be tightly controlled both proprietarily and technically, or just be some loose form of voluntary collaboration. The former typically requires an integrated database or computationally synchronized distributed databases for the whole IS, hence making it a singular IS. The latter, in contrast, would be considered some system of IS. The key point here is that the connectionist definition of IS consistently explains the evolution of IS as an innovator for business designs, manufacturing or otherwise. The concept of human value network uniquely describes this trend.

We will discuss innovations in business designs in general, as IS value creation, in Chapter 2, which broadens manufacturing demand chains to all aspects of human value networks, especially service (e-commerce) and social networking. The following statement draws from the concurrent and converging evolution of IS in all sectors of economics:

The Unification Principle of Information Systems: *An IS is a unifying tool for human enterprises. All IS elements, excepting application programs, are generic in nature and may be useful to any other IS elements for any IS in any functional area and economic sector. Thus, the design of IS should seek the unifying effects by connecting IS elements into systems of IS.*

The history of IS as revealed by the connectionist definition shows something rather impressive: the strong perseverance of IS. That is, information systems tend to evolve rather than do or die; they weather the changes in the volatile IT industry and funnel such revolutions into robust business design innovations. The next section discusses how the continuity may shape the design of IS.

1.5   The Journey of Information Systems: Design for Life Cycle vs. Design for Sustainability

Manufactured products, from personal daily effects to big machinery and buildings, all have definitive life cycles just as biological entities do. Even organizations have legally mandated starts and ends. Therefore, it is fitting that their design and management are often marked with tasks that correspond to the generic stages on their life cycle: product planning, engineering design, manufacturing (fabrication, construction, etc.), sales (implementation, etc.), services (operation/control, maintenance, etc.), and termination (disposal, etc.). Only recently with the rise of the sustainability concerns has the field started to consider the eternal effects of products and promote recycle and reuse. New methods such as design for sustainability and rebirth analysis (Morris, 2011) seek to extend the horizon of product life cycle and design. In a way, the notion of sustainability extends the planning horizon into eternity.

As revealed in Section 1.4, in the spirit of Douglas MacArthur's famous quote, "old soldiers never die, they just fade away", one may say that *information systems never die, they just reincarnate*. Some IS elements (e.g., information resources) may survive the organizations which initiated them and owned them, by being incorporated into other IS (e.g., taxation, Google Web homepages, and archives) as some elements or member systems. For an IS in a continuing enterprise, many of the IS elements, especially the software and hardware, may get replaced or subsumed into other elements many times over, but the real gut of the IS, as defined by its mission (particular value creation), contents (logic and information resources), and connections (persons and supporting resources), tends to perpetuate. It is arguable that the life span of IS is at least as long as that of its host enterprise. A more liberal view may even compare the life of IS to that of a human being which perpetuates into offspring forever. This view in fact regards IS to have an eternal life cycle, which should be recognized as such, rather than limiting its impacts to some terminal life span.

This vision brings this book to *sustainability design for IS*. What is it, however? An intuitive view could focus on the recycle, reclamation, and reuse of IS elements, and strive to incorporate these goals into the design of IS. We have no quarrels with this view. It is good and necessary for a connected world. However, we would rather focus on the design of connections to substantiate the uniqueness of IS sustainability: make IS elements (maximally permissibly) open and scalable for connections, and make the connections of IS elements (maximally permissibly) open and scalable. This is our definition of sustainability design for IS.

This sustainability brings about another dimension of IS innovation. The subtitle of this book, *the connection of people and resources for innovation*, now has three levels of connotation to link IS and innovation: an IS connects for human value networking; an IS connects to become enabling elements; and an IS connects sustainably. They lead to a new perspective to IS design. In comparison, while the traditional IS design methodology categorizes the design tasks in accordance with a terminal view of the IS life span — planning, analysis, design, construction, implementation, and operation — the new design perspective recognizes, accommodates, and promotes an eternal life cycle for IS in a connected world. The innovation comes from the new values enabled by the new connections of people; the new connections of resources; and the new connections of people and resources.

EXERCISES

1. What common IS techniques support the sustainability of an IS? (Hint: think of your PC — what administration apps/functions does your PC have that support its sustainability?)
2. Does the life cycle view still apply to IS that reincarnate? What may categorize the new view away from the old?
3. How can we expand the reincarnation view into an IS design methodology?
4. How do the following concepts of IS planning differ from each other: an IS roadmap, an enterprise IS plan, a phased IS plan, and a specific IS plan?
5. Why does design for connection require more professional expertise than the traditional life cycle design does? Should the expertise reside in-house? Can it become a core competence for the enterprise?
6. What generic IS design methods have proven to be of long-lasting value? (Hint: think, what basic kinds of "things" or terminologies have stayed forever with computers?)

The concept of IS sustainability is actually closer to our survival than many may have thought. Just think what if we lost all the digital data on our PC; all the digital data on our company's PC; all the digital data on all companies' computers; all the digital data on all the government computers; and all the digital data in the world. Or, for that matter, just think what if we can no longer read all the digital data that we have saved. Is there any possibility imaginable at all that Microsoft might all of a sudden be "ruined" and their support to all MS products abruptly stopped (or severely disrupted), thereby compromising the continuing functioning of Windows and Office on our PCs? To be a little more realistic, would it still ruin us if the sudden ruining of Microsoft took place over a period of, say, a month or a year, during a crisis where other vendors were also hard pressed to take over the business completely? In fact, a dark age would not be unthinkable in the worst, oh no, near worst, case of disastrous scenarios on IS.

Luckily, of course, the darkest scenarios seem sufficiently remote as to warrant any loss of sleep at night. However, lesser disasters in IT disruptions do occur, such as those due to terrorist attacks and earthquakes. The IT industry has proven its sustainability during these unfortunate and unwanted tests, by having designed and built some basic sustainability into its systems. These include parallel and redundant systems (resources and applications), backup and roll-back support to systems, and collaboration among (distributed) systems. Needless to say, the sustainability design relied on sustainable connections to work, especially when collaboration among systems is required. The same principles of sustainability (especially recoverability) are commonplace in virtually any PC design, not just for complex computing or IS.

Therefore, the industry has been aware of the defensive side of sustainability design for IS, including saving energy and materials throughout the life cycle of IS hardware manufacturing and operation to cut the cost to customers and society. However, its progressive side still awaits recognition. We argue that when sustainability is linked with the reincarnation of IS, either in the standalone sense or as a member of systems of IS, design for connection has a powerful positive side: It should promote the eternal effects of IS on facilitating value creation for the connected world by incorporating the evolution, or the permissible future networking of IS, into its design roadmap. The key is the strategic planning for the roadmap and the core competence to (adaptively) enact on the roadmap into the future.

That is, an eternal life cycle is still a life cycle except that the planning phase must be a part of the enterprise's long-term strategy, and the operation phase must be oriented to allow for constant renovation. Therefore, we recognize this new life cycle of IS: *strategic planning* (business designs using IS); *specific planning* (accountability for value creation); *analysis* (for IS elements and connections); *design* (of IS elements and connections); system *construction*; and *renovation*, which may lead to revamping, expanding, or merging of IS elements and connections. In a way, the last phase, renovation, may be considered as a recursive or iterative cycle of the previous five phases, driven by new designs of value creation. Compared to the traditional life cycle, the main difference is the scope of IS strategy (equal to the business vision of the enterprise), the extent of IS horizon (societal), and the replacement of operation with renovation as the last stage.

The IS field has accumulated many methods for planning IS from some given mission, which may be mandated by the (top) management without the IS professionals' involvement. Industrial IS planning methods tend to be based on common sense, rather than scientific justification; and vendors have codified many tasks and procedures involved to make their application easier. In essence, these planning methods are some template whose application requires experienced IS professionals to calibrate it on the particular cases at hand. Such software is well-suited for on-the-job training. Strategic planning for IS, on the other hand, requires competence in the development of business strategies for the enterprise. Since business strategy is in and of itself a major subject of study, we content ourselves to investigate the unique and particular perspectives of IS, i.e., how does IS enable a *business design* for the enterprise, and possibly enable its innovation (e.g., new business models; products and services; business spaces; and strategic practices) by facilitating new human value networks? This is the subject of Chapter 2. In this context, the second phase of information system planning, developed in Chapter 3, is the design of the overall IS structure (e.g., the scope of IS elements and the strategy of connection) to implement the overall IS mission in a current IS at the appointed time.

The second phase of IS strategic planning is the planning of an IS roadmap for the enterprise, too. The roadmap may be staged, and be recursively enhanced on specificity, depending on the time frame and the level and scope of development. Its purpose is to knit together long- and short-term IS plans (for particular missions) to yield an overall enterprise IS vision. These plans will feature progressively more specific and narrower definitions of IS elements and connections as the vision moves from long-term to short-term, and from high-end aspiration to immediate budget constraints. The point here is that, IS visions should not be buried in IS reality check. Even an unrealistically ambitious IS roadmap can be accompanied by a realistic time frame for eventual implementation so long as the visions sought are attainable and justifiable. Only the specific IS plan for the current IS is targeted for immediate enactment, and hence it only requires the specification of all goals that substantiate the mission, and of all types of IS elements and connections that constitute the IS, to the point that ball-park budgeting becomes possible.

Another fundamental difference between the eternal life cycle and terminal life cycle views of IS is their last phase: renovation vs. operation. The operation of IS may be outsourced to some application providers or service bureaus, although significant organizations tend to run their IS in-house even if they bought the IS from outside vendors. The reason for in-house operation is the same as that for in-house development: the strategic value of IS. If the value is perceived so high as being a part of the enterprise's core competence or even a strategic competitive weapon, then for control and protection the enterprise would develop the IS in-house, or at least operate it in-house. However, how low the value must go before a company outsources its IS has to be a measure that belongs to individual companies' discretion. Renovation clearly raises the threshold higher, whatever it may be. If a company values the IS so much as to align its business visions with the IS and commissions constant renovation on the IS — or, conversely, if a company finds it necessary to constantly renovate its IS — then the competency on IS clearly belongs in the company's core competency. At this point, it ought to be self-evident that the connectionist definition of IS recognizes IS as residing right at the heart of any enterprise that connects within or across.

The last question of the exercises also indicates the scope of this book: it focuses on such methods for IS design that promise long-lasting value, and leaves the more tenuous ones to on-job training using perhaps the generic skills acquired from one's education. For reasons of specialization, this book also leaves out hardware, operating systems and application programs, human-computer interface (e.g., GUI, Homepage, and natural language), and programming languages and algorithms to other textbooks in the computing discipline. This book will develop the competencies for processes analysis and database design in Chapters 4–7. As such, this book develops the core competences of IS design in strategic planning, system (processes) analysis, and database design. Together, these results constitute a basic IS design science.

The Design for Sustainability Principle of Information Systems: *IS should seek sustainability and innovation in its design, to support an (eternal) life cycle of strategic planning; specific planning; analysis; design; construction; and renovation, for its envisioned value propositions, IS elements, and connections. Innovation comes from value propositions and connections.*

The science and practice of information systems have now been explained.

The rest of the book develops particular theory, methods, and techniques based on the concepts reviewed here. The next chapter discusses the analytic properties of human value networks and on this basis presents a set of generic principles and guidelines for IS strategic planning. This foundation sets the IS design process in motion in the ensuing chapters.

Chapter 2

Strategic Planning for Information Systems: Determine the Mission of Innovation and the Scope of the Human Value Networks Involved

How do we characterize the intellectual nature of connecting people and resources for innovation? This chapter elaborates the concept of human value networks discussed in Chapter 1 to answer this question. It first synthesizes the discoveries from the emerging network science and service science to help understand how humans collaborate to create values and facilitate the process of value creation. The analysis then leads to guidelines for strategic planning of IS. The focus is to determine the players in the networked value creation and how they connect to each other. The rest of the IS design, i.e., determining how to connect the other IS elements as resources to support the players, then follows naturally. Hence, in this chapter, the theory of human value networks is presented first, followed by *a new hyper-network model* to analytically characterize the connected nature of human value creations. The theory and the model are then calibrated on the practices of e-commerce (from the mid-1990s to the present) to verify their empirical relevance. These e-commerce practices also serve as illustrations of the generic hyper-networking strategies and show how particular business strategies may be developed from these generic ones. A set of guidelines for planning innovative IS concludes the discussion, and leads to the next chapter which derives a design science for IS engineering from these guidelines.

2.1   Human Value Networks: Humans Hyper-Networking to Pursue Value Propositions

Human value networks center on persons, and are characterized by collaboration, or value cocreation (see Section 1.3 of Chapter 1). These properties are virtually identical to the definition of service in the emerging service science (Ostrom *et al.*, 2010). In fact, the provision of IS to persons is indeed perceived in the industry as service. Thus, the intellectual nature of IS not only intersects that of networks but also encompasses that of service. This chapter, therefore, develops a unified analysis of all three domains — IS, networks, and service — starting with a review of the established results in network science and service science, as shown below. The review is followed by an analysis of e-commerce and social networking, to show how humans innovate (create new values) by networking in these cases; both of which are direct beneficiaries of innovative IS. The results of the analysis lead to a formal model that characterizes the analytic nature of the connectionist definition of IS, and thereby sheds light on IS strategic planning.

Service science establishes that humans are the end customers that define the value of service; the end workers that provide the service; and the resources that support the service enterprise, in any service system (Maglio *et al.*, 2010). Therefore, value cocreation is all about networking humans in the pursuit of value propositions (Hsu, 2009). We now refer to each value creation enterprise (e.g., a service system) defined on a set of persons as a single human value network. The collection of such networks for many (concurrent) value creations on the same set of persons is accordingly referred to as a *hyper-network* (Hsu, 2009; Chan and Hsu, 2012), where each single network is a layer of the hyper-network. Three possible directions for scaling human value networks are recognized (Hsu and Spohrer, 2009): up to the population (as shown in search engine services), down to persons (as shown in personalization services of e-commerce), and transformationally to new business designs (as shown in the rapid change of Internet enterprises).

From this perspective, the connectionist definition of IS offers a service-inspired particular interpretation:

The Service View of IS: *An IS is a service system (a human value network) that uses the non-people IS elements as resources to support the people.*

We now analyze the network-scientific nature of IS. Analytically speaking, a network is a graph of nodes (set N) and edges (set E) that connect nodes, pairwise. The topology of a network is determined from N and E alone, and may be measured by the average distance between nodes (number of connections required), the distribution of degrees (number of edges connecting at a node), and the like. However, the semantics and dynamics of a network have to do with the properties of nodes and, especially, connections. They include strength of nodes, density of edges, and constraints on connections. A single network tends to be defined on some homogeneous semantics and dynamics that universally apply to all nodes and connections. When multiple such interpretations co-exist on N and E, multiple layers of network WILL result, too, which give rise to a hyper-network (see Section 2.3).

Network science has recognized three main stays of genres for human networks defined from topology and connection laws: random graphs (Erdõs and Rényi, 1960; Newman *et al.*, 2001 and 2002), where a node can connect to any other nodes freely with some uniformly distributed probability; scale-free networks (e.g., Barabasi and Albert, 1999; Newman, 2001a and 2001b), where the degree distribution predicates on some decay power law; and small world networks (e.g., Watts and Strogatz, 1998; Watts, 2003), where the maximum distance may be less than six and/or the topology features long connections. Many other semantics and dynamics have been found from empirical studies of human networks. Examples include connection laws based on some centrality measures for nodes (more even distribution of degrees and/or balanced distances to other nodes from a node; Fefferman and Ng, 2007), exponential probability of connection (Robins *et al.*, 2007), and numerous others (e.g., Caldarelli *et al.*, 2004; Zhang *et al.*, 2006). Many more studied the applications of the network models on socialization, with pioneering efforts from Rapoport (1963), Milgram (1967), and Granovetter (1973).

The opposite of random graphs may be the so-called regulated networks, which tend to be engineered physical systems such as tele-communications infrastructure and highways. Although the use of this infrastructure by humans may constitute logical networks that are different from the physical ones themselves, these logical networks are nonetheless constrained by the physical foundations from which they operate. Therefore, many human networks are considered semi-regular — i.e., they are not really random, nor completely regulated. Social networks on the Internet fall in this broad category since the availability of the Internet itself represents a basic constraint to the network using it. Indeed, access to the Internet is not completely open and free of censorship in many parts of the world. Even for random graphs, one may argue about what really defines randomness: Does random simply mean that the connection is probabilistic, or does it require a uniform distribution? The latter will consider any connection law other than being governed by an equal chance as representing some constraints, such as connection by physical proximity or by logical preferences. Here, we content ourselves with merely stating these views and their implications.

We discussed in Section 1.3 of Chapter 1 the detailed implications of the decay power law degree distribution and the small world topology on connection laws. Now, we present the mathematical rendition of the scale-free networks in Figure 2.1.

We are now ready to analyze the key thesis: ***humans always hyper-network to cocreate values***, from the perspective of network science. Again, the IS is the tool to support this hyper-networking.

EXERCISES

1. How many different social and professional networks do you belong to as a formal member? (Think associations, interest groups, bulletin boards, mailing lists, blogs, Facebook, Twitter, social sites...)

2. Do you think that President Obama may possibly share some common interests or personal attributes with you that may lead to you stumbling into him on the Internet?

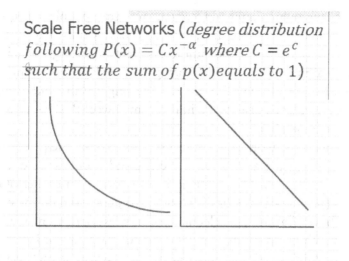

Scale Free Networks (*degree distribution following* $P(x) = Cx^{-\alpha}$ *where* $C = e^{c}$ *such that the sum of* $p(x)$ *equals to* 1)

Figure 2.1: The decay power curve (left) and its natural logarithm line (right).

3. If a clustering of movies suggested to you on Netflix or other similar sites is a network generated from a movie library, then how many such networks (using movie attributes) may be there for all members? Similarly, how many networks (keyword-based lists of homepages) may be there on Google search?

4. Please name some examples of life cycle roles for persons, and explain how these roles tie up (overlap) a person's many networks in life.

5. Do people really collaborate willingly to create value (e.g., resources) on the Internet? Do companies transform their business designs by hyper-networking?

6. When does manufacturing become service (under what conditions)? What manufactured products also sell services?

The answer to the first two questions, when fully played out, may surprise many people. It is not just how many friends or casual contacts one has, but also in how many different contexts one makes connections to them. These networks may be totally isolated from each other, such as a professional association for IS and the fan club for a hometown singer. However, we the people in question automatically serve as the linkage to all the networks that we participate in. Through us, a "wormhole" is created through which an IS professional in another country may gain a peek at an extreme sports star who happens to be a fan of the same singer. Any kind of unlikely connections may be discovered in this "small world". That is, *a hyper-network is a small world.*

The hyper-network concept can be shown from the perspective of products, too, such as movies at Netflix and homepages at Google. The same movies may be clustered in an enormous number of different ways (permutations) for different customers based on the customers' attributes (rating and selections of movies), and so may Websites based on the keywords that users provide. Each of the layers of the hyper-network is a single network in the sense that each carries its own "headlines" and promotions for the particular customers in question. This differentiation of networks from the same collection of titles illustrates personalization of the accumulated resources, and its power (i.e., appeal to customers) for marketing.

Both persons and companies play many roles during their respective life cycles. Examples include child, spouse, parent, and senior for persons, and employer, buyer, and supplier for companies, just to name a few. Are they destined to interact? We consider the next three questions together in a cohesive manner.

We the people have proven our willingness (and indeed, eagerness) to collaborate on creating knowledge (e.g., blogs and open source software), information resources (e.g., YouTube and Wikipedia), and connections (e.g., Twitter and Facebook) on the Internet. One may safely call this manner "all for one and one for all". In industry, knowledge workers have been similarly willing to publish their knowledge resources and support each other in professional undertakings within and even across their organizational boundaries. Open source communities exemplify these powerful professionals' networks. In addition, many organizations also embrace internal social networking as a tool for their employees to boost quality and productivity. Now, all these social networking practices are converging with business, especially e-commerce. Companies enhance their marketing with social networking offerings (comments, blogs, etc.) or with participation in social networking sites. Conversely, social networking sites also develop their own revenue-bearing services for persons and companies.

Note this fact: all these human networks are intertwined by virtue of their common denominator — the (same) persons who constitute the networks — and all persons are intertwined by the roles they play in their life cycles, e.g., being a student, a professional, a spouse, a customer as a parent, a provider as a photographer, and so on so forth. Thus, persons belong simultaneously in myriad networks because these networks belong respectively in a myriad of roles that persons play. Human networks become service value networks when persons pursue value propositions on them, as a customer, a provider, or a resource, either separately or concurrently. For example, hobbies can become businesses and businesses hobbies; and crossing the line between customer and provider can be as easy as uploading and downloading digital files. Clearly, the divides of customer, provider, and resource are intertwined, too, across personal life cycle roles.

All persons consume, thus they by definition are customers. However, many such customers are also providers of the Internet community (e.g., via Wikipedia and YouTube) even when they do not engage in any selling. For formal business, as will be explained in Section 2.2.1, many persons use B2C providers (e.g., e-Bay, Amazon. com, and Yahoo!) and/or set up revenue-bearing blogs or video-blogs on social networking sites. Companies, on the other hand, network through people, too. They either engage executives networking, which is no different from any other social networking, or involve professionals collaborating through B2B practices (e.g., Alibaba.com and GroupOn.com), industrial exchanges (e.g., Covisint.com and Ariba.com), and Internet utilities (e.g., Oasis.com and BBC).

Finally, physical products are increasingly associated with service, beyond the traditional realm of product services (Dausch and Hsu, 2006). The evolution of the iPod, iPhone, iPad, and iCloud illustrates this point, where the manufacturers join forces with service providers (personal apps and information resources) to cocreate values with their customers — i.e., enabling the customers to network, either socially or for any other purpose of life. In general, manufacturing can extend into some human value networks only if the providers are willing to attend to their customers' real reasons for buying the products — i.e., using these products to fulfill their life tasks, by extending provisions to facilitate the use of their products for such customer tasks.

The big picture is that people and companies create, expand, and combine their service value networks by creating, expanding, and combining the human networks underlying them in a multi-dimensional way: *the hyper-networking of customers, providers, and resources.* Taking Yahoo! and Google as examples: Their evolution from providing Web search and email to providing e-commerce and now social networking is a story of this hyper-networking. They scaled up to the population since they had to build the population resources (Web pages) and make their services usable/used by all. They also scaled down to the persons to provide personalized value, in order to compete; and the population resources they accumulated, including the customer base, became a powerful competitive weapon for them.

Ultimately, they pursued fluid business models and designs because their rich population resources enabled them to offer more, and creating new (role-based, task-based) values was not too hard to do at their positions. Similar stories are visible from Amazon.com, which evolved from being a humble online bookstore to now an all-encompassing B2C site with some social networking offerings (e.g., customer comments). The travel industry illustrates well the concept of life cycle tasks. One may expect one-stop sites such as Expedia.com and Hotwire.com to continue evolving and combining more activities involved in the life cycle of traveling. They might provide the information, transactions, and social networking functions required by customers in their roles as a businessman, a tourist, and much more. Finally, it is worthwhile to point out that the story of the iPad portrays hyper-networking across business spaces and industries (e.g., content provider vs. channel provider, and hardware vs. software), too.

The Hyper-Networking Principle of Value Creation: *People and companies hyper-network (customers, providers, and resources) to create innovative value propositions and pursue resources to make them happen. The basic connection laws for hyper-networks are streamlining their respective life cycle roles to reduce the transaction costs and cycle times of life cycle tasks.*

We now review the evolution of e-commerce to illustrate the past and emerging practices of the hyper-networking principle of value creation (Hsu, 2012).

2.2 Innovation in e-Commerce by Hyper-Networking: The Past, Present, and Future

To help shed light on our analysis, we consider the entire Internet community to be a hyper-network for value cocreation. The customers, providers, and resources (including persons/knowledge workers) required for a value creation enterprise may come from connecting any member human value networks of the community, in any way. In fact, the particular way in which they connect defines a category of business designs in our review, as discussed below.

2.2.1 *Internet Commerce: Hyper-Networking Providers with Customers*

This category includes B2C (business-to-customer: individual business sites for direct sales and marketing); B2B (business-to-business: business procurement and supply chain activities); and Collaborative/ Aggregate B2C/B2B (shopping malls, portals, marketplaces, exchanges and auctioning sites, etc.). The B2C and B2B models share common properties, although company customers may present more transaction costs to the provider than persons do. Amazon.com may exemplify a B2C site; but it also represents a shopping mall where individual B2Cs congregate. Many small B2C sites park themselves at popular destination sites, such as Yahoo! and social networking sites including Facebook.com. On the B2B side, Alibaba.com shows a marketplace and industrial exchanges are found in efforts by, for example, PerfectCommerce.com and Ariba.com. Often, the hyper-networking here exhibits the small world topology, clustering around some prime organization with some members connecting to different networks, such as in the cases of marketplaces and industrial exchanges.

Industrial exchanges, including B2C auctioning sites (e.g., eBay.com) and B2B auctioning sites, are powerful examples of hyper-networking buyers and sellers. In theory, this model should excel since the whole economy is a marketplace and an exchange. In reality, however, it saw only a brief heyday at the turn of the new millennium. There are many reasons for this discrepancy, but the idea seems to be still relevant. From the perspective that the story of e-commerce is still unfolding, this book wishes to recognize it as a promising idea, and a possibility for the future.

The hyper-networking principle suggests that this category can benefit from facilitating connections among customers themselves to reap network effects. Examples include allowing for comments and providing blogs (comparable to social networking). Indeed, the field has witnessed such practices evolving over the years, ranging from simple B2C/B2B designs such as online bookstores to portals and auction sites. The former has been proven to be useful for marketing, including clustering products to make recommendations to customers; while the latter was instrumental in implementing self-policing (peer reviews).

The hyper-networking principle also indicates that the B2C/B2B design does not have to be confined to traditional business spaces. Rather, businesses can move in and out of different spaces to pursue complementary value propositions revealed by customers' life cycle tasks. In other words, a B2C/B2B site can sell anything and buy anything on demand, due to the fluidity afforded by the Web. Equally significantly, the digital nature of the Web allows embedding of B2C/B2B into any business design, including social networking sites and personal communications devices. For example, a news article about a book that Amazon.com sells can provide a clickable on the book to link the reader of the article to the precise homepage selling the book at the online bookstore. This idea extends the original concept of hyperlinks from linking homepages to also linking online businesses on the Web in a completely on-demand manner — i.e., hyper-networking customers and providers.

The B2C/B2B design scales up, down, and transformationally, too. Scaling up is shown in the many aggregate B2C and B2B models on the Internet that hyper-network across individual businesses. They include a collection of like-minded sites for one-stop shopping; jointly developed online consortia/communal cooperatives; integration of B2C systems to conduct assortment of transactions in auction/marketplace style; integration of B2B systems for on-demand supply chains as industrial exchanges; aggregated information services as portals for some general or particular life cycle tasks; and aggregated transaction services as portals for particular or general life cycle tasks.

For scaling down, a person offering skills for hire on demand, or acquiring services on demand, or soliciting any activities related to his/her life cycle tasks, is a person amenable to engaging in personal B2C to sell as well as to buy on the Web. It should also be abundantly clear that social networking and personal B2C cannot be separated, and the separation may not even be desirable. By extension, the same can be inferred for the inter-relationship between social networking and organizations to the extent that customers, knowledge workers, and other stakeholders are all persons. In this sense, the hyper-networking principle consistently explains the evolution from simple B2C to embedded B2C and all the way to the business implications of social networking sites such as Facebook and YouTube — they are scaling transformationally.

The big picture is that such hyper-networking can continue to expand and breed new business designs. Not only can one hyper-network among providers and among customers, respectively, one can also hyper-network between these two bases. One can also connect the resources of enterprise systems and integrate them as sharable IS elements for businesses to lease. As we will see below, the story of e-commerce did evolve along this line of hyper-networking. Furthermore, these practices clearly reflected an integration of the *life cycle tasks* and value chains for persons and enterprises (e.g., the life cycle and value chain of the book business: reader/customer, retailer, wholesaler, publisher, writer; and that of traveling: airlines, hotels, cars, restaurants, attractions...).

2.2.2 *Internet Enterprising: Hyper-Networking Resources for Providers*

This category includes practices of Intranet and B2E/B2M (business-to-employee, business-to-management, or company portal for administration activities); e-Enterprise (digitization of pro forma enterprise processes and core businesses); and e-Extended Enterprise (e.g., Globally Integrated Enterprise/On-Demand Business for consulting and real-time custom production and co-production by customer orders). Internet Enterprising is the narrow definition of e-business, which "applies the Internet" to connect enterprise processes, knowledge workers and other resources, and immediate suppliers, for the providers. The hyper-networking principle points out that this connection needs to cultivate pervasive inter-personal relationships among employees, so that a foundation may be put in place to facilitate their collaboration on the job and the accumulation and sharing of work experience (scaling up and transformational). It also advocates the connection of knowledge workers with customers and the customers' knowledge workers, in a value cocreation manner. The practices reflected this principle.

Many people casually refer to e-business as "applying the Internet" to businesses. Evidently, this notion is too simplistic to provide any useful insight into the practices. In contrast, the hyper-networking principle guides e-business to all possibilities of enterprising, by connecting resources within and across enterprises and extended enterprises in accordance to this basic logic: seeking the synergism between the employees' life cycle tasks at work and the life cycle tasks of the enterprise. The original e-business is but the first phase of opportunities. Hyper-networking uniquely places knowledge workers at the center of e-enterprising and this worldview has more momentum to go forward: Knowledge workers could be better networked to enhance the accumulation of knowledge from them, and the accumulated knowledge may be shared among them to support their life cycle tasks on the job. An e-enterprise is a federation of knowledge worker-centered virtual enterprises. Generally speaking, this concept fits especially well for the consulting industry. For this category, the hyper-networking principle uniquely captures the promise of cascading value cocreation along the demand chain and supply chain via knowledge workers, as the objective of e-enterprising.

2.2.3 *Internet Utilities: Hyper-Networking Resources with Customers*

This category includes ISP and tools (Internet Service Provider: basic utilities for persons and organizations to join the Web); ICP (Internet Content Provider: leasing information resources to other sites); and Internet Computing/Resources Provider (leasers of Web resources including technology, hardware, and transaction systems). The sheer size of the Internet community informs the size of its collective users, information resources, and enabling systems; and hence the size of opportunities to make them available for all to use in any imaginable way of application. Business designs have arisen from hyper-networking the users, resources, and systems for on-demand sharing and reusing of them for clients — e.g., bookstores become ICPs and vendors (e.g., Kindle). Some of the most celebrated accumulations on the Web have to come from social networking sites. Again, they prove the versatile nature of business designs on the Web: a social networking provider becomes an Internet utility provider with relative ease.

We submit that the versatile applications and fluid designs of hyper-networking resources and customers are role-based. That is, they target the same persons (and enterprises) to provide different products for their life cycle tasks, as the hyper-networking postulate predicts. The network providers (e.g., Google) and users (all members of Google) tend to exhibit a star-structured small world topology where users are also networking among themselves. The user networking may include B2C/B2B, Internet enterprising, and/or social networking, depending on the users' own practices. Each of these "member networks" may organize according to common types of life cycle tasks, or different roles that a person plays in life. As such, each may be a single layer network (small world or scale-free), with the whole being a hyper-network. In fact, each Internet Resources Provider may inadvertently serve as a hyper-hub, or a "wormhole" to connect these otherwise isolated networks on different layers of roles and life cycles. This category exemplifies hyper-networks as much as the Internet itself does.

Practically speaking, hyper-networking tends to start with gathering Internet users by free services. For example, the early ISPs and user portal sites, including AOL.com, Yahoo.com, and Hotmail.com, all started by giving users free access to the Internet (use, memory, and tools), along with a search engine and/or an email account. Even eBay.com started with free email tools which amassed the initial customer base for it to enable the ensuing auctioning business. Google, Twitter, Facebook and all later social networking sites followed suit.

Obviously, free services and for-fee business are just two sides of the same coin because fee-paying customers and free users are just two different roles of the same people who can switch between them in a split second. The concept of life cycle tasks helps identify these roles and design the embedded B2C (or any other business model) to generate revenues. On this note, we wish to stress that customers and knowledge workers are also just two roles of the same people who can switch between them as easily.

The big picture here is that any owner of original digital content — writings, documents, images, photos, videos, drawings, music, songs, movies, etc. — can become an ICP as well as a B2C, and the threshold of entry is as low as subscribing to an ISP. A freelance writer and an information portal containing original content, for example, can also operate as an ICP for any other sites; and vice versa. Social networking practices, again, can be a very fertile field for developing ICP values, as they hyper-network information resources from virtually all sources.

A generalization of ISP and ICP leads to the category of Internet Computing/Resources Provider. Examples include IBM as a cloud computing provider (running on-demand virtual PCs, etc. on their Internet servers), and companies offering heavy-duty IT systems of data storage, processing, and communications for significant

Internet-based enterprising. These heavy-duty systems are best described as shared IS elements for extended enterprises (e.g., Internet data storage to support globally distributed application systems). Sometimes, the notion of a (resources) portal is also used to describe the concentration of such resources for versatile customers. This design allows specialization, too, where specific IS elements might get accumulated to build up scale; and in turn helps clients reap benefits of the scale. Again, the hyper-networking principle fully describes these concepts, practices, and possibilities.

2.2.4 *Enterprising Services: Hyper-Networking Resources with Providers*

This category includes Online Vendor (providers and consultants of technologies, software systems and solutions); ASP (Application Service Provider: leasing solutions online to clients as their enterprise processes and applications); SaaS (Software as a Service); and On-Demand Service. Similar to Internet utility providers (IUP), enterprising service providers work in the background to enable their clients' systems and provide hyper-networking. However, unlike the IUP, who lease resources to organization customers, the providers in this category lease or sell solutions (enterprise processes, applications, and information systems) to Internet enterprises (who may be providers themselves).

Vendors practice hyper-networking as consulting firms do — on their resources and clients to accumulate, reuse and share them, and thereby gain the benefits of scale. A common necessity is that they practice themselves what they sell in order to excel. For example, IBM preached globally integrated enterprises (GIE); thus, the company itself is also expected to be an exemplary e-GIE. The same comment applies to traditional IT vendors who profit on Web technologies: e.g., Microsoft, Oracle, SoftBank, Apple, Dell, Cisco, and AT&T are also leading Web-based IS users themselves.

The ASP model hyper-networks, too. An example is the airlines' ticketing engine provided by Sabre.com, which is connected to many travel sites as well as airline sites. The ASP model also enjoys the advantage of being able to more readily build up dominance in a particular space. That is, the clients of an ASP naturally give rise to a population in the business space, to allow the ASP hyper-networking them to gain even more leverage. Retrospectively, the ASP model (Tao, 2001) made a leap of business design from sales (software products) to service, and this leap applies to manufactured products, as well. In essence, any online vendor can readily become an ASP if sufficient technology exists.

The original practices of ASP tend to be confined to routine applications and fixed processes. However, newer business designs feature agile and on-demand ASPs, such as Software as a Service: on-demand development and operation of reconfigurable enterprise processes and applications. The newness, i.e., on-demand reconfiguration, is made possible by progress on open technologies and generic enterprise software solutions, to meet the needs of the versatile service providers who meet the needs of their versatile customers. The SaaS class includes Web services, which focus on software objects for enterprise applications.

The big picture here is that these designs provide hyper-networking, and as such they have the ability to "manage" directly their customer population. Therefore, they tend to exhibit a population orientation. For example, vendors all strive to connect their customers' systems to their own in a tight network. Security vendors (e.g., Symantec) install security software on PCs and connect them to their global server, so that they can monitor the population and execute the controls (e.g., the black lists and blacklisted keywords) based on this real-time population information. Such a design de facto allows the global security server to take control of its customers' PCs, just like hackers and zombie computers try to do. The difference is, of course, accountability: legal businesses need to abide by the law. Similar practices are found in Microsoft and many other solution vendors where they update their software installed on client sites, remotely and virtually at will. Such a connection also allows Microsoft to gather performance information in real time and online from the whole population. Hyper-networking describes this population orientation.

2.2.5 *Social Networking: Hyper-Networking Customers and Resources, with Extensions to Connect to Providers*

This category includes P2P (peer-to-peer: individual "walled gardens" of socializing activities); Business on P2P (business use of P2P practices); Business Resources from P2P (Internet utilities: covert or overt customer base and information resource base); and Social Networking as Businesses (P2P as an integral part of regular B2C, B2M, etc.). In a sense, the recent noteworthy stories about the Internet, including the so-called Arab Spring of 2011, all happened here — using venues and provisions from, e.g., YouTube, Twitter, and Facebook. Social networking on the Internet is by definition multi-dimensional. Just ask any user how many social networking sites he/she participates on and this fact becomes clear. Strictly speaking, social networking per se is not a business design. However, it inherently supports people doing business on the Internet, as well as businesses connecting to the general public at large.

Social networking has been incorporated into B2M and other enterprising practices, too. For example, companies practice P2P to link customers, employees, and/or suppliers. This is a natural extension of, for example, the vendor networks discussed above in Section 2.2.4. A company portal (intranet) with a full P2P embedded in it can facilitate its knowledge workers collaborating and hence enhance the enterprise's agility. In fact, the expansion of the previous practices by further connecting itself in all aspects and at all levels is a clear testament to the validity of the hyper-networking principle.

The big picture here is the *person-centered* view of the digital world (Hsu, 2009): we the people employ and deploy everything we have access to on the Internet to conduct our life cycle tasks, be it making a living or living our lives. Our business activities and social activities are but different renditions of the same life cycle. Indeed, social life and business have always intertwined. All social networking sites on the Internet provide free services in order to build customer base and accumulate resources, and compete on this basis. They all have the potential to provide these accumulated resources for business use. Some have overtly linked up with business (e.g., SecondLife. com, MeetUp.com, and LinkedIn.com), and the full potential awaits innovative exploration while preserving ethicality and privacy.

To elaborate a little more, advertisement was the first and primary means for social networking sites to generate revenue. However, advertisements can compromise users' trust in the host. Therefore, more advanced practices have emerged from synthesizing business interests into the socializing activities themselves, such as embedded B2C and embedded marketing by companies participating in such activities. The latter includes exposure, extracting business intelligence, and experiments with massive multi-player online role playing games (MMORPGs). However, the ultimate business value of social networking sites resides in the customer base and information resources they gather. While traditional businesses gain on customer base and resources through mainly business acquisition, Internet enterprises can practice hyper-networking innovatively to open up more possibilities of doing the same than acquisition. They can also make them sharable and reusable by many, to become potential "utilities" to others from which they can garner business values.

The value of these utilities is clearly tied to the life cycle roles and tasks of individuals: The persons at walled gardens (social networking sites) are the same customers at the businesses that they patronize, and the same knowledge workers whom their companies hire. Thus, the information resources about them from social networking are immediately applicable to all these businesses and employers. The social networks they form within the gardens are similarly relevant to their activities outside. They can use these networks to seek professional and business contacts, as can businesses for marketing and recruiting. The hyper-networking principle uniquely indicates this direction of evolution.

Indeed, business designs in this social networking category all came from providing peer-to-peer tools such as search engine, email and instant messaging, and socializing homepages to persons. Then, they quickly evolved into hyper-networking in a person-centered manner. Particular models tend to be driven by particular networking tools, ranging from personal information production such as blogs, Wikipedia, and personal tasks/resource management, to massive group bonding activities. Social networking and e-commerce soon converged in the realm of gaming (including MMORPGs, as well as gambling), mating, and job hunting. Throughout the evolution, social networking has taught businesses a lot about business: how quickly and with relative ease grassroots value propositions can hyper-network and reach the population — i.e., we the people.

We can conclude that the success of social networking of the Internet community confirmed the basic principles of hyper-networking: First, the Web itself is the walled garden for all to play in it. People can exchange, share, and accumulate virtually any digitized content that each owns, for any life cycle tasks that each faces, regardless of the business nature of these activities. Second, the value of connecting the life cycle tasks of persons and organizations across different roles they play drives hyper-networking. Third, hyper-networking results in accumulation of customers and information resources, allowing for reuse and sharing.

The best example of hyper-networking that involves physical products is perhaps the transformational business designs so successfully undertaken by Apple. This IT hardware vendor provided the world with the iPod, iPhone, iPad, and iCloud, which not only integrated personal digital hardware (PC, cell phone, and PDA) with personal application software (e.g., Apps, digital music and books, and e-commerce sites), but also deployed these new personal tools to proactively enable social networking and personal business transactions across the entire cyberspace. All signs point to an even more prolific future for this line of designs.

In sum, the evolution of e-commerce has exhibited a common denominator to all the innovative practices and business designs that it effects: the person-centered integration along person life cycle roles and tasks by hyper-networking. Hyper-networking uniquely explains the dynamics of the e-commerce field: It swiftly broadens, deepens, and transforms business designs by fluidly connecting customers, providers, and resources across business practices and domains. Finally, successful practices all leveraged open and scalable enterprise information systems, which *use societal cyber-infrastructure to connect customers, providers, and resources along the demand and supply chains for persons and/or enterprises.* In a fundamental way, their open and scalable IS elements have also become a part of the societal cyber-infrastructure for others to use — cases in point are search engines, Web resources, and open source technology.

We summarize the above review into the following principle, which paves the way for IS strategic planning as will be discussed later in this chapter:

The Digital Connections Scaling (DCS) Principle of Hyper-Networking: *Hyper-networking builds on digitizing information resources (e.g., text, music, and video) and connections, scaling them up (accumulating, joining force and member uploading), down (personalization, differentiation, and member downloading), and transformationally (e.g., combining business designs, spaces, and partnering) for persons and organizations, in an approach that integrates life cycle tasks for persons (customers and knowledge workers).*

As such, the results of DCS are a hyper-network, and a hyper-network builds on DCS. The next section presents a formal model for hyper-networks and explains the implications of the model on strategic planning.

2.3 The Hyper-Network Model: The Analytic Properties of Human Value Networks

Analytically, a hyper-network is a network of networks. It represents a connected community in which members can link to each other via multiple types of connection channels in multiple types of networks overlaid on top of one another. The channels could use different mechanisms (ranging from digital devices to social and biological bindings) that tie people together via information or physical exchange. In addition, nodes and their connections may have different significance and relative importance in different layers, and hence the degree of connections may have different meaning from one layer to another. In other words, a hyper-network is a multi-dimensional graph with the possibility of "flavors". Below is an enhanced definition of hyper-network:

Define H(B, N, E, M, R), where

B = the *optional* base network, consisting of N and E to represent the physical domain of H.

N = the set of nodes of the base network (size n), consisting of all members of the H community.

E = the set of edges, defining the feasibility of connections among all nodes of the base network (E is of size $n(n-1)/2$ if any node can connect to any other nodes). E is removed if B is removed.

M = the set of community-common roles available to N (i.e., each node has up to M possibilities of roles), where each common role defines a particular layer (or *color*) of networking out of N and E. M defines the dimensionality of H, and its value may be time-dependent.

R = the $(n \times m)$ behavior matrix where each element is a model governing how the node performs each role. The simplest form for an element of R is a $(n-1)$-vector of probabilities that a node may connect to every other node for a given role. R defines the strength of connections, too. The base network represents the physical or regular foundation of the networked community. It is optional to the hyper-network model if the community has no restrictions on connections — i.e., if E is free and random. In general, the behavioral nature of connections between nodes such as feelings and intensity are functions of the R matrixes involved.

The above definition provides a *three- or higher-dimensional graph*, with *m*-layers of edges connecting the same set of nodes over a foundation. That is, an edge between two nodes of a network may have any number of "colors" signifying different roles or genres of channels of connection. The core properties of hyper-networks (technical details and proofs are provided in Chan and Hsu, 2009, 2010, 2012) are: (1) hyper-networks are pervasive in human networks; (2) they shorten the distance for information exchange among people while expanding the degree of direct linkages for each member; (3) randomly adding new nodes and connections to an existing network is equivalent to creating a new layer on top of the network. Derived from these core properties, it follows that scaling human value networks corresponds to building a hyper-network for the base community of the value cocreation domain. In fact, these expansions are commonplace with social networking sites, as they routinely add new tools, applications, or other provisions for socialization. Clearly, business mergers and B2C partnerships are examples, too.

Furthermore, adding to the above three properties, (4) the overall degree distribution of the hyper-network is different from those of its member single networks. That is, hyper-connecting single networks to form hyper-networks will result in new patterns of degree distributions, regardless of how the member networks originally distribute their degrees among nodes. For instance, hyper-connecting all scale-free (or all random, or all small world) networks can change the pattern for the whole community; and so do hyper-connecting layers of different genres of degree distributions (mixing these three). (See Chan and Hsu, 2012 for details.) Finally, (5) the additional *connection laws for hyper-networking* may be derived from *the roles that humans play in their life cycles and the tasks that these roles bestow on them.* Succinctly, the basic law is to *pursue tasks synergism* for people through, e.g., cross-sharing and multiple-use of resources and connections. It follows that some centrality measures may further reveal the significance of nodes in the community as a whole, away from the usual popularity measures, for example. In this case, some otherwise obscure nodes which do not connect to many other nodes, nor provide long connections, may in fact hyper-connect many layers and hence serve as some wormholes for them. These nodes clearly may play important roles in shortening the average distance of overall connections and integrating human and organization life cycles, and may multiply the effects of other significant nodes.

With the formal model established, we can now analyze the possible contributions of the hyper-networking principle to IS strategic planning.

EXERCISES

1. Why does the ability to perform hyper-networking (i.e., implementing DCS) promise to fundamentally change the landscape of business strategies? (Hint: think of the choices available to businesses.)

2. How do the possibilities of hyper-networking impact the traditional dichotomy such as standardization vs. differentiation? (Hint: think of the unity of interests between them rather than the conflict of interests.)

3. How do search engines, e.g., Google, and social networking sites, e.g., Facebook.com, build up barriers to latecomers and compete? Does the hyper-networking principle explain them?

4. What is the analytic growth rate of accumulation of members and member-carrying resources in a hyper-network?

5. What is the analytic growth rate of the so-called "network effect" (word of mouth) — i.e., the number of interactions between members (lateral connections of members)?

6. What is the analytic growth rate of role-based relationships between members (multi-dimensional permutation of members)?

First, how may a hyper-networking strategy differ from the traditional business strategies? The fundamental reason is actually straightforward: Traditional strategies do not consider the promises of hyper-networking because it was not feasible in their time. The new enterprises on the Internet have the unprecedented choice of comprehensively networking with either or both of their external constituencies and their internal production factors, as some extended enterprises. If they have the choice to hyper-network along either or both of the demand chain and the supply chain, even recursively, while their predecessors did not, then they ought to take advantage of it. They may scale up, down, or transformationally by multi-dimensional inter-connections to pursue particular cocreation efforts and value propositions.

These unprecedented abilities to hyper-network have the potential to break down the traditional premises of strategies, such as the well-known exclusive choices presented in Michael Porter's 2×2 matrix: low cost vs. product uniqueness on the one dimension, and broad vs. narrow business space on the other dimension (Porter, 1998a and 1998b). However, service scaling by hyper-networking can abridge Porter's divisions with relative ease. Data analytics have allowed, e.g., Netflix to provide personalized offerings (accurately recommended movies) in a mass market. Many traditional stores (e.g., Buffalo chicken wings and New York cheese cakes) have also used the Internet to do just that: they sell globally, buy globally, and network customers globally (with blogs and other connections). This small example shows that hyper-networking principles can lead to new strategies of service business design.

The strategies of e-commerce reviewed above are all illustrations of the hyper-networking differences. Taking search engine enterprises and social networking sites for example: These enterprises have the entire Web for their business scope and they accumulate customers and resources from the entire Internet as their core competences (scale up). They compete on striving to personalize their products and attend to their individual customers' needs, leveraging the population-oriented assets that they built to create these personal products and services (scale down). At the same time, they respond, proactively as well as reactively, to the customer needs (business opportunities) revealed by how the customers have used their accumulated resources in performing their tasks in life (the life cycle roles that persons play), to combine or transform their business designs (scale transformationally).

The stories of Yahoo (from a search engine to a retailing portal), Google (from a search engine to an all-encompassing person business provider), Facebook (from social networking to business applications), Apple (from hardware to software for person-centered life cycle needs), and other major new service enterprises are stories of hyper-networking. They developed new business designs by pursuing this "simultaneous engineering": accumulation (scaling up)–personalization (scaling down)–life cycle integration (transformation). This pursuit is a story of multi-dimensional hyper-networking, perhaps in an iterative, spiral expansion process.

In a nutshell, hyper-networking leads to accumulation and facilitates reuse, and thereby lowers costs for new applications. At the same time, digital connections allowed for fluid switching and collection of narrow applications and networks by collaboration and acquisition, giving rise to ever broader scope and business design innovation. This is the hyper-networking advantage that successful Internet enterprises have embraced, regardless of how they frame their business designs — e.g., industrial exchange (Glushko *et al.*, 1999), globally integrated enterprises (Palmisano, 2006), and application services provider (Tao, 2001).

In general, hyper-networking may affect traditional strategies by opening up a new dimension to them. A business may pursue product uniqueness by differentiation going all the way down to reach individuals, and thereby effectively turn any product into service, or value cocreation. Conversely, it may also inflate the pursuit of low cost through the benefits of scaling all the way up to cover the entire population of the domain. These two are two sides of an intertwined whole: accumulating, reusing, and sharing the common requirements, resources, and infrastructure built from the collection of personalization. Rather than being mutually exclusive, these two strategies are mutually supportive.

In the pursuit of hyper-networking, the difference between broad and narrow can naturally vanish, and low cost and product uniqueness can converge, in the simultaneous pursuits of scaling up to the population and down to the individuals. The varying degrees of such pursuit can reveal new types and domains of value cocreation that may lead to transformation — as the next section will show, e-commerce/e-business is such a case.

The analytic properties of hyper-networks determine the analytic promises of new strategies pursuing hyper-networking. Based on the hyper-network model presented above, we recognize this ***methodology*** as a way to hyper-network: ***apply the connection laws*** within and across layers to scale service up, down, and transformationally.

It is worthwhile to note that the methodology follows the unification principle of IS discussed in Chapter 1: aiming at both the traditional service sector and the non-service sectors. The big picture is that hyper-networking opens up the possibility of "humanizing" traditional products by connecting the product's utility, design, and usage/operation to its end customer's individual needs. In fact, we see the notion of Apple's "iCloud" pointing to a high-end vision where the whole Web miniatures into a hand-held square, using cloud computing to provide both information and transactions for the users in the way they need and want. For physical products, humanization could mean mass customization of almost anything for almost anyone, from personalized healthcare and design drugs, all the way to household-based alternative energy, micro smart grid, and even homegrown agriculture. In all these, the mass customization relies on hyper-networking of customers, professionals, and the resources in the pursuit of value cocreation. This broad concept describes a new mode of production that features scaling of human value networks for the whole economy.

The hyper-network connection laws are amenable to implementation by DCS — i.e., use digital means to connect persons for value cocreation throughout their life cycle tasks. Digitization reduces the cycle time and transaction cost of connection, and scaling these connections decreases the marginal cost for new value cocreation. The following *generic hyper-networking strategies* are derived from this DCS methodology:

Strategy 1: Create the Accumulation Effects (maximum growth: linear, $O(n)$)

The first level of human value network scaling is concerned with building up the sheer size of N and the resources that accompany the members (nodes). The connection laws of Scale-Free networks — i.e., the broadly defined preference, or the "rich get richer" dynamism — should guide the accumulation. The proven forms of preference include name recognition, opinion leaders, and other competitive advantages. Thus, building such preferences will be the core of the scaling strategies. We submit that scaling down, or personalization for serving the members' individual life cycle needs and tasks, is a general tool for scaling up; and the early reach of the population in the accumulation will effect advantages in preferences and enable new service business designs. The success stories of Yahoo!, Google, and Facebook all testify to this point. The growth is proportional to the number of nodes, n.

In addition to building preferences, another important form of the accumulation effects is the sharing and re-use of the accumulated resources, customers, and providers. They reduce the learning curves of service systems design and the marginal costs of value cocreation. Many e-commerce models, e.g., Internet Service Provider, Internet Content Provider, and Application Service Provider, have shown this type of benefits. The heavy equipment industry also competes on the basis of fleet (population) information to cocreate value in the operation and/or maintenance of the equipment for their clients. The accumulation effects often become barriers to entry against newcomers, as well as the competitive advantages for these businesses.

Strategy 2: Create the Network Effects (maximum growth: polynomial, $O(n(n-1)/2)$)

The second level of human value network scaling is concerned with building up the (role-based) single layer networks for the hyper-networking community. The connection laws of Small World networks may contribute expressly to this scaling; i.e., cultivating long connections to complement proximity (in all forms) of congregation. Proven ways for growing long connections include providing more chances for exceptions and outliers to happen, which may cut across known boundaries of groupings and domains. Examples include the popular marketing designs of B2C sites clustering their products (e.g., by product attributes or customer attributes) as recommendations to customers; and the clustering of B2C sites at some e-commerce portals (e.g., Amazon.com and Industrial Exchange sites). Larger scale of practices is found in, for example, open source communities, open social networking sites, and the consulting industry. The promotions of Software as a Service (SaaS), Service-Oriented Architecture (SoA), and IBM's on-demand represent some of the typical cases of heavy networking in the consulting industry.

Since the core logic here is two-dimensional networking, the growth is fundamentally proportional to the number of pairs among members. Although the concept of network effects is well-known in the field, the hyper-network model goes beyond to call for promoting multiple value cocreation networks and leverage them along the paths of life cycle roles/tasks integration.

Strategy 3: Create Ecosystem Effects (maximum growth: factorial, O(n!))

The third and highest level of human value network scaling is concerned with the *life cycle tasks* that persons and organizations need to undertake. The connection laws of the hyper-network model drive this proposition. As discussed in Section 2.2, information and transaction portals of e-commerce, such as one-stop traveling and online banking, represent harbingers of this proposition. Similarly, the practices of embedded B2C at Facebook, Google, and Meet.com provide empirical evidence supporting the proposition. Based on the connection laws, hyper-networking of customers, providers, and resources can take place if the service value network uses persons' life cycle roles as roadmaps to pursue the integration of tasks. Person-specific roles and tasks can lead to scaling down, while common tasks and roles can lead to scaling up. Furthermore, integrations may show transformation leading to possible new service business designs. The Small World and Scale-Free connection laws may also guide the pursuit of across layers hyper-networking, such as cultivating long connections between layers and promoting preferences with multiple roles (centrality of the hyper-network).

Conversely, hyper-networking may in turn enhance the effects of proximity and preference on single layers. That is, connections of roles may result in additional possibilities of cascading interactions among all members (customers and providers) in the community. This possibility is revealed by the hyper-network property that multiple layers reduce the average distance between people. Since there are indefinite possibilities for realizing roles, the ecosystem effects "inflate" the possibilities of developing value propositions among persons.

Roles materialize in the hyper-network only when some (role-based) interactions among (any) persons take place. Since each interaction is ordered, its chaining forms a particular ordered sequence;

and the possible number of all interactions is proportional to the permutation of all members in a temporal space of the community — i.e., the maximum growth is factorial on the number of members, as shown above. Technically speaking, roles are sequence-sensitive, or even sequence-dependent; and role-based hyper-networking allows asynchronous interactions. Any formula that imposes a fixed maximum of roles on members, such as N to the power of M, is bound to under-estimate the real richness of the role-based human community.

In sum, the hyper-networking view of human value networks is that, *a human community is an ecosystem of value cocreation based on roles.* Any two persons could generate any number of value-propositions in between them, with any one being the customer in some of them and the provider in the others. Such pairings can then coalesce in the community to form single layer networks pursuing congruent value propositions. By allowing such networks to inter-twine and support each other — i.e., hyper-networking — the community can see continued increasing of value cocreation and decreasing of marginal costs.

At this point, the overarching principle for IS strategic planning becomes evident: supporting the generic strategies of hyper-networking by DCS. That is, the IS and the DCS are two sides of the same coin named hyper-networking; DCS shows the way of hyper-networking, while IS walks the way.

The Information Systems Principle of Hyper-Networking: *Implement the DCS principle of hyper-networking of Section 2.2 in IS — i.e., strategize IS to be the way to implement the DCS. The design of DCS ought to be coupled with that of the IS to guide the latter, and the DCS design should follow the generic strategies of hyper-networking: facilitating the connection laws to pursue accumulation effects, networking effects, and ecosystem effects.*

A *corollary* is to review the traditional strategies (before or outside the hyper-networking concept) to examine how the new concept may enhance or contradict them. Apply the generic strategies in the light of the methodology for hyper-networking and identify the intellectual root causes for the enhancement or the contradiction. Seek modification to the traditional strategy, accordingly. (An example is Porter's 2×2 matrix.) Another *corollary* is to do the same for traditional IS strategies: either add the DCS principle to guide the IS strategies and enhance them, or reconcile them with the DCS requirements. The practices of e-commerce reviewed above are a potent source of benchmarks from which the IS strategic planning can draw references to help turn the hyper-networking generic strategies into particular business visions and IS objectives.

These generic strategies have to be translated into the lexicon of particular enterprises in order to make sense to them and be possibly adopted for IS planning. To do so, they need to be re-articulated in terms of the concepts and terminologies with which the enterprises are familiar. For example, this principle may be presented to the *New York Times* as one of building up its libraries of articles and reader comments and making them a strategic weapon for both marketing and new revenue. The *Times* can turn them into searchable and clustered information resources to support customized delivery (iNews?) to personal and organizational readers; marketing research on readership and possible e-news products; and research for their reporters and external fee-paying users who need better cross-referencing to dig out background/history, leads and contacts. These ideas would actually be no different from the DCS practices that Google and Facebook have done. Turning the table around at the businesses, can they see new light on their trusty, rusty old roads that they beat down daily? They may need any help they can get, and hence why not try the generic strategies presented here?

On this note, we move to IS strategic planning using the generic strategies.

2.4 Strategic Planning for Information Systems: Facilitating Hyper-Networking

The first order of business for planning the IS strategy is, clearly, to set the specific hyper-networking goals for the IS. That is, the generic ideas need to be fleshed out in the reality of the enterprise concerned.

Hsu (2009) identifies a set of guiding principles for contemplating the implementation of DCS in IS, or the generic directions for the planning, as follows:

- **The First Direction of DCS:** Build digital connections to reduce the transaction cost and cycle time of performing life cycle tasks for customers and the enterprise stakeholders.
- **The Second Direction of DCS:** Gain economies of scale on customers, knowledge/resources, and values and value propositions.
- **The Third Direction of DCS:** Develop business design(s) for concurrent integration of applications and application domains along demand and supply chains.
- **The Fourth Direction of DCS:** Become a facilitator of the global knowledge economy through the provisions of DCS to the service sector and non-service sectors (a hyper-networking provider).

These generic strategies provide a context for developing the broadest visions on how to deploy an IS to achieve hyper-networking — i.e., setting the missions for the IS. For this purpose, the following four guidelines help orient the analysis in appropriate directions of planning. Together, they frame the scope of IS strategies and specify the properties required of the particular IS strategic plans for enterprises.

Guideline 1: Concerning accumulation by information systems

A basic method for accumulation is to make enterprise information systems open and scalable, to embed them into persons, organizations, and resources and to make the accumulation available as online assistance to customers and knowledge workers.

Guideline 2: Concerning openness and scalability by cyber-infrastructure

A basic method for making information systems open and scalable is to build them on or connect them to common societal cyber-infrastructure, including all open sources and open technologies, as well as the Internet and the Web.

Guideline 3: Concerning benefits through information systems

A basic form of benefits of scale due to accumulation is the reuse and sharing of common service enterprise information systems for concurrent cocreation of value, which decreases the marginal cost and cycle time of cocreation.

Guideline 4: Concerning hyper-networking by information systems

A basic approach to hyper-networking customers, providers, and resources is to connect the information systems along the demand chain and supply chain, either by integrating the IS elements involved (see next section) or by connecting them.

The following methodology suggests some common ways for particularizing the generic strategies, i.e., turn them into business-specific terms for particular enterprises:

- **The Vision-Driven Approach:** First, develop the vision for hyper-networking of customers, providers, and resources for the particular enterprise concerned. Second, develop the requirements that this vision imposes on IS. And third, define the requirements in terms of IS elements and their connections.
- **The Reality-Driven Approach:** First, identify the problems, opportunities, or requirements facing the enterprise, either for the status-quo or for the to-be business plans. Second, recognize how hyper-networking may facilitate resolving, realizing, and revamping them. Third, apply the vision-driven approach from this point on to plan for the IS elements and connections.
- **The Method-Driven Approach:** The IS field is never accused of lacking consulting firms to provide tools or methods for IS strategic planning. Thus, use them if one prefers. The advice here is to add an additional dimension to all these methods and the visions that they produce — i.e., the hyper-networking possibilities, as discussed in the above sections.

How can we put them to work? The challenge is really to translate the abstract concepts into concrete examples. One should attempt this with an open mind and out-of-the-box thinking.

EXERCISES

1. Can you develop some possibilities of hyper-networking for you as a person, a professional, and a (potential) businessperson? Rank-order them according to desirability.
2. Can you develop some possibilities of hyper-networking for an enterprise with which you are familiar — say, your alma mater? Rank-order them according to value and feasibility.
3. How can a B2C company develop its IT expertise to, possibly, become a solution provider (a vendor, an ASP, or a consulting firm) in its expertise area? Or an ICP?
4. Why should Apple, Microsoft, IBM, AT&T, Sony, and GE have unity of interests in framing a new industry that we call Hyper-Networking Providers?
5. What may be an "iWeb" (in the sense of continuing the evolution of iPad, iCloud...)? What functions may it have to offer?
6. What IS strategies can you think of (in terms of what IS elements to develop and how to connect them either as a single IS or as some system of IS), which will support your visions in the first two exercises?
7. Why not formally formulate an alumni IS of strategic value for your alma mater?

These exercises intend to make a connection to the real world. Please contemplate them in the proactive spirit of establishing relevance for the generic ideas of IS strategic planning discussed above. The questions asked are just some leaders to brain-storming, and any reasonable "answers" to them may help, regardless of whether they appear obvious or arbitrary. In any case, the objective is relevancy: do the new ideas of hyper-networking help orient brain-storming and make IS strategic planning (business innovation by IS) more methodic?

An obvious answer to the first question is to put online one's expertise and experience, accumulated either by one's hobby or from one's professional work, by using one's social networks, professional contacts, and plain Web promotion. The B2C model, ICP model, and even ASP model may be appropriate for this potential business, depending on the nature of the particular skills and resources for sale (or rent). Clearly, there may be a large number of possibilities whose realistic values and feasibility vary greatly. The point here is not the valuation of them, but the recognition of them with the unique help of the hyper-networking concept.

In a similar way, the value of making better value-added connections to alumni should be obvious to a university. A university can play many roles in its graduates' life cycle, as the alumni can in the university's life cycle. Without any further expansion, the university-alumni relationships have already shown that alumni are past customers (students); the sponsors of current and future customers; the employers of products (students); the sponsors of faculty research; the donors; and the potential customers for continuing education. In addition, they help market the university; consult on the design of products (curricula); and facilitate the production (teaching and operation). They may be business partners, too. A university has an intricate demand chain (e.g., the high schools, universities, and companies from which the university recruits students; and the government, business, and other universities to which the university supplies graduates) and supply chain (e.g., the universities and industry from which the university recruits faculty and vendors, and with which it develops joint programs in research and education). Therefore, the possibilities for expansion of relationships can be mind-boggling — and such possibilities are uniquely captured by the concept of hyper-networking customers, providers, and resources along their respective life cycle roles. The concept of a person-centered hyper-networking IS uniquely exposes the technical nature of the hyper-network.

A university can explore collaborative, mutually benefitting relationships with alumni in a variety of forms across its demand chain and supply chain, pursuing role-based integration. Not all these possibilities are practically valuable, of course. Co-teaching some courses with another university, for example, may not be realistic. However, there is nothing wrong with recognizing that these possibilities exist and a powerful IS can help make them a reality. Distance learning shows how IS is an integral part of the university's instructional function. In fact, many hyper-networking ideas may be considered the extensions and expansions of distance learning.

The next three questions continue our discussion in Section 2.2 on the evolution of e-commerce. Simply put, if a B2C company has developed expertise in online retailing IS, and accumulated sufficient IT/IS professionals and other IS elements in this field, then what prevents it from making a profit on other (would-be) B2C companies from this expertise and resources? What prevents an author from selling novels or research papers on the Web? What inherent reasons are there that prohibit a significant publisher from expanding its Web bookstore, to carry not only its own publications but also everybody else's, just like other online bookstores have done?

Why do Apple, Microsoft, IBM, AT&T, Sony, and GE all have potential unity of interests among them? The explanation is found in the notion of the whole Web being a hyper-network and an IS (or system of IS): They each provide a major class of IS elements for the whole Web, and hence meeting the needs of hyper-networking for all people favors their collaboration, especially on the inter-operation of their IS elements with each other. Sony is included here to show the provision of information contents (e.g., the population of movies), and GE to show the connections to manufactured products in all sectors of the economy. In this vision, there will be tremendous needs for connection providers, to make the wholeness of the Web work.

We provide some general thoughts on the last three questions, but otherwise leave them open to the reader. A possible scenario is provided at the beginning of Chapter 3. We wish to point out, however, that the notion of iWeb is clearly defined when one fleshes out the definition of its functions and provisions (e.g., apps); which in turn is defined by how one sees the life cycle roles and tasks of people and enterprises. Thus, the key to answering these three questions is to contemplate on exactly what would the IS in question look like in the way of IS elements and connections. These functions and provisions, naturally, will define what should be required of the IS in all the enterprises underlying iWeb. Since an integrated IS for the whole Web is obviously unrealistic, we ought to frame the Web IS as systems of IS that comprise all members of the Web community. On this note, we turn to illustrate the hyper-network concepts more, next.

Please note that the ecosystem concept implies that the divides between any e-commerce business designs and spaces may be an illusion. All designs may ultimately be fused in a common portal of cyberspace. At present, many small businesses sell at both eBay and their own B2C sites; but are there any inherent reasons that perpetuate this separation? Merging these business designs can benefit from the unity of interests across life cycle tasks, such as a common habitat for all customers, person or company. Could Apple Store, for instance, be developed into some person-centered ecosystem of applications along these lines? After all, we the people do see the Internet as one habitat and would welcome a one-stop portal to facilitate this oneness.

To probe further, since any person can become a service provider and engage in B2C or ICP via social networking, the convergence of information portals, transaction portals, and any other forms of collective or collaborative models may get deepened and reach ultimately to the level of individuals. This is why the fluid realignment of business designs would likely lead to a dedicated habitat for people and enterprises to conduct their life cycle tasks. Current trends for the further development of transaction portals (such as financial processing of incomes, payments, and taxation at online banking), traveling, and person-to-person publication are some of the more visible examples. Could the next iPad be based on habitat hyper-networking (an "iHab" or "iWeb")? Both differentiation (on services) and accumulation and standardization (on resources) would occur simultaneously at such a habitat.

The notion of hyper-networking provider may be closer to reality than it appears. For example, such IT hardware vendors as IBM, Dell and Microsoft, and Cisco are arguably seeking to become global Internet/cloud computing providers in their traditional space and new domains. Consistent to the logic of scaling up (managing the population), down (personalization), and transformationally (integration), they have been reinventing their product designs and business models; and there is nothing to prevent them from providing enterprising apps of particular life cycle roles and tasks for all types of users, as Apple has done for personal apps. Would computers become a free-of-charge "set box" offered to the clients of such providers?

In a similar way, large B2Cs have been offering (limited) P2P functions to customers. Not only can they do more to build up customer base, small B2Cs can play the same game, too, by joining forces and leveraging what the ISPs have to offer. The resultant potential for hyper-networking can contribute beyond marketing and facilitate cocreation of value. Therefore, a full circle of connection from Internet Commerce to Enterprising habitat may be realized, where people hyper-network among themselves as customer, provider, and resource, at the level of individual life cycle tasks. As such, businesses would scramble to provide on-demand hyper-networking to fulfill individual roles and tasks.

Again, central to all the above analyses is the concept of life cycle roles and tasks. One may list the top roles and role-based tasks for oneself, and list the services or activities required in them. One may then ask what enterprises provide them, and what is the role of the Internet? What IS applications are involved in all these? Are there any common denominators or possible links between any of them? Are there any ways to develop connections among them? What new business designs may provide hyper-networking and enable person-centered differentiation of products and services? They may come by grouping tasks for people and organizations, and thereby enjoy the benefits of accumulating and reusing resources. They may also come from the integration of tasks along and across life cycles for people and enterprises. Can the reader provide any examples?

The consummation of the IS strategic planning process is the particularization of the IS strategies, in the form of specific IS plans which can be evaluated for feasibility (including cost-effectiveness) and be fleshed out into action plans by an IS design process. The basic logic of such a particularization process is evident, as will be formulated in the next chapter. However, the specific actions of any IS plan would have to be dependent on the details of individual cases.

The following basic IS development principle helps transition our discussion from IS strategies to IS master plans:

The Societal Cyber-Infrastructure Principle of Information System Design: *Embed the IS elements into the societal cyber-infrastructure on which the IS is built, to the extent practical, to achieve maximum sustainability — i.e., the ability to connect and evolve, as shown in openness and scalability, for hyper-networking. As such, the IS strives to incorporate the Web elements (e.g., the use of search engines, Web sites, and open source resources) as its elements, and avail its elements on the Web to hyper-network with prospect stakeholders.*

The best proof of this principle is e-Commerce: the whole story of e-Commerce is one of embedding IS into the societal cyber-infrastructure that we call the Internet and the Web, rather than using proprietary networks. One can argue that much of the B2B ideas had been tried before on third party value-added networks; however, their success pales when compared to B2B on the Internet (see Section 3.2 of Chapter 3 for an example). As for B2C, the whole idea would be laughable if the customers did not have free, open, and scalable access to the retailers, as the Internet afforded them. Therefore, the embedment in societal cyber-infrastructure is really a pivotal, signature aspect of the new IS, and this book recognizes it as such. This principle uniquely distinguishes the connectionist definition of IS and its design science from any others in the IS field (including, e.g., Yourdon, 1989; DeLone and McLean, 2004).

The next chapter continues the above discussion and addresses the design of IS for supporting innovation by hyper-networking. To the extent that any person can conduct business on the Internet, the design framework is relevant to both personal and enterprise IS.

Chapter 3

Development of Information System Master Plans: Identify the Optimal Roadmap to Connecting People and Resources According to the Mission

Once the particular mission of the IS is determined, the next task is to design the overall connection logic for people and resources. This design may be referred to as IS engineering, or the optimization of the analytic structure (e.g., sequential workflows or concurrent processes) of the enterprise IS. The principles and guidelines of the previous two chapters are developed into models of IS engineering to start the development process for the IS. In essence, the design at this stage is focused on the formulation of the scope of all IS elements and their connection strategies. This scope will provide the sound foundation for the ensuing systems analysis which determines the specific IS elements (see Chapter 4). Scientific methods such as the analysis for *digitization, simplification, and concurrent processing* will help guide the design. At this point, construction details such as hardware and software specifications should be suppressed from the investigation, leaving only the total system logic for IS engineering. In other words, the design is targeted on developing *a master plan for the IS* which leads the formal logical and physical designs of the system. This chapter presents the IS engineering methods. In addition, it extends the standard IS design concepts to include societal cyber-infrastructure, and shows how IS can support society-wide service enterprises in a knowledge economy.

3.1 Information System Master Planning for Sustainable Design: A Design Scenario and a Methodology

The previous two chapters have reduced the broad concept of IS (human value networks) to general principles of IS strategic planning. This chapter further reduces the general principles to more specific models of IS engineering. To help the analysis, we adopt a "thought example" to show a design scenario for IS planning. As suggested in Section 2.4 of Chapter 2, one may apply the general IS strategy to conceive an innovative alumni IS, for turning the alumni community into a human value network powered by the university. Simply put, one may envision the alumni to permanently leverage the university, along with all its graduates, as their home base to facilitate their life cycle tasks; and the university does the same on alumni.

Suppose the reader is the IS strategic planner who has crafted out a specific mission for such an alumnus IS and would like to propose it to his/her alma mater. The basic idea is to cultivate and leverage a mutually beneficial life-long active and engaging relationship between the students and the university. The alumnus life cycle tasks may include the following: a new graduate who looks for a job; a matured professional who seeks networking; a life-long learner who takes executive classes; a prospect proprietor who explores business collaboration; an employer who hires promising new graduates; a parent who sends kids back to the alma mater; a buyer who scouts for new technologies and knowledge; an advocate who sponsors new research or new education programs; a philanthropist who donates to higher education; and a mellow senior who reconnects with old classmates and younger days... Please call the proposed IS "iAlma".

Why bother with iAlma? What would it look like? What IS elements should it have? How can it connect to the worldwide alumni community and be linked to the existing IS in the university? Should iAlma be a single system or a system of university systems? How can one optimally scope out its IS elements and define their connections, so as to reduce its transaction costs and cycle times both for the users and for the IS itself? How can one make iAlma easy to grow, change, and transform — i.e., sustainable? Questions like these define Information System Engineering for iAlma, and their answers constitute the master plan for the IS.

The most intriguing potential of this idea may be its potential for evolution: self-promotion of the most prolific relationships and self-identification of opinion leaders and paths of hyper-networking (the "value wormholes"). Both sides of the system, the university and the alumni, may cultivate benefits from the *usage patterns* and develop new applications to further propel hyper-networking. Ultimately, the opinion leaders and value wormholes could bear on both sides and *make the alumni community a human value network* for both the university and the alumni. The university would acquire new resources and create new services for the society, and the alumni would enrich their private and professional lives. Network-scientific analysis of the usage patterns of iAlma would help this evolution.

For illustration purposes, this chapter briefly describes the obvious IS elements and alternative connection strategies, whose choice determines whether iAlma would be a single integrated IS, or a system of separate IS. The first class of elements, People, is the most obvious to see: just use a mirror. However, to connect the people to the system for their daily use, it makes sense to consider creating user interface as smart phone apps, in addition to the usual Web homepages. The Process (software programs and analytics) class of elements for iAlma includes three basic genres: users' access to resources, execution of tasks, and system management tools. The first genre, users' access to resources, may include a search engine, Web and GUI (graphical user interface) facility, and database query language (e.g., SQL) and analytics, as well as iAlma-specific user interface. The second genre, application programs to execute life cycle tasks for alumni, may be conceived as an iAlma apps store, either embedded ubiquitously in the user interface or presented as explicit provisions (e.g., menus) for the users to choose and enact. The third genre, system management tools, provides for performance, security, and integrity of iAlma, as well as its maintenance with respect to its connections to other IS (e.g., transferring of data between systems to assure currency of information).

The connection laws of the iAlma hyper-network need to be planned, as discussed in Chapter 1, in order to guide the selection of possible life cycle tasks to support. In other words, the iAlma master plan needs to identify the most worthy applications to develop first, and the paths of hyper-networking provide an objective analysis to achieve this purpose. For example, survey of the alumni might place job hunting and continuing education by distance learning on top of the candidate list. In this case, the iAlma apps may develop some portal for alumni to network with it, such as posting job opportunities and updating professional contacts. It may also feature connections to certain regular university IS functions (catalog, registration, and degree progress report) and external Web sites (weather, news, and travel) that support continuing education. The small world properties may lead to design of portals for particular classes, professions, or even companies; and clustering of applications for recruitment, such as offering summer internships, authenticating students' credentials (e.g., courses and certificates), and searching for faculty and alumni who possess certain expertise or professional experience. Advanced applications such as extracting knowledge from the repository of university research may be developed to serve as long connections between clusters of continuing education, recruitment, and funding/sponsorship. The design may deliberately solicit hyper-networking by providing a facility to enable the alumni to contribute their own apps to iAlma.

These applications would naturally expose the need for Information Resources, including extensions for university IS such as a searchable repository of research results and advanced online library abstracts system. In a similar way, the vision of supporting job hunting and placement throughout the alumni's career may require changes to the traditional education records. For example, courses may have to be recorded not only as the units of education pertaining to degree programs, as the traditional view holds, but also as professional skills that satisfy personnel requirements in industry. Thus, iAlma may impose additional attributes and summary data of courses as new IS elements, along with flexible applications developed to allow the users' search for course data by professional skills and career requirements.

Generally speaking, the Information Resources class of IS elements represents the information requirements of iAlma. At the minimum, it would encompass student database, alumni database, courses, research projects, library, faculty, and companies. A number of common entities, relationships, and knowledge objects cut across these basic information resources, which tend to reside in different systems of a university. One extreme of the possible connection designs for iAlma to link these disparate information resources is to integrate them all in a single database. The resulting iAlma will be a single integrated IS. Another extreme would be to inter-operate these different systems by data interchange among database management systems (DBMSs), such as using "tunneling" software at the level of application software. The so-called tunneling may be a design of data warehouse which downloads select data in batch mode (non-real time) from the production databases in the university's real-time processes. In this case, iAlma would be a system of IS featuring the specific tunneling software. In-between designs are also possible, ranging from federated databases, data warehouses, and more — see Chapter 5 for an overview of these classes of technology.

The last two classes of IS elements, Computing and Infrastructure, are a function of the connection strategies chosen for iAlma. Cost-benefit analysis would help determine the optimal selection. IS engineering principles including digitization, simplification, and concurrent access and execution (see Chapter 1) can also help the analysis and design of the connection strategies. The core of computing and infrastructure requirements is evident, since the system would have to adopt the IS principle of using societal cyber-infrastructure in order to reach its users (alumni), who are presumably distributed everywhere in the world. Mobile personal communication devices, especially smart phones, are also clearly preferred. Specific details would have to come from technical analysis of the system requirements.

Now, we are ready to review the connectionist IS engineering principles.

EXERCISES

1. Can you outline a master plan for iAlma, including its mission and basic IS elements?

2. What are the unique *design* concepts in the IS principles presented in Chapters 1 and 2? What is their core newness (defining characteristics) *vis-a-vis* any IS that you know?

3. How does the concept of person-centered IS lead to the notion of integrating life cycle tasks and the vision of one-of-a-kind virtual configuration (user interface) of the IS (that the person uses to perform his/her life cycle tasks)?

4. Other than the new design concepts, the hyper-networking IS embraces the same generic IS engineering principles as the IS field does. Can you summarize a brief set of such principles from what you know of the field and/or the discussion thus far in this book?

5. Can you suggest a step-by-step methodology for implementing the above principles and/or for developing an IS master plan?

6. For IS engineering, how does the concept of simplification differ from that of integration? How are they similar?

7. How does the traditional notion of concurrent tasks (value creation) encompass that of collaboration (value cocreation)?

8. How can we "embed" an IS into the Web (making it part of the Web), and why?

The connectionist definition of IS presents some uncompromising requirements on IS engineering, compared to other results in the field. The basic logic is rather straightforward: an IS has to hyper-network people and resources to perform life cycle tasks (value creation); and hence has to be person-centered in design. Yet, life cycle tasks are based on roles in life, which are intertwined and evolve constantly; and hence the IS has to be designed to evolve and connect with others (e.g., system of IS). The best way, in terms of values (transaction cost and cycle time), for IS to extend and expand is once again to leverage societal cyber-infrastructure; and hence IS should best be constructed by using open source software and open source technologies. For example, use the IS to use the Web, and use the Web to use the IS — i.e., embedding the IS into the Web. Thus, the basic, unique connectionist IS design concepts are *person-centered, life cycle role-based (both private and career-related), and societal cyber-infrastructure assisted*, as illustrated by iAlma. Out of the trio, the most straightforward is the last one. Cloud computing is a proof of this principle; and so are all practices of e-commerce and digital social networking as discussed in Chapter 2. These design concepts should be explicitly reflected in the specific IS mission and engineering.

These design concepts also lead to this technical requirement: making the IS capable of one-of-a-kind *virtual re-configuration* to respond to the one-of-a-kind personal tasks. That is, the IS should have the ability to fully employ its IS elements on demand, to respond to any new requests, and it should embark on extensions and expansions only when it does not possess all the necessary IS elements. Technically speaking, this virtual configuration may be as simple as providing ad hoc personal apps, which could be accomplished by coupling the database technology (see Chapter 5) with re-programmable application software. These apps could come from the users especially if sufficiently mobile objects or Web services are made readily available to them, as well as be developed by the IS professionals.

The fourth question demands a brief recap of the design concepts from the IS principles presented above. Here, these design concepts are integrated with the previous results in the field and presented as *IS engineering principles*, or basic guidelines for determining and optimizing the IS elements and their connections:

- Apply the principles of digitization; simplification and/or integration; and concurrent access and execution to basic user interfaces, processes, and information resources, and thereby identify the IS elements and the basic connections required.
- Seek additional connections of IS elements that will promote the accumulation, reuse and sharing of these IS elements.
- Develop additional application programs to facilitate DCS; recognize the required user interfaces, processes, and information resources for these DCS applications; and prioritize them in accordance with the connection laws.
- Identify the appropriate open sources and open source technology for the IS; and maximize the possibility of coding in open source languages, objects, and databases.

- Explore the opportunities for connecting the IS as system of IS.
- Employ societal cyber-infrastructure for computing and infrastructure, wherever possible.

Now, this book is ready to suggest a step-by-step methodology for developing a master plan for an IS such as the iAlma. Its logic is driven by the determination of IS elements, as presented below:

Elements-Oriented Methodology for IS Master Planning

1. First, develop the specific mission for the IS from a strategic planning endeavor (see Chapter 2). Make maximum exploration of the opportunities of person-centered, life cycle role-based, and societal cyber-infrastructure-assisted design in the mission.
2. Determine the basic IS elements that the mission requires and implies. Employ proven structured tools and methods from the industry as appropriate.
3. Determine the connection strategies for the IS elements. Performance, cost-benefit analysis, and technical practicality will collectively discriminate alternative approaches.
4. Apply the above IS engineering principles to optimize the IS elements and their connections, including the possible connections to other IS in a system-of-IS manner. Perform this task iteratively, if necessary. Use the roadmap in the next section to guide the progressive application of IS engineering principles.
5. Finalize and document the IS elements and connections as a master plan for the IS, with sufficient details to allow ensuing IS analysis and design.

Simplification and integration are two important principles for enterprise engineering in general, as discussed in the evolution of manufacturing (see Section 1.4 of Chapter 1). They are particularly important for IS engineering since IT makes them easier to apply. Although closely related, these two concepts are not synonyms. Simplification can refer to redesign of a "unit process" which may not be divisible any further in practice; and yet integration assumes the existence of multiple such unit processes. However, integration does imply simplification of the multiplex of processes, such as the redesign of the connections. In this sense, integration includes consolidation, synthesis, and fusion. An example of simplification is the elimination of typists from office workflows and value chains by equipping every office worker with word processing. The same is also seen in the story of traditional bookstores vs. online bookstores. Such simplifications often take place as a result of automation, or digitization. Integration, on the other hand, may manifest itself in a one-stop portal which optimizes the commonality of all tasks for the workflows or value chains, with or without redesigning of these tasks. Again, digitization often precedes integration since it helps make the latter feasible.

Concurrency in computing sense refers traditionally to concurrent processing, or the simultaneous access to resources by multiple users and simultaneous execution of multiple tasks on the computer. However, concurrent engineering (see Section 1.4 of Chapter 1) extends this concept to a much broader context: collaboration, such as collaboration among design engineers (across parallel CADs) and/ or between design engineers and manufacturing engineers (CADs and CIM). Clearly, a fundamental difference between these two interpretations is the multiplex of systems: concurrent processing requires only one computing system, whereas concurrent engineering requires more than one. We further extend this concept here to refer to value cocreation between any two or more persons, by virtue of the hyper-networking IS. Thus, concurrency here includes concurrent processing on single systems, on multiplex of systems, and most importantly, on the convergence of multiple value creations by a multiplex of people. This interpretation further illuminates the connectionist definition of IS and its design science.

The last question, embedding IS into societal cyber-structure, reflects the iAlma goal of facilitating alumni to contribute their own apps; which in turn represents the intriguing vision of tapping into the resources both inside and outside of the university to grow iAlma. Embedding here means a two-way interaction: the IS employs the open source software, open source technologies, and other public domain IS elements including the Internet itself as a part of its own;

and the IS deploys itself as a part of them — such as consolidating its (select) Process-class resources into an open process library (with certain restrictions if necessary) and putting it on the Web for all to use. While the reason for doing the first, employing open resources, may be cost-related, the reason for the second, deploying to the open resources, is hyper-networking of stakeholders, including alumni, potential customers (e.g., students, employers, and sponsors), and faculty and staff. In a broader sense, building open resources is beneficial to the IS community itself. In essence, the community would be applying the e-commerce practice of Web Services (see Section 2.2 of Chapter 2) to itself, with or without fees, for members to contribute solutions and generic software objects to the open resources, and draw from them.

Next, we elaborate further on the elements-oriented methodology and then analyze IS embedment.

3.2 The Elements-Oriented Methodology: A Roadmap

An IS can be custom designed and developed by using only general purpose methods and tools. In this case, the generic methodology presented here can be applied in its own light, for guiding IS master planning. However, one may also use industrial packages to do the job. The methodology still holds relevancy in this case. To establish the elements-oriented methodology, this chapter now applies it as a valuable reference point to industrial IS planning methods.

3.2.1 *Linkage to Common Methods in the Field*

The IS field is rich in IS design methods and techniques. For strategic planning, the consulting industry has developed proprietary tools to formulate business strategies and transform them into IS solutions. A well-known example is the Common Business Modeling (CBM) approach by IBM. This approach provides for self-reliant and self-contained methodology for IS development. To begin with, IBM would develop some meta-models, or industrial reference models such as the Key Performance Indicators (KPI), for each and every industry from which they recruit clients. The meta-models would particularize for individual clients into the client-specific IS mission. Ensuing modeling work would follow the CBM methodology to create the high-level component business models, simulation and analytic models, and IT implementation models for the proposed IS. Needless to say, the accumulated CBM results from the client base could be deployed as a starting point for the development of the new CBM for the particular client.

The elements-oriented methodology can add to the CBM approach. The conceptual connection between these two is the fact that the CBM results may be readily classified into the IS elements defined in Section 1.1 of Chapter 1. With this conceptual connection, the IS engineering principles are readily applicable to the CBM methodology, too. For example, they may add more dynamism to the otherwise static reference models (e.g., to look proactively for DCS opportunities and innovate by the IS) and broaden the scope of CBM. In particular, Step 4 may be considered as a unique enhancement to the CBM methodology.

Next to strategic planning, a second common theme in the field is designing IS from the perspective of business processes, or process modeling. This approach would first identify and analyze these processes, then re-engineer them if so desired, and finally determine their processing logics to allow for codification. Such process modeling methods tend to be followed by database design and constitute a two-stage process of IS analysis and design. The most venerable and still representative methods include Data Flow Diagrams (DFD) and Structured Analysis and Design Techniques (SADT/IDEF). In essence, these methods are comparable and commonly focus on the identification of process-level activities to determine the IS elements required. This book presents the DFD method in the next chapter, Chapter 4, as an integral part of the connectionist design science that follows the master plan.

The DFD and other process-oriented methods derive the People class and the Information Resources class of IS elements from processes. In contrast, the field also has different design methods that focus primarily on Information Resources to develop data models for database designs. Major examples include the Object-Oriented (O-O) modeling methods (including the Unified Modeling Language, or UML; the OMG/Express Language; and others) and the Entity-Relationship-Attribute (ERA) modeling methods. Incidentally, the CBM results are represented in UML, as objects that connect vertically by aggregation/specialization, and horizontally by relationships. The Process-class IS elements are typically determined in these data models as views and/or application programs of the resulting database designs (e.g., the O-O design or the ERA design). In Chapter 6 this book introduces the O-O and ERA methods, and combines them into a Two-Stage Entity-Relationship (TSER) method that encompasses both the analysis for processes and the design for data models.

The following three models of IS engineering represent a roadmap to execute Step 2 (determination) and Step 4 (optimization) of the elements-oriented methodology.

3.2.2 *The Model of Digitization: Digitizing IS Elements and Embedding Them into Societal Cyber-Infrastructure (the Basis for Hyper-Networking)*

Designing IS for hyper-networking starts with digitization of IS elements, including both the *representation* of elements (for, e.g., persons and physical production factors) and the elements themselves (e.g., shared information resources, IT, and institutions). The digitization must allow for *element-to-element connection either within the same type or between types across domains*, as called for by the connectionist IS design methodology.

The scope of digitization follows the determination of the IS elements required, of course, if one employs a top-down strategic planning approach for the IS. However, in a bottom-up problem-driven manner, the scope may be identified from applying this basic logic: Recognize the *paper trails* (paper workflows and workflows that require paper documents), *file trails* (workflows that require multiple isolated, perhaps even duplicated files), and *decision trails* (workflows that require multiple, perhaps even overlapped chains of decision makers) of the enterprise concerned. Then, the planning could proceed to identify barriers to the connection of business processes for new and old value propositions; and build/expand IS elements to simplify the trails and remove the barriers by digital connections. A "usual suspect" of the barriers, or a proven common candidate for digitization, is the paper-based data resources and manual processes in an enterprise. Their digitization often can inspire ensuing, far-reaching applications (e.g., data integration) beyond what anyone can expect without seeing the conversion.

These elements should be shared and reused for as many processes as possible. If the digitization includes only proprietary elements and employs only proprietary design and technology, then the resultant IS will be completely proprietary, too, and suffers presumably in its openness and scalability. On the other hand, if it is completely embedded using exclusively open source technology, then the IS may become completely sustainable. Any combination in the middle is evidently possible. In any case, the design will be characterized in terms of the element-by-element embedment and connection, within or across the enterprise domain and the public domain. As a rule of thumb, it may always be advantageous to use open source technology to digitize IS elements, when possible, even when these elements are completely proprietary and for internal use only. Furthermore, it may also be advantageous to design process software programs as open source objects, and form an open source community from the stakeholders of the system, including end users and IS professionals, to use them.

3.2.3 The Model of Enterprise Transformation: Hyper-Networking IS Elements Across the Enterprise, to Accumulate, Re-use, and Share Them for Person-Centered Tasks Integration

The milestone following digitization is naturally turning the digitized IS elements into a hyper-networking IS for the enterprise concerned. Thus, this model applies the DCS model to an enterprise to renovate or even transform it as a human value network — i.e., it innovates with a scope limited to the enterprise itself, for now.

The Objective: Reduce the transaction cost and the cycle time of value creation for the whole enterprise — for the customers and knowledge workers performing their jobs, and for their collaboration in new and old value propositions.

The Means/Decision Variables: the mission, the IS elements and their connections required, and the optimization for hyper-networking. The guidelines for the optimization are the connectionist IS design concepts and the IS engineering principles. In addition, for building up the enterprise, special attention should be placed on the accumulation and sharing of resources.

Elaborated IS Engineering Principles (enterprise engineering):

— Implement the digitization model (the first milestone of the roadmap).

— Identify limitations of the digitization (including the means of connection), e.g., exposing current and potential paper trails, file trails, and decision trails by *experimenting with new value propositions for life cycle tasks*, such as new simplifying or integrating processes for performing these tasks — i.e., identify what better ways there are if the digitization goes further.

— Apply the DCS propositions to help discover innovative connections of IS elements and guide for removal of the above limitations, and reduce these ideas to connections of IS elements.

— Accumulate (homogeneous) IS elements by digital connections of the like types, to allow them to be used as common service resources (e.g., customer pools, knowledge worker teams, and information repositories) in different service cocreation.

— Develop embedded or automated capabilities in real-time analytics and data processing to enhance the performance of persons and machines in the enterprise, using societal cyber-infrastructure as much as possible.

— Develop either global or peer-to-peer administration capability to support sharing of digital resources among distributed persons and machines, and enable collaboration.

— Simplify enterprise processes by using the hyper-networking IS (through sharing resources and consolidating sub-tasks and/or sharing results).

— Convert sequential enterprise processes into concurrent by using the hyper-networking IS (through sharing resources and interweaving sub-tasks and/or sharing resources).

— Implement the concepts of teams and virtual organizations, the flexible machinery, and the automated control systems by the IS, to make the enterprise and its facilities more agile.

— Use new business designs on the Web as reference points to seek out new paradigms of conducting business by the hyper-networking IS. For example, the B2E/B2M enterprise portal and Internet Enterprising models may be employed as the analogy to guide the innovation of the IS elements, connections, and designs.

— Seek out the possibility of *using social networking as a collaboration tool* to facilitate value cocreation for both customers and knowledge workers.

— Maximize the use of societal cyber-infrastructure throughout the IS for hyper-networking.

— Deliver the services of the system using personalized open source technology. Web-based user interface should be deployed fully, coupled with possible smart phone apps. The system should be represented as some personable Web pages and be incorporated into the enterprise portal (intranet). Furthermore, all IS of the enterprise should be connected in this way on the intranet to make the community a system of IS for the whole enterprise.

Constraints: availability of the open, scalable, and re-configurable technologies; industrial standards for inter-operation; and costs.

A simple industrial case is depicted in Figure 3.1 to help illuminate the model and its application for enterprise engineering. The story is straightforward (first reported in *Harvard Business Review*): a commercial bank tries to streamline its commercial loan approval process and thereby reduce the cycle time (from application to notification of approval) from an average of a week to within a few hours. The "as is" system involves five isolated "islands of automation", from

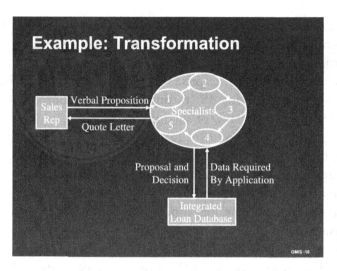

Figure 3.1: Enterprise transformation: The commercial loan example of IS engineering.

the submission of the proposals to digital formulation, to interest rates checking, to credential checking, to final decision, and finally to notification. Each of these islands is in and of itself an IS pertaining to the overall workflow system. Such a situation is commonplace in many enterprises. This particular workflow reflects a file trail and a decision trail that requires further integration. The bank's position in our IS planning roadmap is past the digitization stage but has not yet reached enterprise transformation. Thus, the objective of innovation here is to do just this: transformation by integration.

A "low hanging fruit" of innovation would be to improve each process and each IS island. However, the enterprise transformation model calls for more. Thus, a thorough review would reveal that the information resources of these IS islands could be integrated into an enterprise database, with all processes re-engineered to be applications of the database. This design provides concurrent processing of different proposals. In theory, there are two ways to implement the integration: retool the previous process-specific specialists into generalists who conduct all processes of the entire workflow; or, alternatively, enable these specialists to continue using their previous application programs and doing their previous jobs, with the support of the new database. Both of them would unleash the power of data-bases, but only the second would showcase the unique properties of full-fledged enterprise class database technology. The original case reported followed the first approach.

While the first way is obvious to any IS professional, the second requires deliberate exploration of the virtual configuration capability that the database technology provides. This capability includes the provision of views to connect to the input-output designs (of the previous application programs) in the process-oriented IS islands; and the programming facility that connects the database language to the previous software environments in the islands (e.g., embedded SQL). Figure 3.1 depicts the generalist approach in the big circle, and the specialist approach in the small circles inside it. The database integrates all files from the previous IS islands. In the second approach, the data (e.g., digital proposals) would be modified slightly, such as including additional flags to indicate the progress of proposals in the workflow and to alert the specialists to follow the progress, under concurrent processing. Finally, the societal cyber-infrastructure concept exposes one more possible innovation: putting the loan approval process on the Web to connect directly to the customers. At the minimum, the customers can apply online, track the application online, and receive notification of decision online.

However, the enterprise transformation model points to more possibilities. The customers may get online assistance through embedded analytics in the IS to help them choose among loan products and formulate the final application. In fact, immersing the loan process into the Web leads ultimately to embedding the IS into the Web. With this innovation on IS, the bank could design its own transforming B2C practices to provide better services to the customers and develop more comprehensive business relationships with them. Such an IS would be beneficial for gaining access to prospective customers and accumulating information on them. The person-centered design would become evident once the IS is considered from the customer side.

Many banks have already moved along this line. A consumer loan application may get preliminary approval during the online application right on the spot, enabled by embedded decision logics. This is a major step toward making the embedment principle a standard practice of IS. However, the road of innovation does not end here. Should the information resources of the loan IS be shared with other banking processes? Should value-added smartphone apps be added to the IS? Does the bank have other islands of IS that should be connected? We expect to see the principles of person-centered, life cycle task-based, and societal cyber-infrastructure-assisted IS propagating to all other banking processes.

The commercial loan example of Figure 3.1 in fact represents a wide range of administrative workflows found in virtually any type of enterprises. Examples include personnel management (recruitment, appraisal, and assignment), internal control auditing, engineering change proposals, and much more. These systems probably can all subscribe to the same general logic discussed above — i.e., employing an integrative database to manage these workflow processes and thereby reduce the cycle time (see, e.g., Cho and Hsu, 2005).

Coming back to the iAlma design scenario, enterprise transformation would mean the simplification and integration of all internal processes in the university that have bearing on the new vision. As in the commercial loan case, the focus of this transformation would be on the connection of information resources. The iAlma-specific processes required would support the connection and draw data from the integrated information resources. Value-added apps on the smartphone would invoke person-centered virtual configuration of the databases. To conclude for the model of enterprise transformation, we wish to point out that any enterprise could build an enterprise "portal" which connects all its IS, and a loose system of IS would result. This relatively easy and cost-effective practice often sparks serendipity on stakeholders.

3.2.4 *The Model of Enterprise Collaboration: Hyper-Networking IS Elements Across the Extended Enterprises for Person-Centered Tasks Integration*

The third milestone extends intra-enterprise hyper-networking to inter-enterprise hyper-networking, by connecting the IS elements in different enterprises along the demand chain and/or the supply chain, according to the integrative views of the extended enterprise. Or, simply put: apply the DCS model across the extended enterprise. As is the case for the model of enterprise transformation, the challenge is how to connect the IS elements within homogeneous classes or across heterogeneous classes. The connections aim, as before, at accumulating resources for sharing in (concurrent) value creations to reduce transaction cost and cycle time, but this time by using primarily societal cyber-infrastructure. One could argue that the fundamental difference between an enterprise and an extended enterprise is proprietary control. Therefore, the model of enterprise collaboration is really the transformation of extended enterprises when proprietary control is removed from the concept. For supply chains and demand chains, proprietary controls may also extend to the prime's influence or even mandate on its suppliers, ranging from sheer bargaining powers to stock-holding and some other long-term bonding arrangements.

The Objective: Reduce the transaction cost and the cycle time of value creation for the whole community of collaborating enterprises — for the customers and knowledge workers performing their jobs for the extended enterprise, and for their collaboration in new and old value propositions in the community.

The Means/Decision Variables: the mission, the IS elements and their connections required, and the optimization for inter-enterprise hyper-networking. The guidelines for the optimization are the connectionist IS design concepts and the IS engineering principles. In addition, for building up the extended enterprise, special attention should be placed on the accumulation and sharing of resources throughout the community and the development of collaboration tools. These tools should be built primarily on societal cyber-infrastructure and be embedded into the IS. The IS design should follow a paradigm of (loose) federation, i.e., pursuing the concept of system of IS, across the domain of the extended enterprise.

Elaborated IS Design Principles (enterprise engineering):

— Implement the digitization model (first milestone) for all participating enterprises; and implement the transformation model (second milestone) as much as possible to make participant enterprise IS consistent with the requirements of hyper-networking.

— Identify limitations of the digitization and transformation with respect to collaboration in the extended enterprise, e.g., exposing current and potential paper trails, file trails, and decision trails *across enterprises* by experimenting with new value propositions for life cycle tasks that draw resources from the extended enterprise as a single whole. Then, identify new processes performing these tasks within the community.

— Apply the DCS propositions to the extended enterprise as if it were one, to help discover innovative connections of IS elements and guide for removal of the above limitations, and reduce these ideas to connections of IS elements. Assess their practicality.

— Accumulate (homogeneous) IS elements for the whole community by *hyper-networking the like types across collaborating enterprises*, to allow them to be used as common IS resources (e.g., customer pools, knowledge worker teams, and information repositories).

— Make the digitized information resources (data and knowledge), communication channels (persons and machines), and process resources (control and workflow) compatible for collaboration among participants, either directly (e.g., using societal cyber-infrastructure) or through some intermediary design (e.g., middle-ware).

— Create an inter-operable proxy for each enterprise IS, for connection with other *enterprise proxies*, and thereby construct a system of IS for the collaborating extended enterprise. The enterprise proxy may include processes that are directly connected to dedicated processes at other enterprise proxies (e.g., XML-based data-swapping objects and programs).

— Develop embedded or automated capabilities in real-time analytics and data processing for the collaboration processes, using societal cyber-infrastructure as much as possible.

— Develop either global or peer-to-peer administration capability to enable the virtual configuration of the system of IS, and support sharing of digital resources among distributed persons and machines of the community.

— Simplify extended enterprise processes (e.g., the workflow between the prime and the supplier: forecasting-inventory replenishment-order processing-manufacturing-shipment) by using the new IS to hyper-network previously separated IS elements (e.g., simplifying the workflow by connecting directly forecasting to manufacturing).

— Convert sequential extended enterprise processes into concurrent, by using the new IS to hyper-network resources and by interweaving sub-tasks to share the resources.

— Employ the concepts of teams and virtual organizations, the flexible machinery, and the automated control systems to cover the entire demand chain and/or supply chain, to make the community and its facilities more agile.

— Use new business designs on the Web as possible thought models to seek out new paradigms of conducting business by the hyper-networking system of IS. For example, the Internet Utilities and industrial exchange models may guide the innovation of the IS design.

— Seek out the possibility of *using social networking as a collaboration tool* to facilitate value cocreation for both customers and knowledge workers of the extended enterprise.

— Maximize the use of societal cyber-infrastructure throughout the system of IS.

— Deliver the services of the system to users on a platform that includes personal digital devices with (wired and wireless) connections to the Internet. The user interface should feature "control levers" that trigger the execution of life cycle tasks, such as a "life cycle dashboard". The goal here is to make the IS person-centered at the level of user interface. Dedicated apps on smart phones should be employed to the extent practical, to provide pervasive connection to the system. These apps should be arranged in a life cycle control style, too.

Constraints: business designs; availability of open, scalable, and re-configurable technologies; industrial standards for inter-operation; and costs.

Enterprise value chains can help identify the candidates for process-level collaboration for the extended enterprise. The collaboration model is more involved than the transformation model because it requires inter-enterprise operations, or inter-operation of independent enterprise IS and databases. The model also makes reference to such concepts as enterprise proxy and virtual configuration, which require explanation — see Chapter 5.

The following industrial example (CFAR — see King, 1996) illustrates the collaboration model, as Figure 3.2 depicts.

The case involves a global retailing chain and one of its major suppliers (manufacturers). The collaboration seeks to connect the inventory replenishment processes at the retailer with the manufacturers' production processes for select products. This collaboration reportedly reduced the transaction cost and cycle time for both by more than over 80%. The particular life cycle tasks here include demand forecasting and replenishing at the retailer, and order processing and manufacturing at the manufacturer. The collaboration is achieved by connecting the respective enterprise IS elements in the extended enterprise as if they belonged to one company; i.e., allowing the

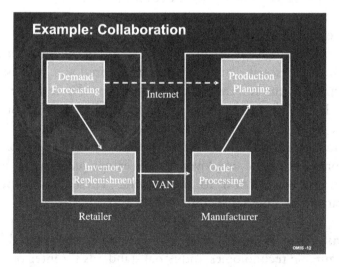

Figure 3.2: Enterprise collaboration: The supply chain example of IS engineering.

forecasting process to feed directly into the manufacturing process, as a single company would no doubt do when it owns both processes. Figure 3.2 shows the "as is" workflow in solid lines, and the "to be" collaboration in the dashed line. In the figure, VAN indicates proprietary value-added network provided either by a third party business or by the prime retailer; which was the infrastructure of the IS before the CFAR project.

The saving on transaction cost and cycle time is obvious. The direct connection between demand forecasting and production planning greatly reduced the need for the previous inventory replenishment processes at the retailer and order processing process at the manufacturer. While the simplification of these processes at each enterprise decreased transaction costs, that of the overall cycle across the extended enterprise removed delays and minimized the global cycle time. In this case, it is the extended IS (a system of IS) that made both reductions possible.

Many B2B practices of e-commerce (see Section 2.2.1 of Chapter 2) have yet to achieve the CFAR level of supply chain integration. Their focus has been to reduce the transaction cost within their own enterprises — i.e., replacing VAN with the Internet and improving the matching of suppliers (e.g., the manufacturers) and clients (e.g., the retailers). The possibility of forming a system of IS across the extended enterprise (even a virtual one) to fundamentally reduce the overall cycle time for all is still awaiting their innovative exploration. Needless to say, this innovation has to overcome organizational barriers and technological limits. Such uphill battles might have seemed insurmountable during the CFAR time, but should have since become more attainable (see Section 2.2 of Chapter 2 and Section 5.3 of Chapter 5).

The big picture of the enterprise collaboration model is that this idea may scale up to include other products, other suppliers, and other retailers; it may even be cascaded through the entire supply chain (suppliers' suppliers). In this vision, some sharable community resources are clearly required. For example, the extended enterprise needs to "drill through" the databases pertaining to the life cycle tasks for every participant from the supply chain to gain the total picture of the supply chain. These participants may need to use some processes library to help them join and play in the community IS, too. Needless to say, the collaboration is in fact a value cocreation process between the constituencies. Embedding the IS into the societal cyber-infrastructure may be the only way to scale up its scope for the population of the (immediate) global supply chain. Concerning the notion of person-centered design, the system may not need it at first glance. However, upon exploring further, the IS could participate in the retailer's inventory tracking provisions for customers shopping online. This customer orientation is naturally person-centered.

Considering the iAlma thought case, again, we note that the proposed IS is an extended enterprise encompassing the university and all external sources that the university may recruit to collaborate for its alumni, according to the vision. Thus, the enterprise collaboration model requires an open and scalable scope of the collaborating sources from outside. Then, it needs to determine the pertinent IS elements, as prescribed in the elements-oriented methodology. Finally, it needs to develop a strategy for connecting these IS elements, with the focus placed squarely on, again, the information resources distributed throughout the extended enterprise. Generally speaking, if the external sources are stable and "offline" from being some production databases at outside enterprises, such as open source documents, data repositories, and the information resources that some Web sites provide for users, then iAlma could develop direct online access to them. Otherwise, the iAlma may want to replicate the select contents from the external sources into a data warehouse that it controls. User interface apps on, e.g., smart phones would have to be determined under the constraints of the industrial settings.

To conclude our discussion in this section, we observe that the roadmap presented above is consistent with industrial practices. That is, it prescribes what should be done from the perspective of the connectionist IS definition, design concepts, and engineering principles; and also describes what is happening in the field.

The next two sections extrapolate the roadmap with conjectures for the future. They analyze some possibilities of what might happen if the progress continues — i.e., they proactively prepare IS engineering for some promising visions. The premise here is *service*, or *value cocreation* between customers and providers. That is, we ask what would be required to fully support the connectionist IS design concepts if the human value networks feature prominently collaboration among persons and enterprises throughout the society?

3.3 The Role of Societal Cyber-Infrastructure

The concept, *embedding IS into societal cyber-infrastructure*, is a little counter-intuitive. It may be required for hyper-networking on the human value networks, but what does embedding mean, and how? The usual notion of leveraging cyber-infrastructure would mean incorporating it into enterprise IS — i.e., embedding the Web, the Internet, and the open source software and technology into an enterprise IS; but not the other way around. However, the latter is precisely the idea. Person-centered hyper-networking is not batch production, as human value networks are by definition individualized. Embedding the Web into IS is a batch-oriented concept which works best for grouping users and processes on the basis of batch resources. Value cocreation by hyper-networking, on the other hand, implies one-of-a-kind IS for one-of-a-kind value propositions. In the ideal case, one would expect numerous concurrent IS operating for numerous simultaneous life cycle tasks. However, even practically speaking, the concept of embedding IS into the societal cyber-infrastructure is not as abstract as it may appear. When all IS are considered parts of the systems of IS of the society, as the Web shows, then the societal cyber-infrastructure is the only "permanent" IS element to them. All others are system-specific IS elements (user interfaces, processes, information resources, computing, and infrastructure), which can be considered the overhead of customizing these systems of IS for individual enterprises. Thus, ultimately, all systems would be inevitably embedded in the societal cyber-infrastructure for other systems to connect to, as the cyber-infrastructure expands.

What does embedding mean? A straightforward example is the embedded error checking on spelling and wording that word processing software offers. Embedded B2C (see Section 2.2 of Chapter 2) offers another example, showing how an enterprise may incorporate its business processes (in the form of Web functions and activities) into the standard operations of other Web sites. Smartphone readable extended barcodes (e.g., the so-called two-dimensional barcode) represent yet another example of embedding Web sites into pervasive and ubiquitous user interface available today. Finally, tools from one Web site may be incorporated into others. This embedment includes practices where open source technology sites provide tools for users to query and process their information resources from their own sites; and business Web sites open some of their enterprise processes to customers — e.g., tracking the movement of parcels. As such, an ordering-receiving process of an enterprise IS can embed the public domain suppliers' information into its user interface by using these tools, and embed the logistic carriers' shipping tracking processes into its own replenishment tracking processes.

Embedding IS into societal cyber-infrastructure is not the same as the traditional notion of Web-based IS design, which often only means Web-based user interface. For one thing, the Web is not the whole societal cyber-infrastructure, which also includes open source information, software, and technology, as we have repeatedly stressed. Moreover, embedding here requires employing these open resources to develop the IS elements, incorporating the Web into the IS (connecting to all the Web resources for the users), and deploying the IS into the Web (distributing IS elements throughout the Web). It is a two-way interaction between the IS and the societal cyber-infrastructure to promote hyper-networking among customers and partners. Using the connectionist definition of IS, this book defines the *embedment of IS* into the societal cyber-infrastructure to be the *employment of the open source IS elements from the societal cyber-infrastructure into the IS, and deploying the IS* (elements) *into them* (open source elements). This definition demands a way to identify the societal IS elements and to connect them.

The above embedment in practice would require virtual configuration, or on-demand connection, of the open source IS elements from the societal cyber-infrastructure, along with other IS elements. Each virtual configuration may correspond to a (family of) value cocreation, and hence a particular way of assembling the resources involved. Therefore, they may incur a considerable amount of over-head which must be streamlined and minimized. In other words, this practice may require some common facility to complement the soci-etal cyber-infrastructure, to help reduce the transaction cost and cycle time of virtually configuring the open source IS elements. This facility may take the form of a common Web front end with built-in utilities for searching, connection, and inter-operation of common IS ele-ments. The (provision of) accumulation and sharing of these utilities may be proprietary, and hence the common facility may allow for proprietary versioning and particularization. The facility itself may also take the form of open source technology, to facilitate the sharing of societal cyber-infrastructure for all systems of IS. A mix of propri-etary arrangements may ultimately be required.

We envision a core *open source facility* to save, administer, and process some *repositories of sharable IS elements* on the Web, as well as *open source utilities and solutions*. In addition, the facility may include industrial protocols and standards to regulate and implement the connections in the embedding and sharing required. Finally, it may also require some ontology for defining IS elements out of the sharable resources on the societal cyber-infrastructure. When an enterprise develops its IS elements in this open source manner and deploys them into such an open source facility, it is embedding the IS into the societal cyber-infrastructure. When the IS in Figure 3.2 would provide a library of open processes on the Web for prospective retailers and suppliers to use, and thereby join in, it is embedding itself into the societal cyber-infrastructure. When iAlma puts up a similar library of open processes so that alumni may contribute new applications and potential apps, as well as generic objects and other process resources, it is being embedded into the societal cyber-infra-structure to facilitate hyper-networking and reaping benefits from hyper-networking.

EXERCISES

1. What are XML, ebXML, XQUERY, and RFID? Please check them out on the Web. Hint: the first three are Web languages for

inter-operating Web-based applications, such as swapping order forms and other documents between Web sites (XML); input and output for e-commerce software programs (ebXML); and portable queries of Web databases (XQUERY). The last one digitizes tags and recognizes them wirelessly.

2. Can you suggest some possible (open source) user apps that alumni might contribute to iAlma (to its open processes library)?

3. Can you suggest some possible open source solutions that your alma mater might develop (from class assignments?) and put in the library of open sources for alumni to use?

4. Can you identify some possible societal IS elements for iAlma and contemplate, exactly what management tools (functions) the open source library needs?

5. Please recognize some basic properties (requirements) for the open source facility.

6. Please suggest some concrete ways to embed an IS into societal cyber-infrastructure.

At this point, this book urges the reader to review the basic concepts that we have discussed earlier. For example, what are B2C/B2B, ISP, and ICP? Why are XML and ebXML necessary tools for B2B? Considering the workflow of inventory replenishment (referring to the solid and dashed lines in Figure 3.2), how would XML and ebXML be used to connect the software programs in the prime to those in the supplier? An obvious answer is that the basic description of orders will be crafted in XML. When more information and functions are required in the input and output of the connection, then ebXML could be used since it provides more standardized metadata and functions about business processes for the coders to use.

In the light of questions 2–4, this book now presents a general model to describe a common open source facility for sharing *additional IS elements from the societal cyber-infrastructure*:

• **People:** Embedded/ubiquitous personal tools, systems, and information for access and interaction; e.g., smart phones, RFID/

ubiquitous coding, personal digital devices, and embedded bio chips. They are in addition to the usual personalized ISP tools.

- **Process/software resources:** Open source facility/technology; open source resources such as tools/analytics/processes (e.g., search engines, B2C/B2B functions and activities, public business process libraries such as XQUERY and ebXML); open standards and protocols; and application-specific enterprise IS processes. The open source facility includes possible management systems to save, administer, and process these process resources in a manner similar to databases; or the "Modelbase" (see Chapter 4 of Hsu (2009) for more details), which integrates generic and open software objects for sharing across the Internet.

- **Information/data and knowledge resources:** Open source information; Internet information utilities and homepages (including files and databases embedded in the homepages); e.g., information portals, meta-models, and repositories of analytics and models.

- **Computing:** Internet computing utilities; e.g., storage networks, public platforms, and Internet transaction portals.

- **Infrastructure:** The usual cyber-infrastructure; e.g., the Internet, telecommunications, and built-in network management.

The last two questions of the exercise have broad implications. Sharing societal cyber-infrastructure for IS is sharing these additional IS elements among systems of IS. Obviously, the job requires significant resources and may be beyond the capabilities of individual enterprises. In any case, the facility of sharing may best be provided on a societal basis since its scale and commonality are societal. We envision that either the public sector or some private providers will assume this responsibility and business opportunity.

A conceptual model is envisioned here, and elaborated in Figure 5.7 of Section 5.4, Chapter 5, to describe what is required of such a facility. This thought model is referred to as the *Web Resources Application System (WRAS)*: a management system for the sharing of societal cyber-infrastructure among systems of IS. A key concept here is the formulation of systems of IS (e.g., an ASP IS for payrolls) as the concurrent users of the societal cyber-infrastructure. Therefore, each value creation is a session (e.g., running payrolls for a client company) of the sharing of the societal cyber-infrastructure. The sharing does not result in a dedicated physical structure (e.g., a dedicated payroll VAN), but a virtual configuration on it. The economy of scale comes from the massive numbers of concurrent sessions performed on the same societal cyber-infrastructure — or, simply, the sharing of digital resources for the society.

This thought model actually describes many e-commerce enterprises. For example, the models of ISP, ICP, and Portal (see Section 2.2 of Chapter 2), along with Search Engines, have thrived on sharing their digital resources among customers, each of whom may customize on their respective uses. This is concurrent value creations using the same societal cyber-infrastructure. This book provides a conceptual design for a possible WRAS management technology to help formulate the technical nature of the WRAS concept. Since it is based on the database model, we defer its presentation to Chapter 5, after the database model has been fully explained in the context of the Internet.

With or without the WRAS, an enterprise can always embed its IS into the societal cyber-infrastructure today, if so desired. For instance, the users who are engaged in, e.g., helpdesk processes, customer relations processes, and payrolls may want to customize the IS for their respective sessions, in a manner in which the IS appears to be custom designed just for the particular job at hand. The ideal control levers would enable this customization by virtue of virtual configuration of IS elements. Again, sufficient openness and scalability are required of them if the IS elements need to be re-configured flexibly with ease. This leads naturally to the maximum usage of the societal cyber-infrastructure available.

This is why the IS master planning guidelines of this chapter envision that an enterprise would acquire an open, scalable, and re-configurable enterprise cyber-infrastructure. On this basis, it would endeavor to design the IS according to the elements-oriented methodology, and employ common Web resources to construct the IS. Finally, it would put, e.g., select processes (software objects) on the Web as some open source library for their current and prospective users to use, to presumably create new functions for the IS. Additional designs would be dedicated to developing person-centered "control levers" for customers and knowledge workers to hyper-network and perform their life cycle tasks. This design promises to bring about person-centered evolution and achieve sustainability for the IS.

The next section looks into the implications of knowledge-based economy on IS.

3.4 The Progress of IS in Service-Led Economy: Additional Implications of Value Cocreation for Human Value Networks

To go another step beyond the previous practices of IS, we ask: does the continuing expansion of the service sector in today's knowledge economy impose additional requirements on IS? Does the vision of the Web's being systems of IS represent an upper bound for IS design? This book analyzes below what service scaling means to IS, and hence requires of IS.

What is service? The answer can come from the question, what is not service? Economic activities that manufacture or cultivate products which occupy physical space are not service. Thus, the economic activities derived from customer (product) services, customer relationships, and helpdesks are services, although the making of the products is not. In a similar way, the facilitation for reaping the utility (benefits) of the products, including the operation and maintenance, is service. For example, GE and IBM can make money from being a manufacturer, making and selling the mega-watts generators and super computers; or they can wear a service hat and make money from helping their customers of these products to utilize them to the fullest possible extent. Leasing products to customers is, clearly, service.

An even larger genre of service is completely unrelated to products: the facilitation of persons' and enterprises' life cycle roles; and the provision of the needs and tasks derived from these roles. Retailing, all sorts of agents and middlemen (i.e., brokers and other transactions providers), healthcare, and social networking are ready examples for persons. Consulting, marketing, and legal activities are examples for enterprises. It is arguable that the entire e-commerce sector belongs to service. A unified definition for service is this characteristic: value cocreation between the customer and the provider.

Conceptually, the connectionist definition of IS has already included any IS that service could possibly require since value cocreation is but a special class of human value networks (see IfM and IBM, 2007; Hsu, 2009; and Maglio *et al.*, 2010). However, technically, service is a more involved class of economic activities for IS to support fully, since it demands *extended enterprise* (customer-provider collaboration), *comprehensive connections* (interactions throughout the course of service, or value cocreation), and *one-of-a-kind tasks* (value cocreations that do not persist, nor repeat) if the service enterprise is to scale its value-added activities. From the perspective of this book, service is the high end of the DCS model: featuring scaling up to the population, down to individuals, and transformationally to cut across business domains, delivered in a person-centered, life cycle role-based, and extended enterprise manner.

What technical capabilities do the high-end services impose on IS? The best way to answer this question is to think about what we all can see surrounding us: social networking. How do people cocreate values on the social networking provider sites? How many users and user sessions are there on the IS involved? What would we wish the IS to provide to facilitate our sessions and our use of other sites? Again, we adopt a forward-looking attitude to contemplate the (future) challenges that the IS field faces, as follows.

3.4.1 *Massively Concurrent Value Cocreations by Customers and Providers*

The first and foremost challenge to IS by service is the massive concurrent service sessions (value cocreations) performed on IS: just think how many thousands, or even millions, of one-of-a-kind networking activities (use of the resources by individual pairs of users) a social networking site may have to support at any one time. The same situation is true for any other service enterprises, be it a helpdesk, a customer relationship IS, an on-demand business site, or the iAlma.

Therefore, let us analyze concurrent processing of requests made by collaborating persons in extended enterprises for distributed resources, to support their value cocreations.

Concurrent processing is about simultaneous sharing of resources for all the tasks that request them. This general concept is well-known in the field. However, we wish to point out that connection of these resources is the key to the sharing. Connecting IS elements per se usually achieves reduction of transaction cost by simplification and integration, as discussed before. Concurrent processing, on the other hand, broadens the connection for repeated and simultaneous use, and thereby achieves further reduction of cycle time. Therefore, concurrent processing always challenges the capacity of the connection. Since service requires comprehensive connections of IS elements throughout the extended enterprise for one-of-a-kind value cocreation, massive concurrent service sessions challenge all these connections *and* the administration (virtual configuration) of the IS elements for use in individual value cocreations.

As discussed in Chapter 1, a job that requires 1,000 man-hours to complete could ideally be finished in one hour if 1,000 men work on it simultaneously. The challenge is how to make all 1,000 men work at the same time on the same job. Resources availability could be a bottleneck and sequencing of work processes could be another. Also, there is the need for coordination and synchronization. For example, how can we share software application programs and analytic models among many concurrent users whose specific requests of them may be all different? Obviously, these programs and models would have to be "normalized" (decomposed) into generic unit modules from which they can be reconstructed, and put into some globally (centrally) administered repositories for system-wide sharing. This would be a new technology to achieve virtual configuration for the Process-level IS resources. Similar breakthroughs are required for virtual configuration of all classes of IS elements. A reference point is enterprise databases. The same database infrastructure drives all virtual configurations of the data resources (e.g., views) to allow all users to run their individual requests (e.g., global queries and applications) against it, concurrently.

The high-end IS would make all processes of all value cocreations concurrent. Thus, the vision faces technical constraints in the physical capacity of the connections and processing, and in the logical control ability to perform concurrent virtual configurations. Some scientific precedents may help the field develop new IS technology and solutions.

Computer science offers some results at the algorithmic level for concurrent processing. Human ingenuity has also provided many intriguing ideas for concurrent value cocreations in various domains (such as the distributed data processing design of the SETI@home project). The field of manufacturing faces the same challenges and contributes some of the most rigorous design ideas that IS can employ. For example, the agile manufacturing models discussed in Section 1.4 of Chapter 1 connect product development life cycle tasks to customer demands, and transform their processing from strictly sequential to partially concurrent. A subset of them, simultaneous engineering, connects the product life cycle itself, such as Design-for-X, with X being anything ranging from manufacturability to serviceability and sustainability. A basic technique is forming *virtual teams* from all stages of the life cycle tasks (e.g., marketing, engineering, and manufacturing professionals) to help execute these tasks, concurrently. These teams configure persons and resources from different stages without having to physically co-locate them, and interweave the detailed steps and tasks of each process with those of others to allow for maximum concurrent processing. The platform for virtual teams is none other than IS.

For service, the virtual teams would encompass the entire demand and supply chains. A team could actually be the persons conducting coordinated value cocreations. In this sense, virtual teams define families of service sessions and hence provide a common reference point for the virtual configurations that these sessions may request. That is, we recognize some relatively stable "views", or virtual groupings, of IS elements from these virtual teams. Virtual configurations may be pre-structured according to these views, leaving only the rest of the requests to the care of on-demand virtual configuration. The grouping may be directed top-down by managerial needs according to organizational structures, or emerged bottom-up from the patterns of value cocreations and IS usage. In any case, the network connection laws that we discussed in Chapter 1 may be applied here for the recognition and design of such views. Finally, the views of virtual configuration may be coupled with the particular applications of the WRAS discussed above. That is, these virtual configuration views may help define the views of WRAS as the core particular enterprise requests of the societal cyber-infrastructure.

The next class of challenges may come from embedding intelligence into the IS to assist persons cocreating values. To be more precise, this book envisions that certain online assistance be embedded into the societal cyber-structure that IS uses.

3.4.2 *Embedded Assistance in Societal Cyber-Infrastructure*

Embedded assistance (e.g., decision logics and analytics) has become commonplace in software design. Examples include the spelling and grammar assistance found in word processors. At the IS level, we also see e-commerce sites providing online analytics to assist customers in picking and choosing products. The newness here is that we further recognize a central role for this concept in high-end IS designs. In particular, the person-centered concept requires that both *the customer and the knowledge worker of value cocreation should enjoy pervasive and ubiquitous assistance from the IS*, such as tapping into the knowledge and other information resources accumulated at the organization and/or on the Web.

Why is it the case? Virtual configuration of IS elements requires deep knowledge of both the IS elements and their connections. Such knowledge may be provided in the form of pre-determined choices, with the required knowledge embodied into the choices at the time when the IS is constructed. However, the person-centered concept of the IS, coupled with support for life cycle role-based tasks, makes it impossible to determine all the applications that the users need at the design time. Thus, prix menu would not be sufficient for the IS. The only alternative is to allow users to make their own virtual configurations on demand, with perhaps the provisions of prix choices to supplement this ad hoc development.

The challenge is, therefore, how can we program the deep knowledge into some pills for the end users of the IS to swallow easily. One can think of a hierarchy of dissemination designs to deploy the knowledge into tools and building blocks. Regardless of how one designs the IS, however, in one form or another certain online intelligence would have to be offered by the IS itself as embedded assistance to, e.g., the user process of virtual configuration. The more the IS embeds, the less the reliance on the variety of tools and building blocks by the users. Why, then, should the intelligence be embedded into the societal cyber-infrastructure?

One reason is that the complexity of virtual configuration tends to arise from the connections of IS elements, and the connections tend to be societal cyber-infrastructure based according to the IS principles and design concepts. Thus, the need for knowledge may concentrate on the points where the connections are supposed to take place. Second, if the cyber-infrastructure is a common denominator to numerous IS, then should the knowledge for their connections be normalized for all at this level (generic and stable intelligence)? Third, it is only nature to embed the intelligence into the common denominator, too.

Generally speaking, an IS possesses information resources and knows what the users need (through usage); thus, it is capable of providing assistance to them in a responsive or even proactive way. This capacity should be exploited to support the users. In a broader sense, the history of the man-machine system evolution is one of "downloading" the burden of mundane operations and analytics, along with their attendant data tasks (gathering, storage, and processing), from the man to the machine. Examples include CATSCAN, Computer-Aided Engineering, Computer-Aided Manufacturing, Computer-Based Information System, and other models of making computers do human jobs (see Section 1.4 of Chapter 1). This potential of downloading continues to march ahead. Therefore, embedding assistance into the societal cyber-infrastructure is only a natural step in the design of person-centered IS for value cocreation.

Ultimately, we see the societal cyber-infrastructure working in the background to provide person-centered embedded assistance through the IS, in the new vision of human-machine interaction. The IS, for example, would provide related experience, benchmarks, or facts assembled from the Web to customers and knowledge workers on demand, while also preparing the connections of IS elements for them. It may assist the users with automatic sensing, monitoring, and adaptive control of the status of the societal cyber-infrastructure used, during virtual configuration. Such an IS, capable of person-centered embedded assistance for virtual configurations, represents the challenges to the field.

We wish to stress here that an enterprise cannot confine itself to proprietary technologies in a knowledge economy, at least not for long. It has to open itself to what the majority in the society is using in order to easily work with its external constituencies. From a cost angle, the societal cyber-infrastructure can support many different uses and can even be customized to support different users in different ways if necessary. An enterprise has little reason to not explore the possibility of tapping into this societal asset. On the necessity side, an enterprise has to be able to continuously expand its systems, without requiring reconstruction or causing major disruption. Such a requirement could arise easily from innovations in a firm's business vision. Next, an enterprise has to provide smooth re-configuration and restructuring of its systems and IS elements, in order to adapt to the changing usage patterns of them by the virtual configurations. Finally, service enterprises are part of the human value networks and hence need to be prepared to connect with any parts of the society, and the fluid nature of service also means that they are in a perpetuating transient state of their business.

An information supply chain scenario is fully described in Section 5.3 of Chapter 5. This scenario shows how owners of proprietary databases in industry, or for that matter, in any possible space of business, may collaborate to cocreate value. That is, new service designs may readily arise from innovative connection of information resources to support hyper-networking even out of ordinary supply chains. Figure 5.6 depicts how ordinary open source technology available today is sufficient to implement innovative designs for turning independent databases into Internet information services, following the IS design principle of embedment in societal cyber-infrastructure discussed above.

The visions of service describe some basic challenges facing the IS field, but they also show that the progress on IS promises to contribute to a new service science. From this angle, IS is a tool that enables new service on the human value networks. This book holds the view that the future of IS can be reflected in the future of a new service science.

To conclude this chapter, we summarize the design ideas discussed above, which promote especially IS that facilitate hypernetworking for value (co)creation into this principle:

The Design Principle for Embedment of IS into Societal Cyber-Infrastructure: *Apply social networking techniques (Web tools and logics) to user interface design; create open source process library as an open source community for stakeholders to contribute to the IS; and connect select inter-operable databases to the open source processes (e.g., include the inter-operation designs in the open library). This principle adds to the general guidelines of using the Internet, the Web, and the open source resources and technology to construct and deliver IS.*

The next chapter will carry IS design beyond the stage of master planning. It presents a process modeling method for determining the core of detailed IS elements required by logical IS design. In the literature, process modeling is customarily referred to as structured system analysis. The input to the analysis is the IS master plan, while the output will be specification of IS processes, along with the data resources and end users implied by these processes.

Chapter 4

Process Modeling: Analyze the Specific Information System Resources Required in the Mission and Master Plan

Chapters 4–7 present the standard results in the IS design field, which happen to focus on resources. The question to ask first is this: How do we flesh out the IS elements and their connections from the master plans of IS? The effort to do this is referred to in this book as process modeling for IS analysis. Its logic is straightforward: gather sufficient and necessary detailed facts from the (ongoing) enterprise, or from the reference points for the (proposed) enterprise, and then map them into IS elements and connections according to the master plans. A method is needed to drive the effort. The analysis is typically an iterative process along two axes: moving from the status-quo (the "as is" system) to the innovation (the "to be" system), and from back-bone sketch (e.g., a black box view) to full refinement (specifications of processes). It terminates when sufficient details are determined from the analysis to allow for the ensuing logical design of the IS to commence. That is, the analysis should meet the requirements of software engineering for codifying the IS elements and connections. This chapter provides a proven general-purpose method, Data Flow Diagrams (DFD), as both a baseline tool that IS analysts can use and a reference point from which they can learn to understand other methods. The discussion features profound logic of structured IS analysis, presented through a set of DFD examples. The analysis will yield the first three classes of IS elements: direct end users, process resources, and information resources.

4.1 Tools of Process Modeling: The Data Flow Diagram Method

The field never lacks IS analysis and design methods. Of the many results, diagramming techniques and graph-theoretic models may represent the bulk that practitioners tend to use. This book adopts from them one particular generic method as the baseline method for determining IS elements and connections: Data Flow Diagram.

Arguably, the most venerable and well-known of all diagramming techniques is the flowchart method of software engineering, which depicts the sequences of controls for executing a computing logic. Mathematically motivated techniques have elaborated flowcharts into such formalisms as the finite state models and Petri Nets, which are applied widely in engineering system designs. These methods tend to be two-dimensional, meaning that they elaborate directly the whole system, without vertically "zooming in and out" of the scope. That is, flowcharts, Petri Nets, and the like do not support a structured methodology which starts with some overview of the system (treating it as a black box) and then methodically expands the system model into iterations of refinement. Incidentally, such structured analysis is often required in practice since details of the whole system may be too overwhelming for any project to undertake at one time. Besides, the details in the real world often have to come from progressive discovery, rather than being raptured or revealed suddenly. In any case, these methods do not differentiate among IS elements, and hence do not support IS analysis well.

For structured analysis of IS, most techniques in the field can be traced back to a few origins. Among them, the ICAM (integrated computer-aided manufacturing) Definitional Language (IDEF), which is based on the Structured Analysis and Design Technique (SADT), is well-vested in manufacturing. For business IS, the Data Flow Diagram (DFD) has motivated many methods that practitioners use today. This book picks DFD as the prototypical method of process modeling for two reasons. The first and foremost is the fact that the DFD logic lends itself more naturally to the connectionist IS definition than do the SADT method and other possibilities. For example, the notions of Activity, Input, Output, Control, and Platform that SADT employs tend to be convoluted, as judged from the perspective of the connectionist definition of IS. In contrast, DFD expressly focuses on the determination of three classes of IS elements — Person, Process, and Information Resources — which constitute the core of requirements for IS logical design. With this core determined, the hardware classes of Computing and Infrastructure will follow in a rather straightforward manner (especially when the IS can be implemented on a single server). All five classes can be shown in an *Enterprise Information Architecture (EIA)*, combining *the DFD* and *the networking diagram* of the IS hardware.

The second reason for the choice of DFD is its generic nature for modeling. The building blocks that it employs — External Entity, Process, Data Flow, and Data Store — apply virtually to any IS and can work complementarily with almost any other IS planning and design methods. That is, DFD can use many forms of master plan as input, complement some other process models, and feed into a variety of detailed system design methods. Although a range of newer methods exist (e.g., CBM — see Section 3.2), which even provide integrated modeling that covers both analysis and design, DFD is still a powerful method that analysts can actually use for IS development in actuality. This book embraces DFD as a suitable IS design method for process modeling.

The DFD method has, as expected, a number of variations that have emerged from its decades of industrial applications. We employ a particular version based on the work by Gane and Sarson (1979), plus some clarifications introduced in this chapter. In general, the DFD method consists of a graphical modeling language and a structured analysis logic using the language. The DFD modeling language is comprised of four basic constructs, three of which are nouns and one verb; and the verb drives the modeling. Although the name of data flow may make one think that the modeling logic starts with data flow, the truth, however, is that DFD is really oriented toward recognizing the processes (the verb). The processes lead to the recognition of the other three constructs (nouns): external entity, data flow, and data store — see below.

Now, this section reviews these four basic constructs and their icons; the iterative modeling (decomposition) process; and the tree hierarchy of DFD models.

4.1.1 *The Graphical Language of Data Flow Diagramming*

Figure 4.1 summarizes the iconic constructs of DFD. An overview of DFD modeling is provided below:

The DFD Modeling Procedure

- Step 1: Develop a Context Diagram, containing only one process — the system — along with all the external entities and their interactions with the system (the external data flows). No data stores should be shown in the diagram, for they belong to the inside of the system, not outside of it.
- Step 2: Expand iteratively the context diagram into levels of DFD model. The process starts with elaborating the context diagram into the System Model (level 0), and then decomposes each process of the System Model into a sub-model (level 1), as required. The level-1 processes of all sub-models will be similarly decomposed as

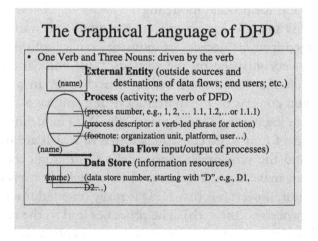

Figure 4.1: The DFD icons for the four basic constructs.

needed into sub-models at level 2, and so on, until concluding with the fully expanded Logical Model at the leaf level of the decomposition tree. Each process at the leaf level is to be fully described with pseudo code type of logical statements.

- Step 3: Describe the full contents of each and every DFD building block in the Logical Model: the logic of the leaf-level processes (in pseudo code or structured English), the data items and their semantic definitions of data stores, the access requirements, information contents, and cardinality of data flows, and the arrangements for external entities. A complete *tree hierarchy* of DFD models will come out after this step.
- Step 4: Repeat the above steps for revision and new design, if necessary (e.g., to progress from the "as is" system to the "to be" system envisioned).

4.1.2 *The Hierarchy of DFD Models*

The process of building the tree hierarchy of DFD models is shown in Figure 4.2.

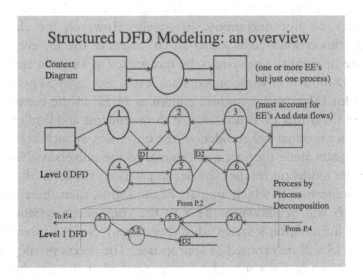

Figure 4.2: The inheritance structure (cross-levels consistency) of DFD modeling.

The modeling of DFD is an iterative decomposition procedure from the Context Diagram moving to the System Model and the Logical Model. The decomposition focuses on processes, methodically expanding each process as necessary from each level to a sub-model in the next level. Thus, the System Model is an expansion of the sole process (the black box that represents the IS) at level 0, and the Logical Model is a collection of many sub-models each of which was expanded from a process in the level immediately above it. The number of levels is completely a function of the scope and the complexity of the system; it could be just one, or quite a few.

4.1.3 *The Grammar of the DFD Language*

External Entity (EE): This is a noun class of construct that *defines the boundary of the system*, by declaring what stakeholders are outside of the system (the enterprise with which the IS is concerned). External entities trigger the processes of the system and represent the ultimate, outside sources and destinations of data flows in the system. Traditionally, external entities are defined at the highest level of modeling (i.e., in the context diagram) and do not change from one level of DFD to the next during the structured analysis process — i.e., they do not decompose iteratively. However, for clarity of design, this chapter advises that all end users of the IS, even when they are internal to the system, be recognized as external entities in the DFD models at some appropriate levels. For example, the DFD model for iAlma will recognize alumni as an EE in the context diagram of the iAlma IS. But it will not show students and faculty, along with other internal stakeholders of the university, as such in the context diagram since they are not external to the university. However, when the modeling reaches (by decomposition) the level of the university's internal IS which are part of the iAlma, then these internal end users will be shown as EE's to the component systems (e.g., student information systems) that they trigger. So, the internal end users of IS will be exposed as appropriate. The access privileges and requirements of EE's should be fully specified at the conclusion of DFD modeling, along with the specification of data flows that connect them to the IS. Evidently, *the EE's give rise to the People class of IS elements.*

Process: It is the *verb*, and hence must have both the subject (input) and the object (output). Processes are the core of the DFD model, and DFD modeling is driven by identifying processes. Since *a process is an activity*, we advise the analysts to force the issue of "focusing on actions" and insist on using only a verb to describe a process. That is, a process should not be named as "the inventory system", "the Latham branch office", and the like. Instead, name them after their missions. A DFD model that follows an organization chart promises little value-added beyond what is already well-known to the organization. An inventory system may focus on a variety of activities and perform different jobs for other processes when it is connected to them; and exposing these IS connections is precisely the reason to conduct a DFD modeling on the system. Using a verb-led phrase as the process descriptor will go a long way towards avoiding "sweeping the dirt under the carpet" and exposing the real system logic. A process must have both input and output; otherwise, it is either an EE or a data store. A process may not send out a data flow (output) and receive it (input) again without any other process working on it first; such perpetuating data flows add no value and show nothing meaningful to IS. Nouns need verbs to connect to other nouns; thus, only processes can connect to any other construct, directly (by data flows). The logic of a process has to be fully specified — this is an original property of DFD. The logic is expressed first in terms of the sub-models into which the process decomposes; and ultimately in the structured or pseudo code style statements for the leaf processes in the Logical Model. These logics are the enterprise analytics of the DFD model and will feed the software engineering effort after the DFD. *The processes from a DFD model constitute the Process class of IS elements.*

Data Flow: A data flow represents some *pro forma* arrangement for *communication of information*, or an informational connection. The word "flow" here is a noun, not a verb. It represents the directional connection between a process and another DFD object of any type (constructs), in terms of the information contents (data) that the connection carries. Thus, a data flow must be named meaningfully to reveal its information contents. Technically, data flows are associated with processes. For example, when a data flow connects a process with an EE, in the direction of (flowing) from the EE to the process, then it is considered as the input (from the EE) to the process, rather than the output from the EE. The EE does not perform anything other than being drawn by the process into the provision of the data flow. Please note that the so-called "bi-directional" data flows are recognized not as one data flow, but as two separate data flows, one in each direction carrying their own unique messages. In fact, strictly speaking, bi-directional data flows do not make any sense, since no system will (should) perpetuate the same message between two processes without changing the content, such as from a proposal to an approved proposal. This book advises never using any bi-directional data flows. Data flows of a process may split (or decompose) in the sub-models of the process — i.e., an input to the process may feed into more than one next-level process in the sub-model. However, this split should be avoided as long as it is possible to consolidate the input-receiving tasks into one process. The information contents of all data flows will be determined and documented for the Logical Model to define the connections. *Data flows pertain to the connections of IS elements.*

Data Store: The fourth basic construct of DFD is also a noun type. It represents the *persistent information resources* of the IS. Please note that processes and data flows may produce and process data at the run time, without having to save them as a part of the IS information resources. These run-time data are called transient and will not be included in any data stores. *Inter-process data flows* are generally considered *transient* even if they eventually get processed into some *persistent data flows* that connect to data stores. Traditionally, a data store may represent a particular (input/output) file conceived for a particular application program which implements the logic of a leaf process. However, for our purpose, this book advises that all data stores should be structured according to the requirements of semantic data modeling in order to assist the ensuing tasks of logical database design for the whole IS. That is, the contents of a data store should be fully specified to reveal distinct global and local data items, their semantics, and constraints (functional dependencies, entity-relationship and object orientations, and other data structures). As such, the definition of data stores is in essence a preparation for semantic data modeling at the high end. These specifications should enable (global) database design for the IS. A global data dictionary should be created to consolidate the semantics of all data items for the whole system, along with the documentation for individual data stores. This important repository also represents the meat of the DFD modeling to support the connectionist IS design method. *Data stores define the Information Resource class of IS elements.*

We wish to note at this point that this book is not concerned with providing any elaborate templates to do "turn-key" identification or documentation of processes, EE's, data flows, and data stores; nor do we endorse such an approach for teaching the basics of process modeling. Instead, this book leaves detailed documentation to the analysts, who can invent their own forms from common sense or choose any from the field as they deem fit. It is the considered view of the author that particular templates may render themselves to particular consulting ventures, and may not serve much intellectual purpose. However, generic templates do exist in the field. If one finds them helpful, then use them, of course. This book only advises that the basic logic of DFD modeling be held firm to guide the adoption, and be blended into whatever templates one uses, to support the sufficient determination of IS elements as required.

Connection Rules: As stated above, data flows are the only and exclusive means to connect DFD objects into an integrated model. The most important connection rule is that no noun class construct may connect directly to another noun class construct without going through a process. Thus, an EE may not connect directly to another EE by a data flow; nor an EE to a data store and nor a data store to another data store. If such a connection is deemed necessary for the system, then it must be a part of the IS and hence some process must be created to make this happen. For example, if alumni want to connect with government funding agencies through iAlma, then the system must provide social networking tools and/or Internet query tools, along with the necessary access to the databases, to facilitate this connection. Such interfacing, then, is a process of iAlma in between these two EE's, Alumni and Government Funding Agencies. Second, connections between any two DFD objects need to be consolidated; i.e., just one data flow per direction per pair of objects. For example, a data flow from an EE to a process is *the* input from *the* EE to *the* process. The article "the" here implies that all the possible data flows between these two DFD objects in this direction are consolidated and shown as just one directional data flow in the model. The only other possible data flow between them is the one of the opposite direction (from the process to the EE). In other words, there should only be one data flow connecting the same pair of objects in either direction anywhere in the DFD model. This rule is necessary to avoid unwieldy representation in the DFD model, but it is also sensible conceptually. If two objects are connected, then they are connected, regardless of how the connection may be used. The actual usage may be ad hoc and task-specific, and hence need not be specified *a priori*. The specification should be confined to the capacity and capability of the connections, and their requirements. The conditions of connections, such as the sending and receiving of data flows by processes, must be included in the logics of the leaf-level processes to which they connect.

Decomposition Rules: Decomposition needs to follow adequate conventions in order to guide the process and preserve the integrity of the resultant models. The core concern here is maintaining consistency across levels of modeling. Since DFD is oriented toward processes, controlling the decomposition of processes is maintaining the consistency of DFD models (from the context diagram to the logical model). A simple book-keeping technique will help: number the processes following the tree hierarchy of models. As shown in Figure 4.2, the processes in the system model (level 0) are numbered sequentially, although the exact sequencing is immaterial (can be changed in any way as long as the sequence makes sense to the analyst). When decomposed into level 1, the level-0 process' number (e.g., Process 5) becomes the name of the sub-model and the prefix to the numbering of processes in this sub-model (e.g., Processes 5.1, 5.2, etc.). In addition, the sub-model must inherit the inter-process data flows from the higher level model to this level (e.g., the designation of "to P.4" and "from P.4"). If some EE's and data stores from the higher level are included in a sub-model, then the sub-model should directly inherit the whole objects without splitting them or decomposing them. If some internal users from the higher level become EE's to the sub-model, then they should be named in a way that distinguishes them from the EE's in the context diagram, e.g., adding the process number under which an internal-turned-EE belongs, as a suffix to the name of this EE. When data stores and EE's are duplicated in the same model, for the sake of simplifying the drawing of data flows, then a slash line should be added to the object to indicate each duplicate. Data flows, as discussed above, may be split or even decomposed if needed; but this practice is not encouraged. In any case, sufficient documentation of all changes is required, and so is an administration process for the entire DFD modeling project especially if multiple analysts are involved.

Transient (run time) vs. Persistent Data Rules: Transient data include phone calls, meetings, emails, memos, and the like. Although some of them may eventually be saved, until then (by the due process) they must be represented as data flows in between the processes (signifying supply and request of information), rather than immediately going to data stores. Transient data flows represent *pro forma* connections (communications) of processes to form workflows. Only the formal repositories of persistent data may be recognized as data stores, and their *pro forma* connections as persistent data flows.

One can now start using the DFD method. It is recommended to use some appropriate drawing software (many are available from the Internet) to create DFD models and help manage decomposition and maintain consistency. What is a good DFD model, and how can we properly model a system using DFD? Such questions beg some heuristics of "good practices", although the field really cannot offer any definitive scientific laws of modeling beyond common sense and experience. This book summarizes a few such heuristics below.

4.1.4 *The DFD Modeling Logic*

The System Logic Rule: enterprise life cycle, task life cycle (workflows), and information life cycle. This rule is concerned with the logical consistency of a model. It may guide the review of DFD models to uncover hidden processes and connections. The basic idea is simple: a system has a life cycle, a task has a life cycle, and information resources have their life cycles, too. Thus, a DFD model must tell a complete story of the system to the extent that its existence makes sense. For instance, an enterprise incurs planning (e.g., budgeting and acquisition), execution (e.g., administration and production), monitoring (e.g., data collection and review), and control (evaluation and adjustment). A task requires initiation (e.g., requests), activity (e.g., purchasing), and closure (e.g., payment). If a customer orders something as an input to the system, then that something should show in some form as an output of the system to the customer. If the library acquires new books according to some budget and review of demands, then such budget and review are expected to be planned or adjusted in some processes. Concerning information life cycle, if a data store is created, then it is expected to be used and maintained. That is, a data store should have data flows in both ways: read (output) and write (input). Without write, it cannot be updated; and without read, it is out of a job. Thus, either the same processes or different processes within or without the immediate scope of the system must provide such read and write. Of course, read-only repositories acquired from outside (e.g., yellow pages) and write-only archives are possible in actuality. But, they are relatively rare — for example, general ledgers will be used in auditing, too. Therefore, applying this rule can at least make sure that no hidden reads and writes are overlooked during the modeling process.

The Decomposition Heuristic I: when not to decompose (stop decomposing)? The answer hinges on the purpose of the leaf processes. A leaf process is meant to correspond to a unit software program such as a routine or even a canned simple application, and the structured description of the logic of the process, such as a pseudo code, should not overlap with that of other leaf processes. Other goals are also possible, such as an app that will be outsourced to external developers or the application of a tool available from some open sources. In any case, when the purpose is achieved, or the process in question is judged to be a leaf process, then stop decomposition on this process. When all processes at the lowest level of DFD are stopped, then the decomposition process is concluded.

The Decomposition Heuristic II: when to decompose? The simple answer is, start leveling when the model has too many processes to fit into one regular page. A heuristic of this heuristic is to use this simple rule of thumb: 5–7 processes per model. This heuristic applies to sub-models, too. Therefore, this book advises the analysts to recognize 5–7 processes for the system model (level 0), and to decompose each process into 5–7 processes for level-1 sub-models, until and unless unit processes (leaf processes) are reached. Or, conversely, if an existing DFD model consists of a large number of processes, then it may improve its communication power by aggregating the processes into higher level sub-models and finally into the system model. The ease of communication is exactly the logic behind this heuristic. A context diagram is a one-sentence description of the IS, and the system model is its executive summary. With a proper tree hierarchy of DFD models, one can choose to communicate at any level as appropriate for the audience.

The Balanced Tree Rule: The "weight" of a model should be roughly equally distributed on all of its processes; or, looking at it from another angle, all processes of the same model should carry similar or comparable significance. Therefore, the decomposition should not take place (be required) only on one or two processes, and the data flows should not concentrate similarly (e.g., converging to the same process). Just imagine a DFD model where only one of the seven processes in the system model is decomposed into level 1, and one of the seven level-1 processes is decomposed into level 2, and so on. This would be a grossly unbalanced tree hierarchy and would inevitably invite questions of the appropriateness of the processes. When this happens, it would be wise to split the super heavy process and combine some of the light processes. Usually, the "transitional" processes, the ones that have only one input (data flow) and one output, are good candidates for consolidation. They may become processes in the next level.

The Connectedness Rule: Finally, the DFD model must not be separated into isolated parts — i.e., any objects of the model must be connected to the rest of the model by some connections (directional reach is not required). The logic is straightforward: if the DFD model does describe a wholly system, then it is unlikely that the system falls apart into different, un-related isolations. There must be some commonality that connects all parts together as a system, and the DFD model ought to reflect on this logic glue. Unsurprisingly, such common glue is often found in the information resources that different parts (sub-systems) share. In fact, one autonomous sub-system may write to some data stores from which other autonomous sub-systems read. This kind of information integration is proven (in, e.g., computerized manufacturing) to be a powerful way to connect otherwise disparate enterprises and improve their effectiveness.

For our purpose, DFD modeling is the analysis that determines the IS elements and connections from master plans. Thus, the following principle shows this approach:

The Process Modeling Principle of IS Design: *Conduct DFD modeling, or the equivalent, to determine IS elements and connections — define Persons from external entities and internal end users; Processes from the system model and, if necessary, the ensuing sub-models; Information Resources from data stores; and connections from data flows. Derive Computing and Infrastructure classes of IS elements (a hardware model) from the DFD to meet the technical requirements of the IS elements and connections defined above. The DFD model, coupled with the hardware model, gives rise to the Enterprise Information Architecture of the IS.*

4.2 The Logic of Process Modeling: Renovating Processes, Data Stores, and Data Flows

The first prototypical example is concerned with the *first processes renovation principle*, which seeks *simplification* of *special-purpose* persistent information resources by consolidating them into a minimal core, and then drawing (assisted by decision analytics) *real-time on-demand data flows* from this core to *replace* as many such special-purpose persistent data as possible. This principle is illustrated in a simple Assemble to Order (ATO) manufacturing system, where the renovation of IS drives its progress. An ATO system distinguishes itself from the traditional Make to Stock (MTS) model by the ideal of elimination of inventory. Thus, the persistent information resources on inventory are removed in the model, reflecting the above principle.

The low end of the implementation for ATO is to shift the burden of carrying inventory to others in the supply chain, as practiced by the major automobile makers — the dealers' parking lots are their inventory warehouse. The PC industry is full of this practice, too. This is really still an MTS mode of business when one evaluates the inventory in the entire extended enterprise (manufacturers and dealers together). The high end of ATO is, of course, customization: assemble to one-of-a-kind orders. The enabling technology for ATO is really IS. The low-end ATO requires the prime (e.g., the automobile makers and the PC makers) to drill through the entire dealer system and be on top of the system-wide inventory situation at all times, in order to optimize its manufacturing. This is an IS job. The high-end ATO, in addition, also requires the primes to possess agile engineering and manufacturing capabilities to mass-customize their products. This is an IS job, too. Thus, a low-end IS gives a low-end ATO, and a high-end one a high-end ideal. This example echoes Section 1.4 of Chapter 1. Figure 4.3 shows the generic core logic of the ATO idea by virtue of a DFD system model (level 0).

The iconic presentation of the figure conforms to the DFD graphical language discussed previously, except that the processes are shown as a square rather than an oval. This slight variation is allowed (an oval, circle, square...) in practice. Please note that the data stores do not include any inventory. Please also note that the EE, shipping system, appears twice to make the drawing (of data flows) cleaner without crossing lines. Thus, a second slash indicates the duplication for the second appearance. For particular ATO systems, this DFD would have to be preceded with particular master plans that define the ATO ideals (requirements and performance criteria) for the system model, and be succeeded by a particular logical model that fleshes out the customization capabilities in all detailed processes. Please also note that multiple workflows exist in the DFD.

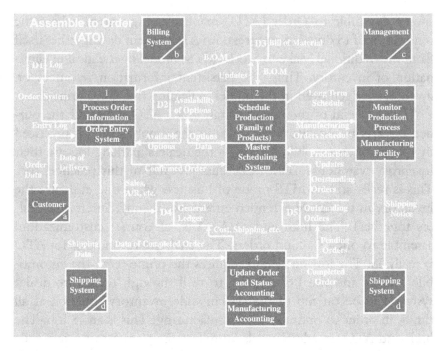

Figure 4.3: A DFD system model (level 0) depicting the logic of Assemble-to-Order IS.

The second example illustrates the *second processes renovation principle: consolidating transient data flows into integrated repository* of persistent information resources. This principle works in the opposite direction of thinking as does the first one. The ultimate guideline is, of course, the value of such renovations: reduction of transaction cost and cycle time. These two principles may work in harmony; but if they conflict with each other on specific design ideas, then whichever turns out more value is the winner. Figure 4.4 shows the case example, which is a traditional commercial loan approval workflow system.

This system features inter-process data flows since the processes in the system model are typical islands of automation — i.e., separate file systems — that could be integrated to simplify their connections and thereby reduce the system transaction cost and cycle time. In fact, the

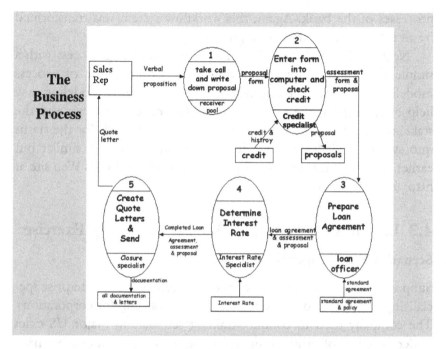

Figure 4.4: The system model for a commercial loan approval process.

system shown in Figure 4.4 is precisely the example of enterprise transformation depicted in Figure 3.1 of Section 3.2.3. Figure 4.4 is the "as is" system, while Figure 3.1 is the "to be" one. As suggested in Chapter 3, this information integration approach often simplifies the connections of processes (inter-process data flows) and achieves the desired improvement on system performance (reduction of transaction cost and cycle time).

Please note that the iconic shape of data stores is slightly varied from the one in Figure 4.1. This practice is also tolerated in the field. Needless to say, the three data stores in the model — credit, standard agreement and policy, and interest rates — have to be maintained by the bank. Since this job was determined to be falling outside the purview of the commercial loan approval process, therefore, they are external to the system and excluded. The data store proposals play the role of an archive here, although it would be used by the management processes of the bank. Again, this workflow system was transformed by an integrative database in Figure 3.1.

Next, we illustrate the hierarchical DFD modeling process with a simple e-business system, following some proven logic of process modeling. This example also demonstrates how DFD modeling may help communicate the innovations by IS between analysts and the stakeholders of the IS — i.e., the use of "as is" models for the status quo system, and "to be" models for the innovation. A similar but earlier version of this exercise is presented on the author's Web site at http://viu.eng.rpi.edu.

4.3 Learning by Example: A DFD Modeling Exercise

Scenario: KnowledgeExchange.com

Suppose KnowledgeExchange.com is an Internet-based enterprise specializing in offering distance learning and e-learning for corporations. The company used to conduct training seminars in major US cities under the name of Troy Seminars, Inc. before the advent of e-business. At the turn of the new millennium, Troy Seminars, Inc. transformed itself to an e-learning provider and changed to the present name. The name change also indicates an expansion of strategy. Although on-site seminars remain its core business, the company is moving rapidly to establish new markets in distance learning and even one-of-a-kind custom training programs. Ultimately, the company envisions itself to become a leader in the business of freelance knowledge workers coops, facilitating the collaboration of members to produce on-demand knowledge products, ranging from research for information to consulting, for all kinds of enterprises. The first step of this innovation is to enhance the capability for on-demand collaboration among the current consultants, who provide customer on-site seminars. The core business processes supported by the status-quo IS are described below.

Each on-site seminar involves a few pro forma processes, which happen to be organized into departments (recall the economic theory that defines the institution of the firm to be a design to optimize information processing and organizational transaction costs — see Section 1.2

of Chapter 1). The marketing department works with the clients and the consultants to plan seminars and close the contracts on them. The acquisition department determines the requirements of the seminar, including the date and city location; confirms with the consultants who will conduct the training; and obtains (new) seminar materials from the consultants and other sources. The logistic department arranges for the seminar meeting facilities, the training consultants' travel, and the shipment of any seminar materials. The sales department deals with external transactions for renting the meeting facilities (e.g., reserving the meeting room(s), planning the seating arrangement(s), and reserving any necessary audio-visual equipment). Finally, the materials handling department prepares and ships the seminar materials required to seminar participants. The company keeps records on seminars, consultants, client companies, meeting facilities, and travel agencies.

To arrange for meeting facilities, the acquisition manager gathers information on possible meeting sites in the scheduled city, and makes a decision based on date availability, cost, type of meeting space available, and convenience of the location. The logistics manager estimates the number and size of meeting rooms, the type of seating arrangements, and the audio-visual equipment needed for each seminar from the information kept on each type of seminar offered, and the number of anticipated registrants for a particular booking. After negotiations are conducted by the sales department with the meeting facility, the sales manager creates a contract agreement specifying the negotiated arrangements and sends two copies of it to the logistics manager. The logistics manager reviews the agreement and approves it if no changes are needed. One copy of the agreement is filed and the other copy is sent back to the sales manager for final closure with the meeting facility. If changes are needed, the agreement copies are changed and returned to the sales manager for approval. This approval process continues until both parties have approved the agreement. The logistics department must also make travel arrangements. First, the logistics manager reviews the consultant's travel information in the logistic file and hires a travel agency to make all necessary arrangements. Then the consultants are contacted to discuss possible travel arrangements, before subsequently the travel agency books everything for the consultants. Once the final travel arrangements have been completed, a written confirmation and itinerary are sent to each consultant.

The logistics department is also responsible for notifying the materials handling department to send out the seminar materials to either or both the participants and meeting facility, two weeks before the seminar date, according to the final list of seminar materials that the acquisition department prepared. Consultants may also have to be contacted by the logistics department if they need to provide additional materials that the company does not have on file. The logistics manager specifies the types and numbers of seminar materials (e.g., lecture notes, power point files, training guides, pamphlets, etc.) that need to be sent to the meeting facility and to the participants. The material-handling department gathers, packages, and sends to the carriers according to the list of request. Once the requested materials have been shipped, a notification is sent to the logistics manager.

How can we develop a DFD model to represent the processing logic described in the scenario, **and** to diagnose it for possible renovation?

4.3.1 *A Brief Description of the Logic of Process Modeling*

The process modeling tasks really begin with identifying the core business processes and gathering facts on how these processes interact with each other; more specifically, do they connect by transient data or persistent data? For example, is the sales manager required to call the logistics coordinator to provide information about the meeting facility, and vice versa? How does the material handling department interact with the logistics department? The description of the status quo system (e.g., about how the logistic manager goes about his/her job) seems to imply certain pro forma procedures for inter-departmental interactions (transient data flows). More facts ought to be collected to flesh out this aspect so that *workflows by transient data flows* can be identified. This is important because IS renovation often comes from improving on these transient data flows, as the above two principles demonstrate. The fact that matters is, IS can easily alter the design of organizational connections (pro forma information flows).

Thus, the core logic of process modeling is to *expose the causes and effects of transient (inter-process) data flows*: should they be replaced by persistent (to and from data stores) data flows; or should they be enhanced in order to simplify the connections and/or to minimize (the reliance on) persistent information resources? Note that the causes and effects may show in the existence of processes and data stores as well as data flows. The two principles of renovation may help the diagnosis of the "as is" system and lead to an innovative "to be" design. The value judgment will be based, as expected, on the measures of transaction cost and cycle time (see Section 1.2 of Chapter 1).

We now illustrate the logic of process modeling below, using the above scenario to go from modeling the status quo to the ideal of becoming a Knowledge Exchange.

EXERCISES

1. Where should we look for renovations to the status quo IS, such that it can help transform KnowledgeExchange.com (KE) from a seminars provider to a Knowledge Exchange?
2. What is an "as is" context diagram? Can you draw one for the KE?
3. What could be a "to be" context diagram for the KE?
4. Can you create a system model (level 0) from elaborating on a context diagram? Is there any general guidance for doing this job?
5. What would the system model look like for the KE, both "as is" and "to be"?
6. Can you decompose a level-0 process and create a sub-model for it on level 1? Any rules?

To begin with, Chapter 3 suggests applying the enterprise transformation model to renovate the connections of the departments and streamline the processes. In addition, the enterprise collaboration model would connect the seminars to the clients' human resources records, to support easy update of the participants' continuing training credits through societal cyber-infrastructure. Finally, the design principle for embedding IS into the societal cyber-infrastructure sheds further light. To begin with, the new IS could incorporate social networking tools from the Web to support consultants and (past) participants of seminars in hyper-networking. Then, it could create open source style repositories for seminar materials, especially those that can be reused, shared, and drawn to support new knowledge product development. It may even simplify much of the work at the materials handling department if it digitizes the seminar materials and makes them integrated with the digital seminar system. Needless to say, a digitally connected and scalable seminar system will not only support distance learning, but also facilitate on-site seminars; and ultimately make on-demand provision of customer seminars possible.

4.3.2 *Draw the Context Diagram — "As Is" vs. "To Be"*

The answers to questions 2 and 3 are shown together in Figure 4.5. Basically, five external entities are recognized for the scenario: Participant, Client Company, Consultant, Meeting Facility, and Travel Agency. Of them, Participant is mainly only implied in the status quo system; but is made active and significant by the renovation envisioned. The figure shows the context diagram for both the "as is" system and the "to be" system in one DFD. To differentiate, the

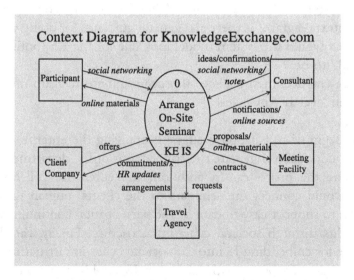

Figure 4.5:   The context diagram for KnowledgeExchange.com.

innovative ideas are indicated in *italic style*, while the generic (traditional) interactions are in regular font. The footnote of the sole process indicates the KnowledgeExchange IS as the platform on which the activity is performed.

A possible alternative representation of the black box process is to name it according to its administrative designation, such as the KnowledgeExchange IS. This is a very common practice in the field. Nevertheless, this book prefers using accurate designation of the IS' mission to name the context diagram process. Just compare a label of KE IS (without footnote) to the process in Figure 4.5 and it becomes clear why the suggested way is better: it delivers more precise and informative communication power.

4.3.3 *Draw the Level-0 System Model: General Guidance for Elaborating the Context Diagram*

The level-0 system model will elaborate the sole process of the context diagram, with the same five EE's. The data flows may be split if more than one level-0 process will receive or originate a subset of them. The question is: how many and what processes constitute "arrange on-site seminar"? There is only one basic approach to answering this question; i.e., following the pro forma business processes. For level 0, we need to recognize, preferably, 5–7 major business processes that conduct the life cycle of the mission with which the (proposed) IS is involved. If they happen to align well with the top-level organization (relative to the scope of the system), as is the case here, then the determination is straightforward. If not, then the processes may either cut across organization divisions, or split them, or do both. To help anchor the processes for better communication and definition, the organizational units that each process encompasses may be included in the footnote of that process.

Once the processes are determined, the information input and output (data flows) to these processes can be determined readily. Then, the decision on the persistent vs. transient nature of the information resources carried on these data flows needs to follow. Data stores will be determined for persistent information resources. A typical way is to designate each major type of (persistent) information resource that a level-0 process uses as a data store, and then combine identical or similar data stores across the system model to allow for commonly used data stores among processes. The transient data flows will have to go to or come from other processes. This way, the data flows will eventually connect every process to the rest of the processes, either through some data store, or by virtue of another process. Again, the connections and the logic of interaction between two processes is a focus of the IS design. Innovation typically comes from renovation of these connections and logics, which in turn come from new designs of the sources of the data flows: processes and data stores.

The status quo system for KnowledgeExchange features five processes on level 0, with each corresponding to a department in the description of the scenario. Four major types of information resources, i.e., four data stores, are recognized: consultants, client companies, meeting facilities, and seminar records (including logistics arrangements and digital materials). Their ownership (the administrative responsibility for maintenance and control) will have to be defined, too, as a part of the DFD model (appear in the logic of the owning process). All preliminary data and negotiations during the planning and preparation for the seminars will have to be communicated by pro forma connections in the form of transient inter-process data flows. Just consider the logistics process: the logistic coordinator would have to connect directly to the sales manager and others by memo, phone, or otherwise in order to make the necessary arrangements for the consultants. Therefore, the "as is" system features intricate data flows among the processes to give rise to the various workflows involved, as well as many line-crossing read-write data flows with data stores in the system model. For the purpose of this book, we only show the system model for the "to be" IS in Figure 4.6. (Can you try the "as is" one?)

The renovated system embodies the IS design ideas suggested by all three models of Section 3.2 of Chapter 3, and the design principle for embedding IS into the societal cyber-infrastructure in Section 3.3 of Chapter 3. In a nutshell, the new design digitizes all seminar materials, knowledge pieces, and other information resources; consolidates them into a single sharable and partially open repository where preliminary data will be included, as well; and connects to the human

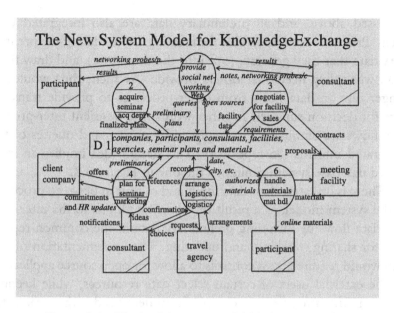

Figure 4.6: The level-0 system model for the proposed IS.

resources inputs of clients' HR systems. All preliminary data on seminar planning, which are transient data in the status quo, are now included in the data store for processes to read and update; thereby removing the need for the inter-process data flows that provide these transient data to processes. In addition, the new design enacts on the EE participants to make them active partners; and provides a new process to enable hyper-networking for consultants, for participants, and for consultants and participants, all with respect to Knowledge Exchange's interests. The new process, along with the open source knowledge materials maintained in the integrated data store, would effectively embed the new IS in the societal cyber-infrastructure for current and prospective participants and consultants to use.

Please note that the *italic names* in Figure 4.6 indicate the renovations of the new design, with the rest inherited from the status quo logic. That is, the italic elements would have to appear as some inter-process data flows and/or data flows between processes and dedicated data stores in the "as is" DFD system model. Please also note that there is only one data store for the four types of information resources discussed above, and all preliminary data are also integrated with them. Processes are responsible for creating and updating the preliminary data that they generate (put into the data store), and draw from it all what they need that others provide. As such, they would no longer rely on data flows from other processes to provide transient data for decision support. In other words, the transient inter-process data flows are eliminated; or, replaced by on-demand queries of the integrated information repository. This design idea implies an integrated database system similar to the one in Figure 3.2.

There is little transient data input and output in between processes in the system model, as a result of removing all pro forma inter-process data flows by including preliminary data in the common repository for sharing, tracking, and updating. The implementation of this idea would require access controls to allow for open source application by the external users of certain select data resources, while keeping others under proprietary control. In other words, the vision for embedding the IS into the societal cyber-infrastructure to support new value creations by hyper-networking will be balanced for the need of business control; and the balancing will become a fundamental requirement for the database design. As will be discussed in Chapter 5, a number of design approaches exist to satisfy this requirement. One obvious design is the created proxy database (partial copy) from the real production database for use exclusively by external users, i.e., the participants and consultants. The proxy database may be constructed as an open source Web database and coupled with Process 1, the social networking provider. This Web process, of course, connects the "to be" IS to the societal cyber-infrastructure and even embeds the former in the latter. In a similar way, Process 6, materials handling, may be eliminated entirely if all seminar materials will be handled online, with the assistance of proper managerial controls.

All level-0 processes should be decomposed into level-1 sub-models to further elaborate on the logic of each process. In other words, instead of verbally describing how to go about each process, we use a sub-model to do the job to reap the promises of the concise communication power of structured hierarchical modeling. For simplicity, only Process 5 is shown here.

4.3.4 *Draw a Level-1 Sub-Model for Process 5*

In the convention of decomposition as shown in Figure 4.2, Figure 4.7 presents the result of expansion of Process 5 in the system model (see Figure 4.6).

A few assumptions are made in the expansion. First, the process has the ownership of logistics data such as seminar requirements and travel plans. Therefore, the top three processes of the sub-model, i.e., Processes 5.1, 5.2, and 5.5, represent the life cycle tasks of processing this class of persistent information resources. In a similar way, the second assumption is that the sales department owns the contracts and the materials handling department owns the materials. Thus, the bottom two processes, 5.3 and 5.4, respond directly to these data (perhaps by flagging them, such as a code of approval or changes) after drawing for use from the data store, D1. Process 5.5, in contrast, may apply rigorous data processing logic to the logistics data concerned. The third assumption has to do with triggers from the data store. That is, we require the system, when implemented, to have the

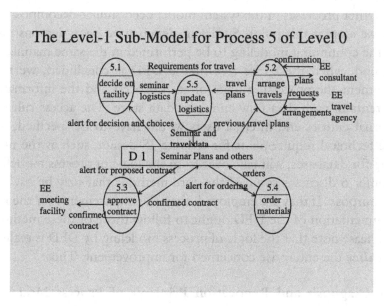

Figure 4.7: Decomposition of Process 5 from level 0 to level 1.

database capability of generating online alerts to trigger certain processes in a workflow. For example, the database may alert the logistics department that a seminar has been planned and the ensuing preparation for logistics should commence. Such alerts may be triggered either by time (e.g., two weeks before the seminar date, to alert the logistics department to order seminar materials) or by each step along the workflows upon completion (e.g., upon the receipt of materials orders, to alert the materials handling department for action).

The information contents of data flows are determined from the case description and common sense (in actuality, common sense has to be based on factual investigation, of course). For example, the data flow seminar logistics will include the number and size of meeting rooms, the type of seating arrangements, and the audio-visual equipment needed, along with the anticipated number of participants and other logistics data pertaining to a seminar. Processes 5.2 and 5.3 may involve iterative negotiations. Only one pair of data flows need to pertain to the negotiation, since they indicate the connections, or channels, not the uses of the connections. In any case, the logic of the negotiation will describe the iteration.

Other processes in the system model need similar decomposition, but we stop at this point. Sufficient details have been demonstrated for the continuing modeling to be performed in the same manner. At the end, when the entire tree of the DFD is concluded, we must document the processing logic of each process and the information contents of each data flow and each data store. The access rules for external entities and internal users would have to be specified, too. The technical requirements for ensuing IS design, such as the modeling for databases, will take over from the logic of process modeling. Chapter 6 discusses some of the core methods that may be used for this purpose. If they are employed, then the requirements for the final documentation of the DFD ought to follow those of these methods.

Please note that the logic of process modeling by DFD is really to *visualize* the enterprise concerned for improvement. Thus:

The Diagnosis and Renovation Principle of Process Modeling:
A process model should expose the causes and effects of transient data

flows to allow for deep diagnosis and possible strategic renovation. The criteria will be how the requirements for these transient and persistent data (by the decision logics of processes) contribute to the overall transaction cost and cycle time of the IS. If decreasing or increasing any particular transient or persistent information resources with some particular designs can reduce the transaction cost and cycle time, then embody these designs in the "to be" process model.

The *first corollary* is the first processes renovation principle discussed earlier; i.e., seek to consolidate special-purpose persistent information resources (e.g., inventory) into a core real-time system (e.g., CIM), and then replace the use of such special-purpose persistent data with on-demand data flows drawn from the core; assisted perhaps by decision logics embedded into the processes that use these transient data (illustrated in the ATO case of Figure 4.3). The *second corollary* is the second processes renovation principle: consolidate both special-purpose persistent data and transient data flows into an integrated repository of persistent information resources to allow processes to form workflows by drawing from (and updating to) this repository (illustrated in the renovation of Figure 4.4 into Figure 3.1).

4.4 Exercises of DFD Modeling

Let us review what we have discussed so far by doing some exercises. Please try your best first. This book provides a skeleton baseline answer after each exercise.

EXERCISE 1: Warm up to process modeling.

The scenario: Troy Rentals, Inc. manages an apartment complex. Whenever it changes rents, the rental roll clerk uses a rental information system to create a rental change form showing the apartment number, the new rent, and other pertinent data. The system then takes the form and updates the company's rental roll file. The clerk also prints out a report showing all apartments that have a rent change, along with their new and old rents and whether they are rented out currently, and sends it to the management.

Tasks: First, construct a DFD model including the context diagram and the level-0 system model, to represent the above rental update process *as described*. Then, please expand your DFD model to include this renovation: the (to-be) system will add a Web presence to it so that prospective tenants can review the rental roll from the Website and apply online. Note that all applications will be saved for the management to review, and notifications will be sent back to the applicants after the review. No further renovation, other than the straightforward expansion with Web homepages, is sought (e.g., no hyper-networking). You may make minor assumptions to clarify the processing logic if necessary, as long as they are consistent with the description. Finally, please determine the IS elements and the connections of the "to be" system from the above DFD, including the computing hardware required. Draw an EIA to show the (networking) configuration of all five classes of IS elements.

The baseline answer should include one external entity (Management), one data store (Rental Roll), and three or so level-0 processes (Create Change Form, Update Rental Roll, and Generate Report). The renovation will add one more external entity (Prospective Tenant), one more data store (Applications), and two more or so level-0 processes (Browse and Process Application), with new data flows and modifications to the baseline DFD. Both transient (e.g., Inquiry and Notification) and persistent (i.e., data store updates) data flows are present. The transient data flows should exhibit two workflows: update rental roll and process rental applications. At least one process should be Web-based (use its footnote to indicate this nature), which can be further extended to embed the system into the societal cyber-infrastructure.

The IS elements are obvious: the DFD shows that the People class includes these two types of external entities and one internal (the clerk); the Process class is made up of the application software programs that you determine the IS should have (e.g., a Perl script running on Apache for the Web process); and the Information Resources class has two major types of data — the rental rolls and applications — which may stand alone or be integrated by your discretion. The Computer (hardware platform) may consist of two PCs, one for the system and another for the management. The Infrastructure is the Internet, basically.

Therefore, an EIA can be readily obtained now. The basis of the EIA is a network diagram, on which are superposed the IS elements of users, processes (application software programs), and information resources. In this simple case, it will be a usual rendition of a Web site powered on a PC which is connected on the one end to another PC, and on the other end to an ISP on the Internet. The external users will be shown, respectively, on these two ends. The Web site PC (the IS PC) will be associated with the application software programs and information resources, along with the internal user.

EXERCISE 2: Multiplex workflows with intricate transient data flows.

The scenario: Troy Tools, Inc. has an accounts payable business process. The process uses an IS to maintain a supplier master file, containing such data as supplier description (e.g., name, address, payment terms, and contacts) and details about transactions with them (e.g., invoice history, payment history, and account balance). After reviewing and approving suppliers' invoices and credit memos, the accounts payable manager authorizes inputting data from these documents into the accounts payable file. The system then issues payment checks, reports on cash disbursement of all checks, and maintains an accounts payable transactions register. It summarizes the total value of the transactions and posts it to the general ledger system, which is not a part of this accounts payable IS; as well as prints summary reports for top management review. The system also audits and makes adjustments to postings or invoice amounts, and prepares reports on these adjustments.

The task: Please develop a context diagram and a level-0 DFD for the system.

The system has two external entities (Vendor and Top Management), not including the general ledger which may be modeled either as an external entity or as an archive (write-only data store). The system model should feature five or so processes and four or so (additional) data stores. It should include transient data flows that represent three or so workflows (payment, registry, and auditing). The accounts payable manager is an internal user, not an external entity to the system. Thus, s/he may be recognized in the footnote of some process.

EXERCISE 3: Please correct the DFD model in Figure 4.8, according only to the DFD rules in Section 4.1. (Ignore the footnotes.)

The DFD model in the figure does not conform completely to the technical conventions and rules of DFD modeling. Basically, there is one process that does not meet the requirements of being a process (having both input and output). Not all data flows are labeled with descriptive names. Some data flow is meaningless (bi-directional), which should be replaced by a pair of related but different data flows. The student information inquiry process is wrongfully modeled. Some data flows are missing and hence rendered the DFD model incomplete for some workflows (review the library update ordering cycle and the computer center software acquisition cycle). Finally, one of the processes seems to be out of the league with other processes, in terms of its workload (number of inputs and outputs) for the overall system in the model.

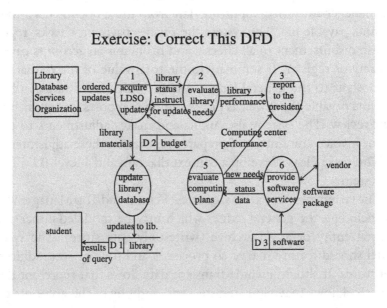

Figure 4.8: A DFD with violations to the DFD conventions.

EXERCISE 4: Please develop a DFD model for the following case and determine the IS elements and connections required/implied.

The case: Troy Music, Inc. contracts local artists (singers, musicians, composers, lyric writers, and so on) to produce musical compact disks of local flavors for local markets. Its planning department maintains a master file for area artists known to the company, including prospective artists as well as those with whom they have conducted business. The file includes the artists' profiles, such as skills, career, and past dealings with the company. Both the artists and the company could initiate a contract talk to plan for a new CD (title). The proposal then goes through a business process as described below.

The new title proposal development process: When the company initiates the contract talk, the trigger is always marketing. That is, either the marketing department received direct requests from institution buyers, or it identified an opportunity from marketing intelligence. Marketing acquires the intelligence by purchasing marketing data from external sources as well as using the company's sales records. In either case, the marketing people need to assess the request/opportunity and prepare a ranked find for the planning department. The planning people, in turn, obtain cost estimates and a production timeframe for the proposed new product from the production department and review the possibility. The production department uses production and inventory data, as well as the artist master file, to develop the required estimates. The planning department next determines the teams of artists and contacts them to negotiate a formal proposal, if the review turns out to be promising. The planning folks use primarily the artist master file in the review, but could check into the marketing and production data resources, as needed. The negotiation produces a proposal that triggers the next phase of contract development involving additional activities such as audition, attorney review, and final approval by the top management. However, these additional activities are exogenous to the New Title Proposal Development process. When the artists initiate the contract talk (for the new proposal process), they contact directly the marketing people, who, then, assess the offers and issue finds to planning as mentioned above. The marketing department is informed of the results of the proposal negotiation in order to notify the artists and institution buyers, if applicable. The planning department also updates the artist master file based on the results of negotiation and marketing finds (for new artists).

This book leaves the exercise to the reader. Just a quick hint: the proper of the system to be modeled is the proposal workflow. Production is external to the system, as is management. In addition, buyers, marketing intelligence providers, and artists are external entities, of course. A few data stores should be used to represent the major types of persistent information resources. Transient data flows can be figured out from the configuration of workflows excluding the interactions with the data stores. The latter are persistent data flows.

EXERCISE 5: Building from a status quo system model.

Suppose Figure 4.9 represents a level-0 DFD model for a university to which you would propose your iAlma ideas. Can you expand the model to reflect on the renovations required by iAlma (see Section 3.1 of Chapter 3)?

Obviously, the current model does not include alumni and the expansion has to correct this (additional external entity). Besides, it must include data stores that support the ideals of iAlma. The rest of the expansion is actually quite open, depending on the specific ideas that you have for iAlma. Please have fun.

EXERCISE 6: Can you suggest a minimalist's list of actions for turning a DFD model into a blueprint for software development (to codify the system)?

Section 4.1 has shown how to determine IS elements (especially the classes of Person, Process, and Information Resources) from a DFD model. Now, we consider the codification of them into an integrated IS. A complete DFD model contains a hierarchy of processes and the documentation for data stores and data flows, as well as the logics of the leaf-level processes in the logical model. If the system

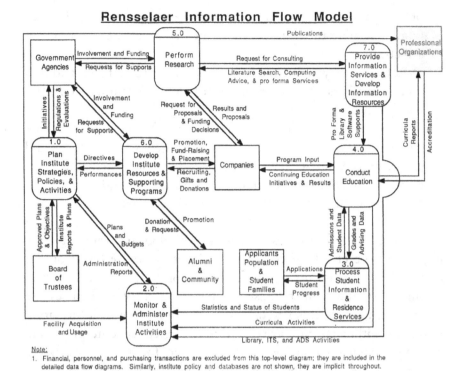

Figure 4.9: An "as is" DFD model for expansion into one for an iAlma.

is relatively straightforward, then the following baseline methodology will sufficiently indicate the approach to constructing an IS from the DFD:

- Leaf-Level Processes (in the logical model): codify the logic of each process as a stand-alone software program, a homepage, or a routine for an enterprise analytics.
- Higher Level Processes (in the tree): use them, first, to guide the aggregation of the routines and homepages into clusters of components, and then to guide the decomposition of the whole system into major applications. Plan the networking of routines and/

or navigation of homepages in accordance with the DFD tree (e.g., designing the front page and the hierarchy of homepages for a Web site).

- Data Flows: they define the I/O components (e.g., forms and user access privileges and requirements) of software routines and database connections.
- Data Stores: each data store specifies an "object" for software engineering, or a "universe relations" for data normalization, and gives rise to database views. Normalize these views to define a data model for the database intended (e.g., Access, MySQL, or Oracle). Then, create the database (e.g., tables) as designed.

Database design is key to IS design. Although software engineering is the core effort for codifying an IS, it has to be based on the logics of information integration, or the connection of information resources for the connectionist IS. The next chapter discusses the design methods for this key task, for the connection of information resources within an enterprise, within an extended enterprise, and within an open community on the Internet, for hyper-networking. Before we leave, the lesson of process modeling is summarized below:

The Enterprise Information Architecture Principle of Process Modeling: *A process modeling endeavor ought to be geared towards determining (the optimal) IS elements, especially the classes of People, Process, and Information Resources. A measure of completeness is whether the results lead to sufficient formulation of the EIA for the IS intended.*

Chapter 5

Architectures of Information Integration: From Single Databases and Distributed Databases to Multiple Databases and Internet Databases

The connection of the third class of IS elements, Information Resources, determines the technical nature of an IS: whether it is an integrated IS, or a system of IS; and whether or not it is open and scalable. Proprietary ownership may determine the nature of purview for an IS, but only information integration can determine its capacity for control and application. Connection at the People class only gives the users access to the interfaces of the (many) IS involved, as the Web does; while connection at the Process class provides inter-operation of individual applications. However, neither connection allows for direct access to the underlying information resources as a whole, nor the use of them with an integrated view and tool. Only integrative connection of Information Resources gives users the full-fledged database capabilities. The baseline database model was devised originally for integrating disparate files of application software systems into a single repository under company control. But the same principles were soon being extended and applied to integrating all kinds of disparate data resources, or islands of automation, across extended enterprises (e.g., federated autonomous distributed databases), and even across massive numbers of independent databases on the Internet. This chapter presents these database models as design methods for connecting massive information resources of an IS, or systems of IS. It progresses from single enterprise databases to federated databases of multiple organizations, and finally to collaboration of vast amount of independent Internet databases. It also shows how the design ideas support the principle of embedding IS into societal cyber-infrastructure, including a proposal for designing a WRAS system (see Section 3.3 of Chapter 3) from these ideas.

5.1 The Baseline Database Model: The Three-Schema Concept

In a nutshell, the core logic of the database model is this divide and conquer: first, separating user (application) views, common semantic core (entities, relationships, and/or objects), and the structure of storage (e.g., access methods for mass storage hardware) from each other; and then consolidating the last two to support the first. For example, a manufacturer may operate an inventory system, a production scheduling system, and an engineering design system. These systems may use different software and maintain their own files which all contain their own versions of product (part) data. The production file may view products in the context of bill-of-material; while the inventory file arranges them according to the views of stocking (sorted by types) and procurement (related to suppliers). The engineering file, in a similar way, focuses on CAD requirements and solid modeling. Clearly, these three systems cannot swap their product data and are bound to have duplicate or even inconsistent data on products.

Another perspective to this data integration is revealed in DFD: different data stores may exist in a DFD model to be maintained and shared by multiple processes. These data stores may each contain some data items unique to it, but may also contain some data items common to some other data stores or to all of them. The way each process sees the data (how they use them) may be different, even for the common data items. Thus, some normalization of all data resources across the data stores is naturally needed, as a part of the IS implementation design.

The most straightforward way to integrate different versions of information resources is to replace them all by a single, integrated version; e.g., consolidate the above three file-based systems into one and require all three types of users to see the data in a unison way, regardless of their different needs and contexts. This approach does not work since it puts the cart before the horse, demanding that the need for data be dominated by the convenience of data processing, rather than the other way around. To make the integration work, the consolidation of data resources must not destroy the user views, or the natural/required ways of using the data. The solution is the separation of the user views from the core semantics of the common data — the views will be individually derived from the common core, which is independent of any particular applications, including possible future applications. The database will implement the common core and provide the derivations to support both the user views and the application software programs that run on these views. This is referred to as *data independence*. With data independence, the common core may be modified without necessitating the corresponding modification on application programs (only the derivation of views need to be adjusted), and vice versa. In addition, new views can be constructed from the common core on demand. Thus, certain openness and scalability for the repository of data resources are achieved.

This principle of data independence can also be applied to the physical storage designs of the computer that processes the database. That is, a set of logical designs will be abstracted from the common access methods of computer storage, and the actual storage of the common core will be structured according to these logical designs. The results will be a portable database that can migrate from one hardware platform to another with relative ease. Data independence includes these two types of separation for the common core at these two ends. This book refers to this design of data independence and its attendant requirements of data modeling (i.e., how to represent the common core for flexible derivations of views) as the *baseline database model*.

Please note at this point that the baseline database model requires physical integration of data resources into a common core, as well as a logical one to represent the common core. In the example of the three islands of product data, all three versions of product files would be replaced by a common one. This replacement represents a limitation to the baseline model since it is not always possible, or at least not always preferred. A reason is differences in the native data models that these islands use. The CAD system, as a case in point, may use object-orientation to structure its application and data management, while the other two systems may employ the relational model. For the CAD, the separation may not be feasible in its current technology, and even if it is, it may not run effectively if it has to import product data from a (relational-object hybrid) database that it does not control directly. The same may apply to bill-of-materials processing, which tends to require specially structured data and logic. Needless to say, if these three islands happen to belong to different organizations which collaborate on the same product data, then physical integration is really infeasible and impractical. Therefore, the baseline model has evolved over the past decades since its conception in the 1960s, to better support integration without strict physical consolidation. The rest of this chapter will review these extensions.

The baseline database model is formally presented in Figure 5.1, which is a reconstruction of a previous rendition of the concept by Date (2004). The figure shows five layers and one administer software. From top to bottom, the first layer is external to the database albeit defining its purpose: the end users and machine (application software programs) users. The next four layers constitute the database system. The facility layer provides interactive query languages to end users (e.g., SQL, see Chapter 7), embedment of the query languages in common programming languages (e.g., the SQL library for Perl, PHP, C, C++, etc.), and (links to) common programming languages that the machine users require (the applications may be coded in these languages).

The sets of external views — the External Schemata — represent the pro forma data that particular applications use (and that the end users routinely use). Each set may correspond to a particular file in the island IS that the database integrates, such as Inventory or Scheduling. Each set may also be considered as corresponding to a data store in the DFD model. The conceptual view, or the Conceptual Schema, is the logical definition of the common core normalized and

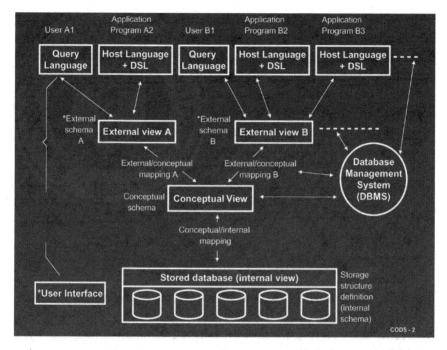

Figure 5.1: The baseline database model: three schema, DBMS, and user facility.

consolidated from all the views (see Chapter 6), and from which all (new) views derive. Finally, the Internal Schema (storage structure definition) defines how the common core is mapped to storage structures by which the raw data are stored. The physical raw data of the common core may or may not be included in this bottom layer, depending on how they are controlled by the administer software: the database management system (DBMS). The DBMS creates the schemas, manages the facility, and generates the mappings between schemas for the users. It controls all four basic types of operations (insertion, updating, retrieval, and deletion) requested of the data in the database by the users, and conducts the processing.

Please note that the notion of an external schema has broad significance: it both conceals the conceptual schema and rhapsodizes it at the same time. Modern databases tend to open the conceptual schema to any users and hence do not require external schemas, technically. However, an external schema is a virtual representation of the database crafted particularly for a user (group). External schemas can make end users' queries easier and correspond directly to application programs. Moreover, an external schema can restrict and masquerade the scope of data that a user group can see. Thus, different masquerades may be presented to different user sub-communities as "the" database for them to use while protecting the real thing. An external schema is really a rhapsody that works, to connect users to the database. This idea is important for the extension of the baseline model as we will see later.

EXERCISES

1. Is Microsoft Access a database or a DBMS? How about Oracle and MySQL?
2. What are the three schemas in an Access database (a database managed by Access)?
3. How does Access connect to another database (managed by a different DBMS)?
4. What facility/programming environments does Access provide/support? VBA and Excel?
5. How does Oracle differ from Access (other than the price tags) — i.e., what classes of capabilities does Oracle provide and Access does not?
6. How does the three-schema model explain why an integrated database as shown in Figure 3.1 can support the different applications in the workflow processes shown in Figure 4.4?
7. How do you compare the three-schema concept to the software engineering principle of View-Model-Control? (Hint: the software engineering principle advises abstracting the semantics of software objects, called views, into a common logical model, and provides controls to process the objects for their individual purposes but manage them globally according to the model.)
8. Can you suggest some general design principles for connecting disparate information resources in any environment — i.e., what does the baseline model teach us?

9. Can you think of some possible extensions of the baseline model to cover for (the integration of) multiple databases? By using the connection facility?

Microsoft Access is a DBMS that manages and processes databases. It is not a repository of the raw data themselves. Generally speaking, Access consists of a number of basic types of constructs, including Graphical User Interface (GUI)/Form, Page, Report Generator, Macro, Query, Base Table, and some facility. What it calls Query is actually external views defined from the base tables. Thus, a Query in Access is a virtual table consisting of pointers to data items (fields) in base tables. Needless to say, (the definition of) base tables constitute the conceptual schema of an Access database. When one creates (defines) base tables, one is creating the conceptual schema. When one defines Queries, one is creating an external schema. The internal schema is not exposed to the users, nor controllable by the database owners. Access supports end users by virtue of its GUI, especially forms; but it also provides the facility to run SQL in batch mode as well as applications coded in Visual Basic (VBA). Excel is an external environment that can import from and export data to Access. The facility is integrated with the Microsoft Office environment. Also included in the facility are tools of connection with other database environments, such as Link and ODBC (open database connector). These tools work as views (virtual tables) except that they are exposed (readable) to other databases, with ODBC catered to Web technology while Link not. This is a very powerful feature for connecting Access and other DBMS that have the same provision, in a system-of-IS fashion.

A full-fledged enterprise class DBMS such as Oracle and DB2 distinguishes itself from Access and other personal class DBMS, including MySQL, in the capability of running (massive) concurrent processing jobs, huge volume of data management, and sophisticated database administration (DBA). A lot of the capability comes from the fact that the enterprise DBMS runs from the platform of heavy duty computing servers, while Access operates on PC. However, even when Access and MySQL are implemented on a server that supports concurrent processing, only one job can really run at any one time, with other "concurrent" jobs being put in a queue by design. In contrast, enterprise DBMS may share processing among millions of database jobs. Volume of data reflects on similar design limits: millions of entries of thousands of tables on the enterprise side versus thousands of entries of dozens of tables on the personal side.

The DBA capability is critically important to enterprise databases. It needs to support database design. It must provide integrity control (to safeguard data quality and consistency across the large user community) and security control. In addition, the ability and capacity to back up the database or roll back transactions to some known points in time are treasured, too. Finally, the DBMS may also need provisions to expand into distributed environments across a number of geographical locations. Such is the unique capability of enterprise class DBMS which earns its price tags.

The answer to Question 6 should be evident at this point. A full-fledged, enterprise class DBMS will structure the files in Figure 4.4 for the previous commercial loan approval workflow (islands of automation) into a normalized conceptual schema, and physically consolidate these data resources into one database. However, the original files will be mapped to external schemas (one set for each file) and thereby be "kept" as virtual files. The original application software programs (coded in C, C Sharp, etc.) can continue to run against these virtual files through the programming facility. Any changes to the applications or to the database will be managed as changes to the mapping between external schema and conceptual schema (and perhaps between conceptual schema and internal schema, too). For example, in a SQL database, the mapping is accomplished by virtue of "define/create view" expressions; which can be easily modified and re-interpreted right away, or re-compiled the next time the database is opened again.

Question 7 has in fact answered itself: the View-Model-Control principle is another rendition of the data independence principle. Both call for views, separated from the common core logic (conceptual schema vs. model), with the ability to map between them and process according to them (DBMS vs. control). This comparison intends to sensitize the readers to the broader implications of the baseline model. Questions 8 and 9 follow up on this point.

Concerning Question 8, the baseline database model achieves the connection of information resources *within an enterprise*. It proves the following general design principles. First, data independence is the key to achieving openness and scalability of the connection. Second, metadata (the three schemas) provide information integration. Third, a common open query language may be the best way to connect people and processes with information resources. And, fourth, an information regime (implemented in the baseline model by the DBMS) is needed to define and maintain the integration. The baseline database model may be extended to provide connections between enterprises and across the entire Web as Question 9 asks. Various extension designs typically reflect various interpretations and implementations of these principles.

Now, this chapter follows Question 9 into the next sections.

5.2 Multiple Databases: Distributed Database, Federated Databases, and Metadatabase

The scope of connection discussed in this section is integration of information resources *within an extended enterprise*, where proprietary purviews of databases exist through perhaps some oversight authority. The extended enterprise may include a number of databases located in different locations, but the number is in dozens and at most hundreds, rather than thousands or millions. According to the technical nature of the distribution, three classes are reviewed here: (1) distributed database (singular), where an intrusive single DBMS controls all the distributed data; (2) federated databases (plural), where an administer mechanism coordinates multiple databases in a fixed federation structure; and (3) Metadatabase, where a logical integrator uses metadata (data models and logics) to provide open and scalable connections of multiple databases. All of them are direct extensions to the baseline database model.

5.2.1 *Models of a Distributed Database: Extending the Single DBMS to Connect Multiple User Systems, Data Storages, and External Data Sources*

The signature property of this class of designs is a single DBMS that manages the distribution of data and synchronizes the processing of the distributed data. We recognize three sub-classes: a number of *user systems drawing from a central database* (e.g., Access databases draw data from an Oracle database); a number of distributed *component systems* making up an overall database; and a number of independent databases providing select data to form a surrogate database for particular applications. The first case is commonplace in actuality but seldom formally recognized. The second is the classical *distributed database*. The third describes *data warehouses* and variations such as history databases and summary databases. All three classes support database query and batch mode retrieval; but only the classical distributed database also supports distributed synchronization. They are direct extensions to the baseline database model, with each featuring their unique designs and hence properties, as shown in Figure 5.2.

In the figure, the baseline database model of Figure 5.1 is extended in three different ways. The external user systems may be any databases that the end users use, which draw data from the enterprise database in the background with or without the users' involvement. The arrows signify online exporting of external schemas from the DBMS to the user systems. Specifically, both systems will create identical views for the data (e.g., tables) that they share in their respective environments. Then, the user systems will declare these views in their linkage facility (e.g., Link or ODBC) and draw data from the prime DBMS. The facility may provide automatic feeding in some cases (including Access). The symbol "DB" represents external databases from which the data warehouse (or equivalent) draws data to save into its own system by the DBMS. The two-way arrows for the distributed database design indicate indigenous control by the DBMS of the distributed data resources as if they were physically collocated. The controls include data definition, management, and

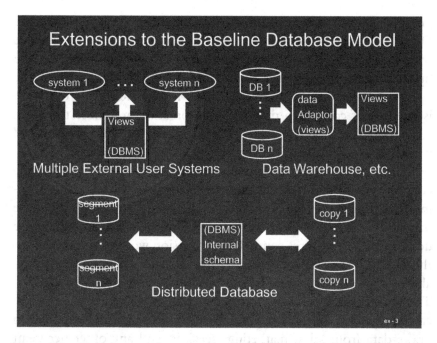

Figure 5.2: Multiple external user systems, data warehouse, and distributed database.

synchronized processing for both read and write. The distributed database may save different segments and/or copies of the data in different locations.

The first class may be illustrated by an office environment where many professionals of different trades maintain their own spreadsheets and Access database applications (e.g., VBA programs) on their own PCs. If an integrated enterprise database exists (using, e.g., PostgreSQL) to manage all these office-related data resources along with other production data, then the multiple external user systems design can apply. The PostgreSQL database will export data according to the external schemas defined for the professionals, and as drawn by the Access links on their PCs when Access is opened. The tables in the link can then feed the professionals' applications. This process may not be reversed automatically. To feed data into the prime database, the professionals would have to go through PostgreSQL in the due process of the DBA. However, the "due process" may be automated for the external users. For example, the DBA can design some professionals' update template which embeds with required SQL expressions and other analytics to check on the updated data, send them to the prime DBMS, and execute the update, with or without the DBA's direct involvement. Improvization is needed, of course, to design the automation and close the read-write loop, based on what the DBMS and user systems really are and what they have to offer. The point is that this can be done, usually.

The data warehouse design also makes use of the external schema concept, except that it works virtually in the opposite direction: feeding data from the external systems to the prime (the data warehouse database). Although the basic logic is similar, the data warehouse design typically requires some data conversion work to smoothen out the heterogeneity in the various external data sources and thereby allow data from all sources to run on the prime in the same manner. The adaptor design, as expected, depends on the particulars of the case in question. Examples include a customer data warehouse, which draws data from sales, marketing, services, and any other pertinent sources to provide the enterprise with a 360-degree view of the customers. The sources of the data may be production databases engaging in real-time actual business transactions for the enterprise; but the data warehouse may not need such real-time data, and hence does not need to be a real-time online indigenous user of these systems. It may only require batch-processed offline data in the same timing. Thus, a variation of the data warehouse concept is the general notions of history database, summary database, and more, where offline, batch-processed data are saved separately for particular repetitive query. By definition, this class of designs does not require feeding data back to the external sources.

The distributed database class involves some of the most rigorous database technology in the field since they require real-time and online synchronization of data processing across all storage systems. The typical premise is that these distributed storages are homogeneous in their design and using the same technology. The DBMS provides uniform access to the distributed storages so that the users need not be aware of the distributed nature of the physical data resources.

For users, the distributed database might as well be a traditional single database. In addition, the segments and copies shown in Figure 5.2 may have their own local users whose access to the database is limited to the local segments. Today's DBMS industry tends to blend the distributed database technology into their single enterprise DBMS products. If the homogeneity premise does not hold, then the situation becomes one of multiple databases, no longer a singular distributed database. This situation is discussed next.

5.2.2 *Models of Federated Databases: Logically Connect Enterprise Databases*

How can a supply chain connect the suppliers' production and inventory databases to the IS at the prime? Such a connection would empower the operations officer at the prime (e.g., Cisco, Boeing, GM, and Wal-Mart) to drill through the suppliers and obtain sufficient understanding on the status of their production schedules, such as whether or not they can meet the deadlines of their products' delivery. This is but one obvious example why connecting different enterprise databases may be a good and necessary idea. Equally obvious is the fact that such connection begs for advanced designs to overcome the many complex issues involved. Foremost is, naturally, the problem of proprietary control. It is no small issue to open a company's production database to others, even if the other is its prime customer. Then, there comes the technical problem: How can the supply chain reconcile schemas, define and enforce consistent data semantics, and synchronize processing across a wide range of DBMSs and computing platforms located possibly in different places, regions, or even countries and continents? If a technical solution exists which also allows the participant companies to maintain the necessary proprietary control and security, then it would help solve the proprietary problem, too.

Researchers in the field have developed many different designs, each of which offers a different level of information integration, ranging from connecting only the users to also connecting processes, and ultimately to connecting databases. Accordingly, they impose different degrees of intrusive coordination across these participant databases. The early approaches tend to either improvise or extend directly the three-schema model. The latter would impose some global conceptual schema over the local databases for all DBMSs to follow, and employ application program interchanges (API) to translate queries and swap data among these databases. The challenges are apparent: Even the loose form of a common schema requires global definition and maintenance, which dictates what and how data from one local database can be used in another. This level of intrusion and infringement on the autonomy and proprietary control of local databases may be unacceptable to many, and hinders the performance, too.

Over time, the field has largely settled on the general notion of federated databases as the norm for connecting multiple databases within an (extended) enterprise (see, e.g., Litwin *et al.*, 1990; and Stonebraker *et al.*, 1996). This approach does not require a global conceptual schema but replaces it with a (loose) collection of schemas from all participant databases. These participant schemas describe what they routinely request and offer as views for others to see. Any change to these requests and offers (related to external schemas) will cause re-definition of views, or schema updates. Therefore, participant schemas really represent pro forma connections rather than on-demand requests and offers. They use a common query language, which tends to be the ANSI SQL, to process global queries, and a system of APIs to prepare them for execution at local DBMS. The rest of the operation is standard DBMS processing.

Although many variations of the federation concept and technology exist today, this book presents the one shown in Figure 5.3 as a baseline design (Litwin *et al.*, 1990). In the figure, Import Schema represents the inputting connection (requests) and Export Schema the outputting connection (offers). Please note that these requests and offers have to be determined *a priori*, in order to be coded into the schemas. They really define the pro forma external connections conceived for the local databases. Each of such schemas represents the whole user community at a local system. This design requires rigorous maintenance of the system of Import Schemas and Export Schemas, as well as query translation and data conversion APIs. In any case, federated databases in actuality tend to focus on information retrieval

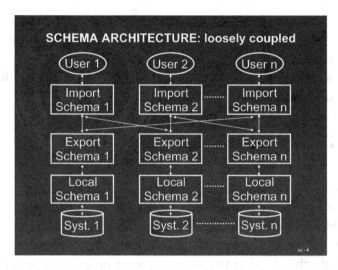

Figure 5.3:   Federated databases: inter-operation by connecting external schemas.

and leave out database updates. In other words, users from one local system in the federation will be able to query the databases in any other local system per the export schemas, but may update only their own databases. No global synchronization is provided, other than the maintenance of the global schema system depicted in the figure.

However, the maintenance of the schemas, along with the requirements to design and enforce a global ontology for the federation, tends to be a majorly involved task if the federation is not trivially small or simple. This is the first problem that still challenges the field. In addition, database updates may increasingly become a must since extended enterprises (e.g., the Cisco/Boeing/GM/Wal-Mart supply chains) are increasingly closely knitted. Supply chain integration leads to overlapped information resources, which in turn lead to the need for cascading database updates. Some improvising designs may work readily here, such as using database triggers to propagate selected updates, without having to require a wholesale DBMS capability of distributed synchronization. An example is to trigger an email carrying database update objects upon the occurrence of the event that certain data fields are updated. To do so, the logics of the triggers need to be modeled and managed globally, although a DBMS facility already exists (e.g., PL/SQL) that can implement them. The global representation and management of such logics is another problem still facing the field.

These two problems lead to the Metadatabase design that this chapter discusses next.

5.2.3 *The Metadatabase Model: An Open and Scalable Database of Schemas and Logics*

This book presents the Metadatabase model as an alternative design to the usual federated databases that holds promise for resolving some of the problems discussed above. In a nutshell, the Metadatabase model attempts to achieve openness and scalability for the connection of multiple databases, while still assuming some proprietary purview. The main difference stems from the design of the global schema system and the provision of efficient updates. Although particular technology has been developed to implement the new design, this book attempts to separate the implementation of the design from its design ideas that hold broad implications, and discusses only these general ideas.

The Metadatabase model is the result of years of research at Rensselaer — see, e.g., Hsu (1996) and Levermore *et al.* (2010). It is not a commercial system, but the concept and design have been proven in industrial settings. Although the whole model can be implemented using commonly available technology, including open source technology, this book presents it as some general design ideas for information integration. The model was motivated by resolving some of the hard challenges in the field of federated databases.

Simply put, the Metadatabase is a database of enhanced "integration schema" and logics to play the role of the global schema system in the federated databases design. The integrated schema is in essence data models and their correspondence to the schemas of the participant databases. The logics are in general not included in federated databases, but are added here to facilitate database updates for the whole community.

The first design idea to make the federated designs more open and scalable is to turn schemas and logics into metadata that a DBMS can process. We note that schemas come from data models such as relations and objects — e.g., a base table in Access or Oracle is the implementation of a relation defined with the primary key, attributes, and other semantic constraints such as foreign keys and cascading rules. The data models, in turn, are data specifications of some semantic definition of the information world concerned. These definitions may express the information resources in terms of entities, relationships, and their attributes; or the inheritance hierarchy of objects. Thus, although schemas are tightly embedded in particular DBMSs, the definitions of semantic models and data models are nonetheless generic and may be represented as metadata for a DBMS.

Furthermore, if these metadata are further typed according to some ontology (e.g., the categorization by the concepts and constructs used in data models, such as Entity, relationship, and so on), then the DBMS of metadata will be able to tabulate, subset, and perform all four basic types of database operations on them. In this way, an unlimited number of such definitions can be uniformly managed by the DBMS as ordinary data do, for all platforms and implementation environments. When database logics such as triggers and alerts are represented as rules, or the first order predicate logic, they can be represented as metadata for the same DBMS to manage in the same manner. Thus, the second basic design idea is to employ a simple but encompassing ontology of data modeling to structure the DBMS of metadata, or the Metadatabase. In the literature, the Metadatabase model uses the Two-Stage Entity-Relationship (TSER) method for this purpose (Hsu *et al.*, 1991), which is discussed in the next chapter.

How does the Metadatabase achieve openness and scalability for the global schema system? Suppose a participant database is represented as a group of metadata indicating one member, four applications, ten entities, twelve relationships, twenty relations, thirty-two rules and constraints, and so on. Then, the corresponding tables of metadata in the Metadatabase (the DBMS that manages the metadata) will have one entry in its Member tables, four in Application, ten in Entity, twelve in Relationship, twenty in Relation, and some entries in the tables for Rules and so on. Other participant databases will be similarly added to the Metadatabase. In the end, the Member table may include ten entities representing ten such participants. This is only an illustration, of course, since the details will be dependent on the specific design of the Metadatabase, and the specific design has to account for the ontology of data models and semantic concepts. The TSER-based design in Chapter 6 is a reference point for such design.

As stated above, the Metadatabase model brings more openness and scalability to the global schema system, since it can add, delete, and modify the participant databases' connections to the federation (requests and offers) by performing ordinary database query on their metadata. Compared to the usual federated databases, the Metadatabase does not require any schema restructuring that is disruptive to the operation of the federation. In addition, the Metadatabase can coordinate the processing logics (required by, e.g., the trigger APIs) for the entire federation in the same manner; thus, it can assist on a rule-based system for database updates.

Figure 5.4 depicts how the Metadatabase adds to the federation of databases. The context of the illustration is a CIM (computer-integrated manufacturing) environment, where multiple databases exist in the enterprise, each of which uses a different information regime and a different DBMS to run it. Some of the multiple databases may be distributed in nature, such as the concurrent engineering environment, and hence the Metadatabase may distribute to it, too.

It should be noted that all participant databases in the figure continue to operate with total proprietary control as if the Metadatabase did not exist. Only added functionality will require specific additional actions on the part of the participants. Compared to Figure 5.3, the Metadatabase contains the definitions and logics for the pro forma connections among the participant databases; and hence is minimally comparable to the system of Import and Export Schemas. However, more metadata contents from participants may be put into the Metadatabase to increase its functionality, all the way up to the inclusion of the whole models. At the bare minimum, the Metadatabase works as an online metadata repository for any participant to tap into; and next it can provide global query (Cheung and Hsu, 1996). At the full scale, with rule processing (Babin and Hsu, 1996), the Metadatabase joins global updates for the federation.

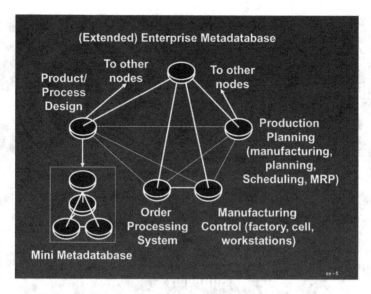

Figure 5.4: The Metadatabase as a global schema system.

Figure 5.5 illustrates how the Metadatabase model processes database updates. The context is an industrial supply chain. The double circles in the figure signify a system of APIs that assists in the triggering of updates and the translation and data conversion of global query processing. The logics of these APIs are managed by the Metadatabase and hence are open and scalable to changes.

The Metadatabase model responded to the two major problems of federated databases that Section 5.2.2 points out, but did not address the following issues: How can we support "on-demand" collaboration among participants, i.e., allowing the participant databases to post select data resources to the Metadatabase — flexible and dynamic requests and offers, rather than always following a wholesale permission? How can we scale up the federation to open communities on the Internet, with a size of possibly thousands and millions of databases? How can we embed the Metadatabase in the societal cyber-infrastructure? In short, we ask how can we effect hyper-networking of information resources to enable value cocreation on the Web?

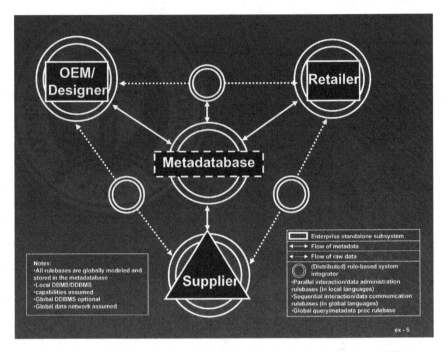

Figure 5.5:   Information integration by virtue of the Metadatabase.

The next section describes how the design ideas of Figure 5.4 may be further generalized to respond to these challenges, and to help implement the design principle of embedding IS into societal cyber-infrastructure.

5.3 Connection of Independent Internet Databases: The Hyper-Networking Provider

The connectionist IS definition suggests hyper-networking of IS elements up to the scale of involving the entire Internet community. Arguably, the first class, people, has been hyper-networked. The second class, processes, has also made significant progress towards this end as long as no information integration is required, by virtue of e-commerce (see Section 2.2 of Chapter 2). The third class, information resources, is a major drag, at least not at the scale of thousands, tens of thousands, and millions of Internet databases. Is it feasible? This book summarizes proven results in the field that support this goal, and couples them with design ideas from the research literature, to establish some conceptual possibilities in this section. We will try to rivet these possibilities in concrete analysis (see also Hsu *et al.*, 2007; Levermore *et al.*, 2010).

First, why bother? Answering this question will lead to the database requirements of hyper-networking that go beyond what the field has to provide today. To this end, let us consider a well-known context for hyper-networking databases: a large supply chain community where vast numbers of companies from different industries transact with each other on demand and thereby form massively extended virtual enterprises along both demand chains and supply chains. For simplicity, we refer to the need for hyper-networking information resources as the *information collaboration* problem.

As discussed before, these virtual extended enterprises come into being by digitizing and connecting IS elements across multiple enterprises. Each particular connection (configuration) of these IS elements gives rise to particular (feasible) information supply chains in the community. Thus, information collaboration is characterized by on-demand information supply chains. The core of such information supply chains consists of the enterprise databases that support them. Because enterprise databases are proprietarily designed and controlled — i.e., they are independent of the supply chains — their connection inherently requires open and scalable designs that afford maximum flexibility with minimum disruption for collaboration.

For example, the transaction phase of supply chain integration requires, ideally, the independent databases in the participating enterprises (e.g., those of retail forecasting, retail inventory, suppliers' ordering, suppliers' production, suppliers' delivering, and other life cycle tasks) to work together as if they were pertaining to one organization, and coalesce using one data management regime (e.g., "drilling through" these databases for global scheduling). This oneness reduces the global transaction cost and cycle time of the extended enterprise of the supply chain. Clearly, the integration regime that achieves this oneness needs to be able to reconfigure its connections and respond to new demands, as the oneness is bound to evolve. To help our analysis, we use the following scenario to illustrate the requirements of design.

The supply chain scenario: A manufacturer makes different products to supply multiple primes in different industries (including, e.g., Boeing, Cisco, GE, and Wal-Mart). These products share common raw materials, some common parts, and certain common fabrication facilities. All data are controlled under the same enterprise resource planning systems throughout their production cycle; but they are subject to different (simultaneous) supply chain regimes (e.g., data interchange protocols) imposed respectively by these primes. Each prime also promotes its own goals of (on-demand) collaboration and information sharing throughout its own supply chain, such as e-engineering for design and global coordination of demand-supply schedules. Each chain is in fact recursive, since the prime has its own customers (e.g., the prime defense contractors who subcontract to Boeing) who, in turn, have their customers; and the manufacturer has its own suppliers who have their suppliers as well. The situation goes on until it reaches end users and individual production-factor providers at the level of people. The manufacturer needs to reconcile these differing regimes, configure and reconfigure its enterprise databases' roles in these collaboration relations, and minimize the impact of disruptions due to any changes or failures in any parts of these concurrent supply chains. Furthermore, the manufacturer wishes to solicit as many new buyers and select from as many new suppliers as possible from the global market. In all these cases, it wishes to reap the maximum benefits of shared data resources throughout the extended enterprises to coordinate its production and inventory schedules and reach maximum quality and productivity. Thus, there are numerous potential information supply chains just like there are numerous potential supply chains. An open and scalable design for connecting the manufacturer's enterprise databases to any supply chain is required.

The above scenario illustrates what is hyper-networking of information resources and why it is desirable. This book notes that supply chains in practice tend to use fixed protocols (or "workarounds") to connect independent databases. This approach is often associated with asymmetrical business relations, where the dominating primes promote asymmetrical sharing of information to their advantage, such as retrieval of on-demand information from supplier databases, but not the other way around. While it may also allow the suppliers (e.g., Warner-Lambert) to gain access to select information at the prime (e.g., Wal-Mart's sales forecasting on Listerine), this approach typically presents major obstacles to the suppliers who are subject to multiple concurrent supply chains — e.g., the manufacturer in the above supply chain scenario.

More fundamentally, hard-coded designs by nature do not respond well to disruptions such as connection failures. They do not facilitate flexibility dictated by shifting demands, evolving requirements, and new technology, either. In addition, application-based proprietary protocols tend to be intrusive and costly to change. Open technologies such as XML, ebXML, and UDDI help to an extent, but their effectiveness may be limited. The latter is generally dependent on how standardized these databases are in their design and semantics, since interchanging data is not the same as understanding the data. Often, as shown in present B2B practices (see, e.g., Alibaba. com, Ariba.com, and PerfectCommerce.com), only basic file transfer (using, e.g., fixed format) is enabled, not database queries.

The model of information collaboration will allow an enterprise to simultaneously participate, on demand, in many collaborating relations across many supply chains, as the manufacturer in the aforementioned scenario wishes to do. The best characterization of the model may be the ability to offer/sell as well as request/buy random information from all participants. This on-demand request and offer ability benefits all parties involved since it delivers cost benefits from flexible processes and accumulated data resources, as well as global coordination. Therefore, the general notion of hyper-networking information resources is reduced to the particular analysis of the on-demand requests and offers on the Internet. Establishing the technical feasibility of providing this ability helps prove that hyper-networking at the information resources level is not infeasible.

What has the field established for information collaboration, towards providing the ability of on-demand requests and offers?

Generally speaking, the field has achieved massively distributed process inter-operation which stops short of database collaboration. Take the e-commerce practices of Exchange and ASP for example (see Section 2.2.4 of Chapter 2): the Exchange model expands pair-wise relations of B2B procurement into open and scalable marketplaces for all buyers and sellers to meet and transact and thereby gain possible economies of scale (by virtue of competition as well as consolidation of transaction supports). The Exchange can either be public, in the style of the New York Stock Exchange; or private, led by some prime companies in a particular space such as Convisint.com for automotive. The model entails a technical "federation" design linking the global market servers and the massively distributed information systems of the participating enterprises. Each meeting of buyer and seller forms an on-demand B2B connection, and connecting inter-related B2Bs results in an on-demand supply chain.

The Exchange model promotes new IS design paradigms that employ matchmaking at a global site (to establish the requirement of connection) and proxy servers at local/enterprise sites (to execute the connection at the level of processes/applications — e.g., swapping XML objects). However, it does not support buyers and sellers querying each other's databases. This is an unfortunate limitation since, at the least, buyers and sellers need to match their information requests and offers in order to help establish the requirements of a supply chain. At the execution phase, they also need to match information for mission-critical tasks.

The ASP model, on the other hand, turns a software vendor into an online global processor/server of the software for the clients. Therefore, IS designs of the ASP model promote shared data and transaction management, featuring client-side computing as well as strong server capabilities. These practices continue to expand and result in further design paradigms including the employment and deployment of open source technology. New models and business designs such as service-oriented computing and computing/software as a service (e.g., SaaS) have also developed. Incidentally, the SaaS practices have proven that it is practical to make massively distributed process inter-operation open and scalable, not just technically feasible.

In fact, from the perspective of information collaboration, all these models also proved the need for openness and scalability in their connection of processes (see, e.g., UN/CEFACT, 2003).

How can we extend the state-of-the-art for full-fledged information collaboration? This book recognizes this basic approach: combining the Exchange (and perhaps ASP, too) model with open and scalable federated databases, using the societal cyber-infrastructure. The first order of business is to further open up the previous results to inter-operation on the Internet, and then the field needs to couple them with select results of process inter-operation to facilitate information collaboration. Figure 5.6 represents a particular design along this line of research (see Hsu *et al.*, 2007; and Levermore *et al.*, 2010).

This IS design synthesizes certain open and scalable results of the Exchange model with the Metadatabase model; namely, integrating the matchmaking methods of the former with the Metadatabase global query methods of the latter. However, the Metadatabase in the figure may be less controlling than it is in Figure 5.5. It may distribute some core metadata to participant sites to support peer-to-peer collaboration, and control only the maintenance of such metadata.

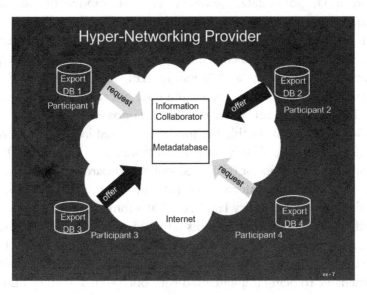

Figure 5.6: A hyper-networking design for connecting Internet databases.

It may also reply entirely on an open registration process to populate itself from participant sites. It may also confine its operation to the support of the Information Collaborator.

The Information Collaborator in the figure is an information exchange (matchmaker) that connects information requests with appropriate information offers. These requests and offers come from the Export Databases of participants, which are registered with the Information Collaborator. Export Databases represent participants. It is a proxy of the real production databases at the participants' sites, created expressly for information collaboration. It is both a firewall and an import and export facility for the community of collaboration. Each Export Database defines the connections (comparable to the Import and Export Schemas of Figure 5.3) for the participant's enterprise databases. It is populated with "images" of real production data from the enterprise systems, and hence is comparable to data warehouses in this sense. It executes the actual information interchanges with other Export Databases. An Export Database can make requests (issue queries) against other Export Databases, just as it can respond to others' requests in the manner of traditional global database query. The data models of the Export Databases are integrated in the Metadatabase (see Figure 5.4), which supports the Information Collaborator. The Metadatabase may also distribute some core metadata, such as the semantic equivalences of data items and possible API logics, to the Export Databases to assist them in executing data interchanges. The participants have full control of their Export Databases.

Two new designs enable the model (provided in Levermore *et al.*, 2010; Hsu *et al.*, 2007; and Levermore and Hsu, 2006): the Information Collaborator (called Global Blackboard in the cited literature) that performs information matchmaking; and the extended Metadatabase global query language that submits requests and offers. Together with the previous results adopted, they give rise to a hypernetworking provider for connecting massively distributed independent databases on the Internet, for information collaboration. All elements are amenable to being implemented with open source Web technology, and the performance requirements are generally consistent with the proven capabilities of these Web resources. In fact, the Information Collaborator is meant to operate as an Exchange on the Web.

With such an exchange in place, the earlier supply chain scenario will see the manufacturer's business space connected, including ready extensions to all other willing participants from the population of manufacturers, retailers, and contractors. The Information Collaborator will establish information supply chains by posting requests (for buyers or sellers) and finding the partners who fit. Then, it will support the transaction phase of a supply chain by its ability to execute database tasks. A virtual sequential supply chain is formed when sequentially inter-related B2B pairs (overlap at either end) are identified and connected at the exchange. Sequential information supply chains are formed by following some ordered list of database executions for transactions (e.g., forecasting, tier 1 supplier production, tier 2 supplier inventory, and so on). Concurrent processing of all these chains is supported since all pairs are connected at the exchange in parallel. Configuration and re-configuration are achieved by arranging for these connections through on-demand matching.

The manufacturer in the scenario can connect to different pairs pertaining to many parallel virtual supply chains. When additional managerial controls are added, such as certification of suppliers for particular prime companies, a virtual supply chain can become as binding as desired by the participants. In addition, the design consolidates all changes at the common infrastructure for all to use, and thereby provides economies of scale.

The full model will support any number of providers from any type of information repository, anywhere in the digitally connected community. A far more modest model will assume a pre-defined community regulating the participants and imposing certain (open technology) protocols to make the model practical. The practices of global supply provide a lower bound to the vision and an upper bound to the requirements for implementing the vision. From this perspective, information customers (users) are comparable to traditional global database queries (subscribing), which will be satisfied either by using single individual information providers or by joining multiple such providers on an as-needed basis. The information provider is, on the other hand, a new type of query (publishing) representing the proactive and dynamic provision of ad hoc data resources, which will be satisfied by single or multiple customers. The matching also involves satisfying rule-based negotiation and other matching conditions from each type of query. Finally, both the information customers and the information providers search for their counterparts on demand; the matching can occur over a prolonged period per demand; and the matched queries are executed automatically to complete the transaction.

The big picture is that information collaboration is a significant class of databases connection, and the Information Collaborator is actually a *hyper-networking provider* for Internet databases, period. It both helps illustrate the vision of systems of IS on the Web and helps implement it. We see that the notion of information integration for an enterprise is implemented in the single database regime, which requires both read and write under tight control. Then, we see the same notion reduced to largely read-only in federated databases for extended enterprises. Now, the meaning of information integration for Internet databases evolves, again.

That is, if it is astronomically hard to permanently connect information resources from all enterprise databases on the Internet, then the information collaboration idea simply suggests that maybe the adverb "permanently" is unnecessary. With this premise removed, the connection can be simplified to meeting mission-critical information needs, on demand. This is a much simpler task to perform and yet still fulfills a lot of the vision for hyper-networking.

To see this, let us think of a thought model: "an eBay for information resources." In this vision, a large number of information customers are matched with a large number of information providers on a concurrent and continuous (24/7) basis at an information exchange. Unlike eBay, however, the information eBay can construe the information resources in many different ways from the same physical data to create more values. Information resources can be used, re-used, and shared by many without diminishing their value (i.e., not be physically "consumed"). Finally, almost any person can possess information resources that others want at any time. Therefore, a participant can post ad hoc requirements to look for suppliers of particular tasks as a buyer, and simultaneously offer multiple views of its databases for use by prospective suppliers as a seller. This is hyper-networking for people and enterprises at its fullest.

It is worthwhile to note, again, that the baseline database model still drives the thinking here, as it did distributed database models and federated databases. The next section concludes the design of connections for information resources.

5.4 Design Principles for Connecting Information Resources for Systems of IS

The evolution from single databases to distributed databases and finally to Internet databases shows unequivocally a trend, a drive to connect information resources from anywhere in the world. This drive is evidently powered by the fact that doing so delivers business promises, and technically progress followed suit to make the strides. By extension, this evolution also vindicates the notion of promoting systems of IS to facilitate innovation, since if databases can be connected at this scale and in this manner, then IS can, too. The connectionist definition of IS describes accurately the intellectual movements in the field.

An important observation of the evolution of databases is this: the scale of information integration and the scope of control move in opposite directions. As the former soars up, the latter adjusts down. This phenomenon seems to reflect the philosophy of constrained optimization, i.e., seeking the objective within the feasible region. For intra-enterprise integration, since full proprietary control of enterprise information resources exists, the feasible region includes full range of tightly managed database operations. The DBMS industry is capable of providing single databases to almost any sized enterprises. Thus, we can conceptually equate enterprise information integration to single databases, with the qualification that large-scale enterprises need multiple single databases for their different businesses and divisions.

Extended enterprises with significant proprietary control may employ federated databases. Examples include supply chains where the primes have the ability to impose certain information regimes on suppliers to bring about connection of multiple databases throughout. Endeavors with lesser control can reduce the scope of global query to select contents, and enact only pinpoint updates on an even smaller set of mission-critical information resources. When proprietary control is completely removed, then the information integration mission becomes similar to information collaboration. The point is that building systems of IS is feasible.

EXERCISES

1. You have suggested some principles for database design in Section 5.1 (see Question 8). How will you generalize them for the design of any class of information integration?
2. Figure 5.6 is an example of embedding IS into the societal cyber-infrastructure. If you are responsible for the embedment, can you use some "Web resources clearing house" type of services on the Web?
3. The scale of participation in the information collaboration example of Figure 5.6 may be significant, and the possible number of similar examples for different business spaces and user domains can be large, too. Can you generalize your ideas for Question 3 and suggest some global reference model (maintained, say, by some public sector authority) for everyone to use? What should the model contain?
4. What other services should such a public sector facilitator provide?
5. Can you consolidate your suggestions into a mechanism and design it after the baseline database model — i.e., using the three-schema concept?
6. Please review Section 3.3 of Chapter 3 and abstract a WRAS figure to show your design. That is, please create a three-schema model for the WRAS.
7. How can you determine what exactly should go into a database, and what should the schemas contain? How can you create the conceptual schema and the external schema? Please suggest a step-by-step process for designing and creating a single database.

In any case, we recognize a few design lessons for connecting information resources at any scale, towards providing database class of functionality to the IS. These lessons are a generalization of the discussion in Section 5.1 for the baseline database model, as follows:

- **Pursue Data Independence:** In practice, the concept of external schemas (Figure 5.1) is a very potent tool for creating data independence for any environment of disparate information resources. It can be upgraded to external/ODBC connections (Figure 5.2), Import/Export Schemas (Figure 5.3), and Export Databases (Figure 5.6). The possibilities are limited only by one's understanding of the technical possibilities.
- **Explore Metadata:** Metadata come naturally for the definition of information resources and their connections; therefore, they ought to be put to use in the actual execution of these definitions. The Metadatabase model shows how metadata, including control logics, may be managed, processed, and used in all classes of database functionality. The objective here is to achieve operational openness and scalability for the integration design.
- **Develop Global Query Capability:** The real meaning of this principle is to equate connections among information resources to the global query of them. The ability to update selected data items across these information resources is included in the global query capability. Communication for user actions, such as information requests and offers, is also defined to be part of global query. The Information Collaborator design (Figure 5.6) illustrates this idea.
- **Facilitate a Community Information Regime:** Loose or tight, information integration cannot work without some common definition of the information and the mechanism for integration. The single DBMS model may represent the high end of tight regimes. At the other end, a loose regime may embrace an open registration mechanism, using ontology and embedment in societal cyber-infrastructure to allow participants to self-police their own conformity to the community.
- **Design Surrogates for Proprietary Control:** This is the positive interpretation of the notion of trading functionality for proprietary

control. It reflects on proactive optimization rather than reactive compromise. The design ideas of the Metadatabase model are an example: focus on global query but also support mission-critical updates. The information collaboration idea shows how innovative conception may help reduce an impossible job to a feasible one.

With the database knowledge, we are ready to revisit the concept of Web Resources Application System (WRAS) discussed in Section 3.3 of Chapter 3. The core logic of WRAS is best illustrated in the spirit of the baseline database model, as shown in Figure 5.7. The figure features a common facility (the WRAS) to assist users (people or enterprises) "subscribing" to elements of the societal cyber-infrastructure and configuring them as some virtual cyber-infrastructure for their own IS, to support connection of IS elements. The WRAS is envisioned to be an integral part of the societal cyber-infrastructure, just like a DBMS is to

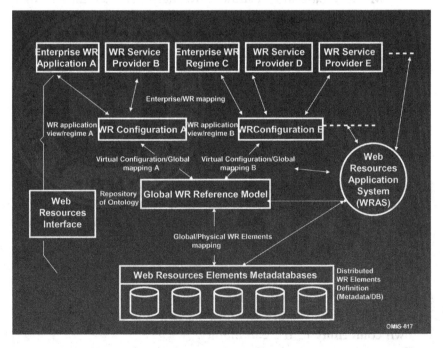

Figure 5.7: The concept of Web Resources Application System: a three-schema model.

the database. Therefore, it should be created and maintained at the level of the public domain authority responsible for the societal infrastructure (e.g., a government similar to the FDA, FCC, and NSF). Open sources, open source technologies, and all sorts of Internet services are examples of Web Resources (WR). They would be defined in the Global WR Reference Model, which is a Metadatabase-style repository for the WRAS. This reference model may be construed to be some public domain Internet clearing house, and may best belong to the auspices of the Internet-overseeing authority (e.g., ICANN). The notion of WR Configurations represents specialized prototypical reference models for particular industries, segments of the market, or user communities. The WR Elements Metadatabase contains the metadata connections (or, the IS) at individual Web Resources sites that the global reference model can use. The top layer of the model corresponds to value-added cyber-infrastructure service providers who connect the end users to the Web Resources. Finally, Web Resources Interface reflects on the embedment of the WR elements in the societal cyber-infrastructure.

It is worthwhile to note that as more global metadata are embedded into the societal cyber-infrastructure via something such as the WRAS, Internet databases may rely less on global models such as a federation Metadatabase, and become more completely peer-to-peer in their connections. Broadly speaking, databases at all levels might have already been embedded into the societal cyber-infrastructure as long as they code their global query language in open source technology and implement the community information regime on the Web. For example, a database is embedded if it executes the ANSI SQL through Web homepages. Figure 5.6 is, again, an illustration of this embedment. It also explains why the WRAS concept is relevant, since the potential number of such embedded databases can be as large as the Web itself.

Finally, we note that the baseline database model also implies a design methodology for the development of a single database. Starting with the output: the physical database results from population of raw data into its constructs (e.g., tables and views); the constructs are created according to the conceptual schema (e.g., table definitions and relationships) and the external schemas; the external schemas are derived from the conceptual schema in accordance to applications (e.g., data stores and software objects or programs); the conceptual schema comes from the data model (e.g., normalized relations or objects); and the data model originated in the recognition of the "information world", or a context that formulates the enterprise information resources and their applications (e.g., data stores, entities, relationships, and object hierarchy). Of course, the context comes from the IS master plan. Extended database models typically just add to this baseline methodology. They may apply their own methodology to develop their additionally required elements, but single databases are still the foundation.

Fundamentally speaking, two mutually exclusive but collectively exhaustive approaches exist for developing IS from the master plan: process modeling and semantic data modeling. The first has already been explained in Chapter 4; i.e., define data stores in the DFD and feed them into a data modeling process, such as data normalization, to design relations. The second reviews the known (as given) sources and applications of enterprise information resources and then organizes them into some generic abstractions of data for the entire IS. Data normalization may either be embedded in the semantic modeling or be conducted afterwards to refine the semantic models. The difference is that semantic modeling globally defines data items to achieve data independence, but it does not analyze for the processes that determine the information requirements. Process modeling, on the other hand, defines the data resources within the local, individual context of data stores and processes, one data store at a time. They converge at the point of data normalization. In practice, large IS projects often use both approaches simultaneously to cross-reference each other.

We now summarize below the overall logic of database development to help transition to the next chapter:

The Process of Developing a Single Database

- **Step 0:** Obtain a master plan for the IS, for which the database is designed.
- **Step 1:** Either conduct process modeling to obtain data stores and leaf processes (or their equivalent), or perform semantic modeling

to fully formulate the enterprise information resources; or do both.

- **Step 2:** Define the full semantic definitions, constraints, and logics that need to be embedded in the DBMS (e.g., access privileges and triggers) either for the data items in the data stores or for those pertaining to the semantic model. Each data store becomes a "universal relation" for data normalization and each semantic construct a possible sub-model for further refinement by the concept of data normalization.

- **Step 3:** Perform data normalization: either decompose the universal relations or refine the semantic model, until the results are ready to be implemented as conceptual schema.

- **Step 4:** Create the conceptual schema according to the fully normalized relations or the refined semantic model on the DBMS chosen for the single database. Customization may be needed to reconcile the model with the particulars of the DBMS (relational, object, or otherwise).

- **Step 5:** Create external schemas (views) to correspond to the data stores and/or the application programs required by the leaf processes; or to the hierarchy of constructs in the semantic model. Also, create all other logical elements (security, integrity, and other DBA requirements) as part of the schemas (conceptual or even external).

- **Step 6:** Populate the database (using SQL and/or other DBMS provisions). A combination of manual data entry, digital data scanning, and batch processing (editing and file conversions) is typically required, dependent on the nature of the input data sources.

- **Step 7:** Connect the application programs to the database by virtue of DBMS facility. These application programs may be inherited by the database or newly developed.

The next chapter develops semantic modeling and data normalization for steps 1 and 3. Before moving on, the design lessons from this chapter are summarized for systems of IS:

The Metadata Principle for Connecting Systems of IS: *Use metadata to connect independent databases across massive systems of IS and achieve data independence on the Web.*

Chapter 6

Designing Databases: Data Normalization and Data Modeling Using Entity, Relationship, and Object Hierarchy

Database systems nowadays tend to use relational technology. They define relations (base tables) as the core of the database and derive processing logics and other constructs from this core. The relational philosophy reflects such basic semantic concepts as entities, relationships, and attributes (ERA). However, other philosophies exist, too, and the prime case is the object-oriented (O-O) paradigm. The object philosophy bears well on engineering data and open software resources on the Web. A relational system may need to reconcile with the object model if it needs to store and manage complex engineering design objects and/or open Web services in the database. Theoretically speaking, ERA, O-O, and Relation are inherently consistent and all share a common logic of data normalization. Data normalization is, technically, concerned with consolidating data resources and controlling redundancy and enforcing integrity (consistency). All data models, regardless of their semantics and worldviews, must pass the test of data consolidation before their designs can be implemented in a database. Therefore, the general notion of data normalization is considered the basic database design logic in this book, regardless of the particular modeling approaches adopted. For this reason, data normalization is presented first, before the discussion progresses to ERA, O-O, and their modeling in Unified Modeling Language (UML). The Two-Stage Entity-Relationship (TSER) model is introduced at the end of this chapter, along with the specific design of the Metadatabase model discussed in Chapter 5.

6.1 Data Normalization: The Design for Relational Conceptual Schema and the Baseline Knowledge for Semantic Data Modeling

Section 5.4 of the previous chapter revealed two alternative approaches to organizing data into a database: process modeling and semantic data modeling. Most database textbooks focus on the second approach. As such, they treat data normalization as a tool for logical database design, where the normalized relations from the design lead directly to the definition of base tables in a relational DBMS. Semantic data modeling is a design stage preceding this logical design; therefore, data normalization methods tend to be covered in the context of semantic models such as ERA and O-O. This book takes a broader view. We develop the concepts and methods for data normalization here as a follow-up to process modeling — i.e., normalize the universe relations which are data stores into relations that can be implemented as base tables in MySQL, Access, SQL Server, Oracle, DB2, or any other relational DBMS. After the competency is established in this context, we then use this baseline knowledge to help us understand some intricacies of semantic data models while moving to this modeling approach.

6.1.1 *The Need for Data Normalization: What Problems Can Un-normalized Data Cause?*

Four basic types of problems have been highlighted as anomalies of database processing due to insufficiently normalized design (e.g., Atre, 1980). Each is associated with a particular type of basic database operations, as follows:

- **The Retrieval Problem:** Two sub-types of this problem exist; i.e., inconsistence and convolution. The first is the result of inconsistent data in the database, so that different users can get different information from the repository for exactly the same query, under exactly the same conditions, and at exactly the same time, without any deliberate (i.e., managed) manipulation. This is arguably the most serious problem that a database can have since it effectively renders the repository untrustworthy. The second is the difficulty to sort out data, to identify the right data to retrieve with minimum transaction cost and cycle time.

- **The Update Problem:** To update one single data item, the user/system needs to search for multiple possible copies of the data from the (entire) database and update them all repeatedly. This is the result of redundant data. The problem leads directly to significant transaction cost and cycle time for updating, but more seriously can cause inconsistent data values since one single slip in the search for all copies will lead to more than one value for the same data items.

- **The Insertion Problem:** One may need to include additional, unintended (and unfamiliar) data in the insertion if one wants to add certain data items into the database. For example, it is problematic if the user who just wants to add new supplies from a supplier to the inventory data must also indicate the supplier's level of certification and other business data, as well as the past history of how the parts in the new supplies had been used.

- **The Deletion Problem:** One may automatically remove more information than one intends to when deleting some records from the database. And the inadvertently removed data items may be the only ones of their kind in the system. For example, removing a part from the bill-of-materials data would remove its design details, too, if these data are stored together.

All these problems are rooted ultimately in (uncontrolled and unmanaged) redundancy in data items that a database is designed to save; or simply put, resulted from insufficiently normalized (consolidated) conceptual schema. A relational design needs this consolidation; an ERA one needs it; and so does an O-O database. We use an example to shed further light on why a database has to be normalized.

The Hospital Scenario: Suppose a hospital wishes to integrate its islands of automation. It has conducted a process modeling project using the DFD method. Two data stores have been selected for a pilot study of database design. The first is the patients' charts and the second the patients' insurance claims; both are considered a universe relation and shown in the table form. Table 6.1 shows some header/summary data of a small portion of the patients' charts. (Please note this scenario is inspired by a similar example in Atre (1980), with significant extensions and modifications such as the inclusion of insurance in the scenario. In particular, Table 6.1 modifies the previous example by adding new columns and upgrading the data, while Table 6.2 is completely new, representing original work of this book.) Naturally, the data are designed to illustrate the concepts of normalization, rather than the complete adherence to medical data.

Table 6.2 similarly demonstrates a header for patients' insurance claims. The claims themselves are referenced to by a log number, pointing to the actual (digital) records of the claims. Table 6.2 includes additional data items for the patients and the insurance companies. As expected, an insurance company may provide multiple products (plans), each of which has its own unique provisions and coverage.

EXERCISES (Refer to Table 6.1)

1. How can you retrieve the insurance data for patient Alan Smith? How many records (rows in the table, also called tuples of the relation) will you have to use? Note that you do not need to think of any query language or formal logic; just use common sense.
2. How can you update the table if patient Jane Keyes has changed insurance to MVP family plan, with an ID 402444352? How can you add new side effects to a drug, say Cephaldsporin?
3. How can you insert a new surgeon who has not operated on any patient yet to the table?
4. What information would you inadvertently lose if you delete the record for the surgery on Kevin Atari by Lou Louise on July 31, 2011 (07312011)?

Table 6.1: The patient charts relation of the hospital scenario.

Patient No.	Patient Name	Insurance Plan	Insurance ID (SSN)	Surgeon License Number	Surgeon Name	Date	Surgery Name	Drug	Usual Side Effect
44659	Abe Jewison	CDPHP Family	110213214	12410	Joseph Higgins	09 12 2011	Prostate Exam	Demicillin	Rash
44659	Abe Jewison	MVP Traditional	110213214	12410	Joseph Higgins	01 23 1999	Stomach Exam	Penicillin	Rash
31256	Alan Smith	Blue Cross Single	102896745	97284	Lou Wayne	03 01 2012	Open Heart	Cephaldsporin	—
31256	Alan Smith	Blue Shield HMO	102896745	12410	Joseph Higgins	08 31 2004	Kidney stone removal	—	—
31256	Alan Smith	Blue Shield HMO	102896745	57274	Ray Kim	02 28 2000	Cholecystectomy	Demicillin	Rash
63981	Jane Keyes	CDPHP HMO	402444352	32475	Beth Steiner	09 24 2009	Endocrinology Testing	Tetracycline	Fever
55728	Kevin Atari	MVP HMO	301577329	88216	Lou Louise	07 31 2011	Gall stone removal	Tetracycline	Fever
20160	Mary Brown	CDPHP Traditional	401760751	69325	Jorge Lucero	05 09 2012	C-section	Cephaldsporin	—

Table 6.2:   The patient insurance claims relation of the hospital scenario.

Patient No.	Patient Address	Insurance Plan	Insurance ID (SSN)	Claim Date	Claim Log#	Company	Company Address	Plan Copay
20160	14 15th St., Troy	CDPHP Traditional	401760751	05 09 2012	050912-009	CDPHP	CDPHP Plaza	$100
31256	3 Jay St., Albany	Blue Cross Single	102896745	03 01 2012	030112-112	Blue Cross	210 Main St., Albany	$15
44659	230 Rt. 9, Latham	CDPHP Family	110213214	09 12 2011	091211-086	CDPHP	CDPHP Plaza	$20

5. What is wrong with this data entry (adding a new row) by the Surgery Administrator: "63981, Jane Keyes, Blue Cross, 402444352, 69325, Jorge Lucero, 05092012, C-section, Cephaldsporin"?

6. What "identifier" would you use for the table? How do you know that it is appropriate — what does it mean to be "appropriate"?

7. Would an automatic key such as the Row ID (or Object ID) that Access customarily creates for each table solve any of the above problems?

The first question of the exercise requires first a search on the keyword "Alan Smith" (as value of Patient Name), and then reading the Insurance and Insurance ID fields out of the records pertaining to this name. Any of the three tuples in this example may be used for the search; or, just use the one from the latest record in the database. This search logic does not command pinpoint precision in the general case. It may have to use a somewhat involved program to do the job due to the fact that multiple records of the patient may exist.

The second question is a little tricky. The hospital does not need to retrospectively change the patients' insurance data as long as these data were accurate at the time of surgery (billing). Thus, no update is needed until Jane Keyes is having a new surgery with the hospital under the coverage of the new insurance policy. In which case, the job is an insertion of new records rather than an update of the present ones. However, if we ask the same on updating the pharmaceutical-published usual side effects of drugs, then the answer is different: one has to go through the entire table and change the side effect field for the drug Cephaldsporin everywhere in the table.

For Question 3, inserting a brand new surgeon into the table may not be permissible in this case since some of the key fields would be missing (patient number and date); unless of course the DBMS were to use a system-generated ID to represent every row and give the new surgeon a new row with a new ID, while leaving all other fields "empty". However, even in this case, such rows would become dubious for database search to locate them.

Question 4 shows the case of deleting a surgery which happens to be the only record for some entities, be it the surgeon, the patient, or the drug (i.e., they appear only once in the table, which is this surgery). Clearly, doing so would result in losing information about those particular entities — as is the case here for the patient Kevin Atari and the surgeon Lou Louise.

Question 5 may be answered by simply blaming the Surgery Administrator, who entered the insurance data wrongly for Jane Keyes (assuming that the patient is under the same insurance plan). However, a deep investigation would reveal that the blame is really the database designer's. The reason is "user ergonomics": the database is unnatural for the users to use it right. Why should the Surgery Administrator be expected to enter business data such as insurance when his/her job is really only about surgery? By the same token, if a registration clerk would have to enter drug data as part of the job of creating a row for a patient, then the data entry could be expected to be error-prone on that part. This error would lie in the setup by the database designer.

The above five questions illustrate the four anomalies of database processing. They are all rooted in the fact that the table is not sufficiently normalized for consolidating data and removing (uncontrolled) redundancy. That is, putting all data into a single table is unwieldy and convoluted in this case, against the natural ways of use of the database. Thus, what is appropriate? The appropriateness has to be judged by users' natural ways and needs; which have to be globally consolidated and reconciled for all users. Data normalization does the job for relational databases. It also achieves the same for O-O and other genres of databases, as it has been embedded in the basic logic of the O-O and other methods.

Please note that data normalization culminates in the identification of appropriate primary keys and foreign keys for all tables (see the next section). They define the technical soundness of a database in design and in operation. If the keys do not meet the technical requirements, then the database will be vulnerable to the anomalies discussed above, no matter what. Thus, the keys must be determined from rigorous technical analysis by normalization methods, not just by one's preference, or "your word against mine" type of arbitrary choice. System-generated ID certainly would not suffice.

Question 6 will be answered below as the data normalization method is fully developed. For now, we simply alert the reader that the right answer has to be the technically sound primary key, not an automatic ID such as a row number for each record.

Question 7 is very telling: automatic ID does not convey any semantic value, nor does it identify any natural ways of use for the table. We could add an ID column to the table and all the problems would still remain — we would not need to change a word. No one can use the automatic ID in any pinpointed search. Worse, totally inconsistent data or even wrong data can still be added to the table and cause wholesale loss of any ability to audit the data and maintain their integrity. This book advises strongly against using any built-in design wizard that creates tables for dummies, unless you take the word literally: by the dummies, of the dummies, and for the dummies. Automatic IDs can be useful only when they are used to supplement semantically based proper primary keys. For example, use the ID as the automatic key for processing while design integrity controls the underlying semantic, real keys.

It is worthwhile to note here that any persistent artificial ID in the database must be anchored in some concrete semantic definitions that the IS recognizes, so that all such IDs can be audited, and made meaningful for the users to use. Social Security Number (SSN) is such a meaningful and concrete ID. A managerially mandated log number for forms (e.g., invoices and claims), which is used routinely in internal data processing, auditing, and control, is a meaningful number, too. An arbitrary "customer number" that a receptionist can create on the fly during a phone conversation or an e-commerce session is not. The SSN can identify a person because it is nationally defined *and* maintained; and the same goes for the log number for the enterprise. The arbitrary customer number is meaningless since it is arbitrary and not quality-assured. No one can entrust the arbitrary customer numbers for any purpose of identification since a customer may have many obsolete numbers created in the system. Conversely, no customers in their right mind would ever use (remember) them to do business, either. To make an artificial ID meaningful, the IS needs to put it under a rigorous regime to assure its integrity (uniqueness, correctness, etc.), such as defining a lookup table for these numbers from semantically meaningful data items, such as names, dates, and SSN.

6.1.2 *Functional Dependency: The Language of Data Normalization and Relational Design*

How does one uncover the users' natural ways of using the data? The answer is to uncover the inherent semantic structure of the data — i.e., how data items are grouped together to pertain to semantic concepts such as (the applications of) data stores, entities, relationships, and objects. Two things need to be determined: the members of the group and the representative of the group. Functional Dependency (FD) provides such an analysis. Figure 6.1 summarizes the graphic representations of FD.

A methodic, technical way to group data items is to analyze for functional dependencies: what data items appear together; and of

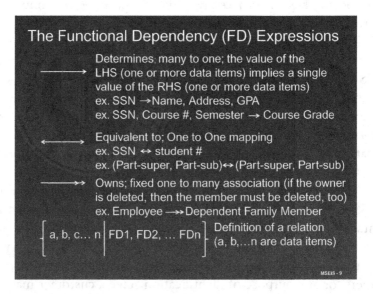

Figure 6.1: The iconic definition of functional dependence expressions.

them, whose appearance determines who else's appearance — i.e., what data items are associated with what else? For example, a person's SSN, name, address, and the like appear together as the group that describes the person per se. Of these data items, the SSN is the leader with which others are associated; or, the SSN gives the uniqueness to other data items in the group and hence determines their appearance.

There are ten data items in the Patient Charts relation and nine in the Patient Insurance Claims relation. How many (non-redundant) FDs are in each? A non-redundant FD is one that cannot be derived from others. For example, a → b and b → c imply a → c. Thus, the third FD is redundant when the first two are included. In a similar way, self-to-self mapping for individual data items, e.g., a ↔ a, and b ↔ b, is considered trivial and redundant, and hence is not included in the analysis. Please note that self-to-self mapping for a set of data items (e.g., two or more data items grouped together to map to themselves as a group) is not only allowed but also important, since it represents multi-valued associations of data items (see below).

Now, we do some exercises. We add Figure 6.2 (inspired by Hawryszkiewycz, 1984) to the two universe relations discussed above to help the exercises.

EXERCISES

1. Please identify the FDs for Table 6.1.
2. Please identify the FDs for Table 6.2.
3. A bottom-up way to identify FDs is examining data records. Figure 6.2 shows two logs: Shop Floor Cell Worker data and Position Occupancy data. Can you identify some FDs that conform to the data (i.e., there is only one single data value, or none, on the RHS for a given data value on the LHS) in Relation B?
4. Can you identify some FDs that conform to the data in Relation A, Figure 6.2 *and* also make sense in the usual business settings?
5. Can you identify some FDs that conform to the data in Relation A, Figure 6.2 but do *not* make sense in the usual business settings?

Relation A: Shop Floor Cell Log

WORKSTATION	MACHINIST	ITEM TYPE	DATE	WORKHOURS
Station 1	Smith	Leather Jacket	090711	8
Station 2	O'Keefe	Safari khaki pants	090811	7
Station 3	Chang	Cowboy Hat	090111	10
Station 4	Lambardo	Dress Skirt	090111	8

Relation B: Positions Occupancy Log

EMPLOYEE	POSITION	DATE–STARTED	DATE-ENDED	DEPT.
Jose Romer	MGR 071	010109	123110	MFG
Lopez Woods	CLK 164	073008	113008	MKTG
Jill Leung	ENG 102	122311	---	MFG
Jose Romer	MGR 203	040412	063004	MKTG
John Watts	ENG 164	040412	---	HQ
Jose Romer	MGR 071	070104	---	MFG

MSEIS - 10

Figure 6.2:   Two logs of data records for FD identification.

6. Please formulate FDs for the following condition: "a machinist can work only on one workstation on the same day, and a workstation can have only one operator working on it on the same day," with respect to Relation A, Figure 6.2.

The relation of Table 6.1 is composed of ten attributes and a few FDs associating these attributes into groups which may overlap. We recognize five FDs:

- Patient No. → Patient Name, Insurance Plan
- Patient No. ↔ Insurance ID
- Surgeon License No. → Surgeon Name
- Drug → Usual Side-Effect
- Patient No., Surgeon License No., Date → Surgery Name, Drug

The first four FDs should be rather straightforward to recognize, since they make sense to us. To be absolutely certain, we need to double-check them against the technical definition of FD: does each of them conform to the requirement that there is only one value of the data items on the RHS for any single given value of the LHS, according to both the sample data and the business practices of the hospital (our common sense)? The second FD, equivalence between Patient No. and the Insurance ID (SSN), is kind of hidden by the fact that the hospital chose to maintain a Patient No. rather than using directly the SSN. However, recognizing it is important to the ensuing normalization of data.

The last FD with plural LHS is the FD that defines the essence of the relation in Table 6.1. It says that a surgery is uniquely identified by the combination of patient number, surgeon number, and date: who performs the surgery on whom, on what date. The business rule here is obviously that a patient may have seen many surgeons, and a surgeon may have many patients; but on the same date a patient may have just one (distinct) surgery by the same (head) surgeon. What if this rule is relaxed so that a patient may now have multiple surgeries by the same surgeon on the same day? The "fix" is to append time to date: at any one point in time there is only one surgery by the same surgeon on the same patient. In all FDs, the LHS is the representative of the grouping, and the RHS the ordinary members of the group. Semantically speaking, the RHS shows the attributes of the semantic concept to which the group of data items pertain. For instance, the semantic concept of the fifth FD is surgery, whose representation (the key) is the threesome LHS and whose non-key attributes are surgery name and the drug administered during or after the surgery. Other complexities are possible, of course.

For instance, multiple side effects usually exist for a drug, and they may have to be individually recognized in the database so as to allow search, such as find all drugs that have certain side effects. In this case, the drug FD should be replaced by this one:

- (Drug, Usual Side-Effect) ↔ (Drug, Usual Side-Effect)

In practice, this kind of FD corresponds to a multi-valued all-key table (see the next section) containing individual combinations of drug and side-effect. Each row is identified by the combination of both values. For example, if three drugs have respectively three, four, and five side effects, then the two-column table (drug and side-effect) will have three rows for the first drug, four for the second, and five for the third. The table will be represented by both fields combined. A glamorous generalization of this class of relations is the well-known Bill-of-Materials (BOM) structure, which will be discussed in Section 6.2. Can you think of a fix if a surgery may administer multiple drugs? Hint: a straightforward extension is to add a new plural self-to-self FD; i.e., the group of Patient No., Surgeon No., Date and Drug maps to itself, as the sixth FD. In this case, Drug would be removed from the RHS of the fifth FD, for it is no longer a humble attribute of the threesome key.

Similar analysis will reveal the following five FDs for Table 6.2:

- Patient No. $\rightarrow$ Patient Address, Insurance Plan
- Patient No. $\leftrightarrow$ Insurance ID
- Insurance Plan $\rightarrow$ Company, Plan Copay
- Company $\rightarrow$ Company Address
- Patient No., Claim Date $\rightarrow$ Claim Log No.

In the old days, the claim log number may have corresponded to a hardcopy insurance claim form filed by the hospital. The digital version of the file may be optical documents stored external to the database. Or, it may even point to some database external schema (forms) to construct the claim online according to the insurance company's format. It is also possible for the hospital to "tunnel" into the insurance company IS and to craft the claim forms there. The database designs of Chapter 5, especially the ideas in Section 5.2, may apply readily here. Thus, the data item Claim Log No. is only a generic placeholder for our illustration.

It may also be worthwhile to note that the third FD, Insurance Plan $\rightarrow$ Company, could be somewhat counter-intuitive, since one would think that it is the company that determines the company's plans, not the other way around. However, this is precisely the point of FD: once the plan is specified, the company that offers the plan is determined (implied), too; but knowing the company does not help one nail down the specific plan among the many that the company offers. For a many-to-one (or one-to-many) mapping, it is the many that determines definitively the one.

An FD has to conform to the observations; i.e., the empirical data from the current practices. However, it also represents a business rule and hence must make sense in the big picture. Relation A in Figure 6.2 supports these FDs which also conform to common sense:

- Machinist, Date → Work Hours, Workstation
- Workstation, Date → Machinist

This is an answer to Questions 4 and 6, too. However, the following two FDs, and their kind, do not make sense since they are way too restrictive:

- Item Type → Date
- Machinist → Workstation

The first FD — Item Type determines Date — implies that a type of item is made for one day, only, never before and never after. The second, in a similar way, says that a machinist can operate only on one particular workstation (while, incidentally, a workstation can be operated by more than one machinist, according to this FD). All four FDs seemingly conform to the current data, but not all four make equal business sense. Thus, one can expect future data to show violation of the two FDs that do not make much sense, as the story continues to unfold itself.

Relation B in Figure 6.2 seems to suggest that an employee may occupy only one position at any one time, but may return to the same position at a different time; while a position belongs to a particular department. Both make sense, although they would need to be confirmed if this exercise were a real design project. The first condition indicates the need for a "time stamp" to represent the notion of point in time. (What was the time stamp in Tables 6.1 and 6.2?)

- Employee, Date-Started → Position
- Position → Dept.

Why doesn't one use the other possible time stamp, Date-Ended? Why is only one needed?

Once all FDs are determined, data normalization is more than halfway through. For relational systems, normalized relations can be almost readily defined from the FDs (which give rise to the conceptual schema of a relational database).

6.1.3 *Normal Forms: Decomposition and Synthesis*

Data normalization starts with FD analysis and ends in turning the FDs into relations. The proper relations must represent collectively the full semantics of the data resources, and incur only properly controlled minimal overlaps. There are two basic approaches to do this relational design from FDs: decomposition and synthesis. As its name suggests, the decomposition approach starts with the universe relation and goes through a logical progression to turn it from the first normal form (1NF) to the second normal form (2NF), third normal form (3NF), and finally the Boyce–Codd normal form (BCNF). Each step along the way may yield more and more decomposed relations which conform to the ever higher level of normalization. This approach requires the determination of a *primary key*, along with all other possible *candidate keys* each of which may be used alternatively as the primary key, for the universe relation; which is already put into the 1NF. Other FDs may be determined along the way according to the definition (requirements) of 2NF, 3NF, and BCNF. Please note that the BCNF reduces to 3NF if the universe relation (1NF) has only one candidate key — i.e., there is no other technically permissible alternative to the primary key.

In a similar way, the synthesis approach requires a comprehensive set of FDs to be determined first, and then builds relations from these

FDs that conform to the definition of BCNF. Generally speaking, it may be easier for an experienced designer to use the synthesis approach, since an FD typically gives a BCNF relation if it is recognized properly. The challenge is to recognize the need for combining FDs, in order to minimize overlaps (under control) and allow non-loss recovery of the original universe relation from these (decomposed) BCNF relations. *Non-loss recovery*, which is required of any data normalization, may be best described as performing the join operations of relational algebra (see Chapter 7) on the resultant relations to exactly undo the decomposition, nothing more and nothing less. This requirement assures that the FDs of a universe relation do collectively represent the full semantics of the data resources (e.g., a data store), and are mutually consistent with each other.

The following is a summary of the key concepts of normal forms:

Candidate Key (of a relation): a singular or plural set of data items (i.e., one data item in the set, or multiple data items in the set) in the relation that functionally determines all other data items in the relation. The set is the LHS of the FD which covers the entire relation, and the others are the RHS of the FD. The candidate key (CK) may be referred to as a *singular key* if the LHS contains only one data item; or a *composite key* otherwise. Please note that a relation may have more than one CK. In Table 6.1, two CKs exist: (Patient No., Surgeon License No., Date) and (Insurance ID, Surgeon License No. and Date). What is/are the CK(s) for Table 6.2?

Primary Key (of a relation): the CK designated for the representation of the relation. In Table 6.1, the first CK is obviously preferred to be designated as the primary key (PK) since the hospital recognizes patients by Patient Number. Thus, the PK is not arbitrarily determined, since it has to conform to the technical definition of being able to uniquely identify everyone else in the relation. A PK (CK) may consist of the LHSs of more than one FD. The PK implies a rigorous *key integrity* control regime on its data field(s): the value (combination) must be non-null and non-duplicate. The DBMS usually automatically enforces these rules once the data fields are declared to be a PK. Additional CK(s) may be subjected to the same integrity control by using other DBMS provisions. If so, then they are in effect some additional *alternate keys* for the DBA to use. Such alternate keys can be very useful when it should become necessary to use values other than the regular PK; or when cross-referencing is needed such as for auditing.

Foreign Key (FK): the attribute group (one or more data items) in a relation that corresponds to the PK of another relation — hence it is directional. Foreign keys relate relations in a relational database. They are the logical glue that connects relations together to achieve non-loss recovery. The FK imposes *referential integrity* on its data field(s). That is, the values of a FK in a relation must be consistent with the values of the PK in the other relation to which the FK refers. Thus, a PK value must exist first in the referred-to table before the FK field in the referring table is allowed to have that value. The Relationship diagram of Access is actually a diagram of FKs, and virtually all enterprise DBMSs available today support directly the declaration of FK.

Prime Attribute: a member of any CK. Table 6.1 has four prime attributes: Patient No., Surgeon License No., Date, and Insurance ID.

Key Attribute: a member of the PK.

First Normal Form: a relation that is representable as a disciplined, well-structured table where each cell contains only one value (e.g., a number such as Patient No., or a string of characters, such as address and name). Note that a string of characters is considered a single value if it is always used together as a whole value. Thus, multiple side effects that are always used together, without being individually searched for, can be considered practically as a single value. Both Tables 6.1 and 6.2 satisfy the definition of 1NF.

Second Normal Form: a 1NF relation where only the whole PK, not any proper subset of it, can determine any non-prime attributes — i.e., no attributes outside the collection of CKs may be functionally dependent on any part of the PK. In the literature, this requirement is also phrased as the non-prime data items being fully FD (FFD) on the PK. In Table 6.1, Surgery Name, Drug, and Side-Effect are FFD on the PK, but Patient Name, Insurance Plan, and Surgeon Name are not. Thus, Table 6.1 is not in 2NF. (Is Table 6.2 in 2NF?)

Third Normal Form: a 2NF relation where no non-prime attributes determine any other non-prime attributes — i.e., there is no FD among non-prime attributes. The FD of Drug determining Side Effect in Table 6.1 is one where a non-prime attribute determines another.

Boyce–Codd Normal Form: a 3NF relation where all LHSs of FDs are a CK. That is, if a BCNF relation contains more than one FD, then every LHS is a CK. Conversely, if an FD has a LHS that cannot determine all non-prime attributes in the BCNF, then it is not allowed to be in the relation. Clearly, Patient No. in Table 6.1 is a LHS, but it is not (in and of itself) a CK. The same holds for Insurance ID, Surgeon License No., and Drug.

This chapter now presents a ***methodology for data normalization*** from the perspective of developing relational database design from a process model; as follows:

- **Step 0:** Obtain the full definition of data stores (or their equivalent) as universe relations (1NF). Then, perform data normalization using either of the following two approaches, data store by data store.

The Decomposition Approach

- **Step 1:** Define the whole relation as a FD and determine its LHS(s) — i.e., the CK(s) and PK of the 1NF relation.
- **Step 2:** Apply the 2NF requirement to the 1NF relation to recognize discrepancies due to the violation (if any) of the FFD on the PK — i.e., recognize the FDs led by some prime attributes. Remove these FDs from the relation and define each of them as a new relation. Purge duplicate rows in the new relations. Retain the PK of each new relation in the original table as attributes, while the new relation duplicates these attributes as its PK in it. Declare such retained PKs as Foreign Keys in the original table.
- **Step 3:** Apply the 3NF requirement to the relations from Step 2, one by one, to recognize FDs among non-prime attributes. Remove

these FDs, define them as new relations, purge duplicate rows, and declare FKs, in the same manner as Step 2.

- **Step 4:** Apply the BCNF requirement to the relations from Step 3 to recognize all FDs where the LHSs are not a CK. Remove the violating FDs, define them as new relations, purge duplicate tuples, and declare FKs, as do Steps 2 and 3. Continue on to Step 5 (see below).

The Synthesis Approach

- **Step 1:** Determine all non-redundant FDs (see Section 6.1.2).
- **Step 2:** Tentatively define all FDs as relations, with the LHS becoming the PK for each.
- **Step 3:** Recognize FKs among these relations and relations that do not connect to other relations by FKs — all relations should be inter-connected since they pertain to the same universe relation. Thus, by definition, they are semantically associated.
- **Step 4:** Connect gaps and remove duplicates of relations — i.e., combine relations whose LHSs are identical, and combine LHSs to define new relations (typically self-to-self mapping between a plural set) if such new relations are required to achieve non-loss recovery of the original universe relation. Declare additional FKs for the new relations. Continue on to Step 5.

Conclusion of Either Approach

- **Step 5 — Grand Integration:** Globally synthesize the relations in all sub-models obtained above. That is, combine those relations whose PKs are identical, and recognize the FKs across relations from all sub-models. Finally, form new relations as needed to create flexible connections for the global users and applications.

The above methodology has two loose ends: how to determine the overall LHS (PK) for the universe relation (Step 1 of the decomposition approach), and how to recognize and connect gaps (Steps 3 and 4 of the synthesis approach). The answer involves rigorous mathematical analysis at the high end (Ullman, 1982; Ullman and

Widom, 2008); however, simple heuristics also exist. A useful simple heuristic is presented herein:

Determination of Primary Key (or any CK): Recognize the largest LHS of all FDs in the relation, or the FD that covers the most data items of the relation. Then, expand the LHS' coverage by transition using the FK concept; i.e., following the attributes on its RHS that play the role of LHS for other FDs to transition to these FDs and cover their RHS, until all connections are exhausted. If all data items can be covered this way, then the LHS is the PK (or a CK). Otherwise, group the FD(s) of the remaining data items and connect them among themselves in a similar way. Finally, combine the LHSs of these isolated groups of FDs.

The largest LHS in Table 6.1 is the one of the fifth FD. We test it: it can determine all other data items by transition via other FDs, and hence is declared to be the PK. For instance, given a value (combination) for (Patient No., Surgeon License No., Date), the RHSs of Patient No. are determined via the Patient No., and so is the RHS of Surgeon License No. Drug is determined by the combination, and via transition, the usual Side Effect is, too.

Either the decomposition or the synthesis approach will normalize Table 6.1 into the following BCNF relations (the boldface indicates PK, while italics the FK):

- Patient Relation (**Patient No.**, Patient Name, Insurance Plan, Insurance ID). The table includes five tuples, each pertaining to a unique patient. The field Insurance ID may be declared to be an alternate key by subjecting it to the same rigorous integrity control (non-null, non-duplicate) as the PK, Patient No. With this alternate key, the hospital has an additional assurance for the integrity of the patient data.
- Surgeon Relation (**Surgeon License No.**, Surgeon Name). As one will expect, six unique tuples (surgeons) are included in this table.
- Drug Relation (**Drug**, Usual Side-Effect). Four tuples represent four drugs here.

- Surgery Relation (***Patient No.*, *Surgeon License No.*, Date**, Surgery Name, *Drug*). The table contains eight tuples representing the core, non-repetitive information of all eight surgeries; which are the reduced version of the original Table 6.1 after the removal of the above three relations. Three FKs are defined, with two levels of integrity control. The first two FKs, Patient No. and Surgeon License No., are a key attribute (part of the PK), thus they must satisfy the requirements of both PK and FK: be non-null, non-duplicate as well as matching the value of the PK of Patient and Surgeon, respectively (finding their values in the PK of these relations). The third FK, Drug, is a non-key attribute, thus it only requires that its value, if any, must be found in the PK of the Drug relation. Note that each PK is the combination of three key attributes, and hence its value is the combination of the values of these attributes. These combinations are unique in the table, as required by the normalization theory.

EXERCISE: Can you show the contents (data instances) of these four tables; i.e., Patient, Surgeon, Drug, and Surgery? Can you normalize Table 6.2?

The normalization of Table 6.2 follows the same logic and results in a similar collection of smaller BCNF relations. They are shown below:

- Patient Relation (**Patient No.**, Patient Address, *Insurance Plan*, Insurance ID).
- Insurance Plan Relation (**Insurance Plan**, Plan Copay, *Company*).
- Company Relation (**Company**, Company Address).
- Claim Relation (***Patient No.*, Claim Date**, Claim Log#).

If the claims themselves are digitized and saved as normalized relations in the hospital database, then there should be FK to link Claim relations to the Insurance Plan relation. In any case, two sub-models have been developed at this point, with each containing four relations. The hospital database will include, therefore, all eight relations as base tables. Clearly, since the Patient relation in each sub-model has the identical PK as the other, they really represent the same entity type Patient and hence should be combined. Combining these two versions of Patient relation results in the following full extension for the entity type Patient:

- Patient Relation (**Patient No.**, Patient Name, Patient Address, *Insurance Plan*, Insurance ID).

Thus, the database contains only seven distinct tables, not eight.

To conclude the hospital scenario, the pilot study will have two sub-models developed from the two data stores; and the integration of these two will result in seven relations, all of which conform to the BCNF requirement. Integrity rules will be identified as key constraints to connect all seven tables. Now, we do a few exercises to reinforce the normalization concepts.

EXERCISES

1. What BCNF relations will result from the normalization of the following relation — by the way, what is its PK and what is the highest normal form that it satisfies?

$$R1 = \{a, b, c, d, e, f \mid a \rightarrow b; c \rightarrow d; e \rightarrow f\}$$

2. Please determine the PK and the highest normal form for each of the following relations:

$$R2 = \{a, b, c, d \mid a,b \rightarrow c; a \rightarrow d\}$$
$$R3 = \{e, f, g, h \mid a \rightarrow b; b \rightarrow c; c \rightarrow d\}$$
$$R4 = \{w, x, y, z \mid w,x \rightarrow z; w,y \rightarrow z\}$$
$$R5 = \{m, n, s, t \mid m,t \rightarrow s; m \leftrightarrow n\}$$
$$R6 = \{u, v, y, z \mid u \rightarrow v, y, z\}$$

3. Please determine all CKs for the following relations:

$$R7 = \{i, j, k, l \mid i,k \rightarrow j, l; l \rightarrow i; k,l \rightarrow i\}$$
$$R8 = \{o, p, q, r \mid o,p \rightarrow r; o,q \rightarrow r, p; p \rightarrow q\}$$
$$R9 = \{i, o, u, m \mid no\ FD\}$$

The first question introduces a new concept, the ***all-key relation***, which has the whole table to be the PK and contains no non-key attributes. An all-key table typically serves to associate otherwise isolated data items and/or relations. Its very existence owes to the fact that these data items pertain to the same universe relation. The PK of R1 is the group of (a, c, e), since no other attributes or groups of attributes smaller than it can determine everything else in the relation. R1 is in 1NF, only, since none of b, d, and f is FFD on the PK. As a result, the normalization of R1 will see four BCNF relations: {a, b}, {c, d}, {e, f}, and {*a, c, e*}. The last BCNF relation is an all-key, where all three attributes together constitute the PK. It serves to associate all data items and help the non-loss recovery from these four relations for R1. Incidentally, an all-key relation is already in BCNF. The plural self-to-self mapping for groups of data items always results in this kind of all-key relations, as illustrated by the (drug, usual side-effect) multi-valued table discussed in the earlier section for the hospital scenario. One expects to see all-key relations in large-scale complex databases.

Question 2 is rather straightforward. For R2, the PK is (a, b) and the highest normal form is 1NF. R3 has (a) for PK and is in 2NF; while R4 has (w, x, y) for PK and is in 1NF. R5 has two CKs — (m, t) and (n, t) — and is in 3NF since both m and n are a LHS and yet neither is a CK by itself. R6 is in BCNF, pure and simple.

The last question is also a FD manipulation exercise: there are two CKs for R7, (i, k) and (k, l); and two for R8, (o, p) and (o, q). Both are only in 1NF. R9 is an all-key relation with the PK = (i, o, u, m), and is in BCNF.

To put a capstone to this section, we suggest conducting a FD analysis exercise which leads to the synthesis approach to logical database design (relational data normalization). The answer is provided at the end of the exercise.

The e-Commerce Scenario: Suppose an e-commerce site sells outdoor gear to customers. The company runs a Web site as the front end to the company's production database, through a firewall protection. The site shows an online catalog (e-catalog) of products, which provides product information such as the product code, name, general description, picture, price, maker and the like. Pertinent data about the makers, such as address and contact telephone number, are also included. The e-catalog organizes products into an "on-demand" hierarchy of categories; which means that hierarchy is virtual and can be re-versioned on the fly, according to what the customers want to see — or what the IS thinks the customers want to see.

Each category may be a sub-category (child) of one or more other categories (the super-category, or parent), as well as a super-category of other categories. Both the categorization and the number of levels of categorization are flexible, and they change frequently to respond to the marketing needs. That is, the super-sub category hierarchy is not fixed and there is no telling how many levels of decomposition the categorization may go. Furthermore, a category at a level of categorization may be used as a sub-category in another "branching" at a lower level. Thus, the categorization is more a network than a tree. Each category has a title along with some general description and other information about it. A product may belong to different categories, each of which in turn may include many different products.

The e-commerce site takes customers' orders online and interacts with the company database. When a user requests to order some products from the e-catalog, the user ceases to be a browser only and becomes a customer. At this point, the IS asks the user to register, which involves the selection of a unique user name, password, and authentication data; and entry of the customer's name, address, zip code, and telephone number. In addition, the IS provides rewards to allure the customer into providing information that it can use in personal marketing, such as email, age, gender, and income range. The IS then generates a customer ID from the combination of telephone number and name to recognize her/him, since it is inappropriate to ask for SSN. The IS also associates the customer's user name with the customer ID, and uses the ID in internal audit. It calibrates the ID's correctness (phone number and name) with the customer's other data such as financial (payment). A returning customer could either provide his/her user name or enter the combination of phone number and name to go directly to personal online shopping.

The personal marketing data will be used to recommend products for returning customers, as well as for new customers who have purchased a product. The e-commerce business may expand this marketing design to include customer comments, blogs, and other social networking provisions. Although there are many possible designs for enacting the idea of online recommendation, the IS chooses to employ personalized logic for individual products. That is, the recommendation logic (to show additional products for the customer) is dependent on the customer and the product. The logic may be referenced in the database by some pointer to a library of such logics. The IS creates a personalized logic after a new customer has made a purchase, and regularly updates the logic after the customer's transaction session is closed.

The registration marks the beginning of the transaction session for the customer, while the session ends when s/he leaves the site. A customer uses a form-building process called Shopping Cart to place an order, which could contain one or more lines. Each line indicates the product code and quantity ordered for a name and address to which the product is to be shipped; and different lines may contain the same products. The customer completes an order when s/he clicks the "submit" button and confirms it, and can order again (new orders) in the same session. The system determines automatically the starting time and the ending time for each order, within the session. It records the elapsed time of each order, along with other usage data, for analysis purposes. The system also records the customer's payment method for each order, such as the type of credit card, card number and the like. The IS maintains active information (name, address, rating, etc.) about credit card issuers whose credit the company accepts. The payment method has to clear against this information before the transaction is completed and accepted.

To continue the exercises:

4. How many e-commerce applications does the Web site provide, and hence how many external schemas must the company database support?
5. How many universe relations are implied in the scenario?
6. Can you formulate all the FDs implied in the scenario?
7. Can you complete data normalization and arrive at a relational design for the database in the scenario by using the synthesis approach? Any rules?

One can recognize these three perspectives, or enterprise applications, for the company database: e-catalog (on-site marketing), user registration (customer relationship), and ordering (sales). Each requires particular software programs supported by an external schema. The connection of the external schemas and the application software is a subject of further design, to take into account the firewall requirements. However, it is conceivable that a full-fledged enterprise DBMS is capable of providing such Web applications through its facility (see Section 5.1 of Chapter 5). The FDs for each perspective are listed below:

The e-Catalog Perspective

- Product code → name, product description, picture, price, maker, etc.
- Maker → address, contact, etc.
- (super-category, sub-category) ↔ (super-category, sub-category). (Note that this is a generalization of the multi-valued Drug and Side Effect relation that we discussed earlier for the hospital scenario. It is directly comparable to the BOM structure that we will discuss next in Section 6.2.)
- Category → title, category description, etc.
- Product code, category → remark

(Note that these three data items — category, super-category, and sub-category — are to be defined on the same domain, or declared to be equivalent.)

The Customer Registration and Marketing Perspective

- (Customer address, phone #) ↔ Customer ID. (Note that this FD will be combined into the Customer ID FD when they are implemented as relations; with the combination of customer address and phone # being defined as an alternate key using DBMS provisions.)
- Customer ID → address, zip code, personal marketing data, etc.
- Customer ID → → customer user name. (The user may have registered multiple user names over time, any of which may be used. The fixed association, → →, imposes removal of all user names from the database if the owner Customer ID is removed.)

- Customer user name → password, authentication data
- Customer ID, product code → recommendation logic

The Ordering Transaction Perspective

- Customer ID, order end time → elapsed time, usage data, payment method, payment instrument # (Note that if the method is credit card, then the instrument is credit card #; if the method is check, then the instrument is check #; and so on.)
- Customer ID, order end time → → line # (As shown in Figure 6.1, → → represents fixed association, meaning that the lines are part of the order. If an order is deleted, then the lines associated with it must be deleted, too.)
- Line # → product code, quantity, shipping address, receiver. (Note that when this FD is implemented as a relation, then its PK will be augmented by the PK of the owner FD — i.e., the Customer ID and the order end time in this case.)
- Payment instrument issuer → bank, address, rating, etc.
- Payment instrument # → type, expiration date, issuer, customer name, etc.

The above list of FDs is amenable to the synthesis approach of relational database design — see Section 6.3 for a semantic graphical representation of the overall database. The discussion on super- and sub-categories is an illustration for the general concept of BOM, too. This chapter will elaborate on this in the next section.

In fact, all FDs correspond directly to a BCNF relation, with the LHS being the PK. Some additional work is required: the FKs must be defined globally, and the fixed association between order and line must be enforced by using, e.g., appropriate ANSI SQL provisions (such as cascading delete on order); and so do alternate keys and any additional integrity control measures. Please also note that a new data item, Order #, may be defined from customer ID and order-end-time to facilitate database programming, at the cost of additional auditing concerns. The reason that order end time is used as the time stamp over order start time is business-based — an order is not really an order until it is completed. In any case, please note that the designs for virtual categorization and personalized marketing logic support hyper-networking for customers.

6.2 Semantic Modeling: Entity, Relationship, and Object

The FDs of the hospital scenario clearly reflect on some semantic concepts that describe the business of the hospital: patients, surgeons, drug, insurance, and the like. In fact, grasping these hospital semantics is evidently helpful for recognizing FDs for data normalization. Therefore, conversely, can we start with such semantic modeling to recognize directly normalized relations? An obvious advantage of this semantics approach is that it is more appealing (and less overwhelming) to people than FD formulation, and it is amenable to top-down structured analysis: starting from generality and progressing gradually to specific fine details, similar to process modeling. This is fine as long as FD level of analysis is still conducted at the end of modeling to confirm the technical quality of the results.

This book recognizes two basic methods of semantic modeling — the ERA (entity-relationship-attribute) and the O-O (object-orientation) — and discusses them together from a single paradigm of relational database design. The reason is simple: in the field, entities, relationships, and objects all correspond to relations, and all need to conform to data normalization. Since many versions of ERA and O-O conventions exist, this book goes back to the originals; i.e., Figure 6.3 summarizes the baseline concepts of ERA and O-O.

These two sets of concepts also form the basis for a particular modification in the next section, the Two-Stage Entity-Relationship (TSER) method, which combines the essence of process modeling and semantic modeling for relational database design. This book recognizes the ERA model due to Peter Chen (1976) as the origin of much of today's semantic modeling concepts and methods, including O-O and TSER. The ERA method was inspired primarily by the need for relational database design, although it also encompasses the concepts of object (used to be called the CODASYL design). For our purpose, we simply connect ERA to the relational model and consider

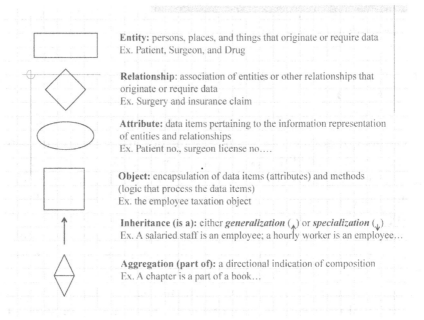

Entity: persons, places, and things that originate or require data
Ex. Patient, Surgeon, and Drug

Relationship: association of entities or other relationships that originate or require data
Ex. Surgery and insurance claim

Attribute: data items pertaining to the information representation of entities and relationships
Ex. Patient no., surgeon license no....

Object: encapsulation of data items (attributes) and methods (logic that process the data items)
Ex. the employee taxation object

Inheritance (is a): either *generalization* ($_\wedge$) or *specialization* ($_\downarrow$)
Ex. A salaried staff is an employee; a hourly worker is an employee...

Aggregation (part of): a directional indication of composition
Ex. A chapter is a part of a book...

Figure 6.3:   The baseline concepts of entity, relationship, and object.

it the higher level abstraction for relations. Figure 6.4 shows a simple ERA model that covers all core conceptual constructs.

Please note that the ERA model includes some cardinality information for each relationship, to indicate whether they are one-to-many, one-to-one, or many-to-one. The "has" relationship, for example, indicates that a department has many consultants; while the project relationship may involve multiple consultants, clients, and tasks. Each entity and plural relationship (many-to-many mapping) is expected to include a primary key. Finally, the double square, Dependent, represents the so-called Weak Entity, where the owner's existence determines that of the member. In this example, the dependents of the consultants are included in the company database simply because they are part of the consultant employees' fringe benefits. If the consultant leaves the company, then all his/her dependents must go, too, from the database.

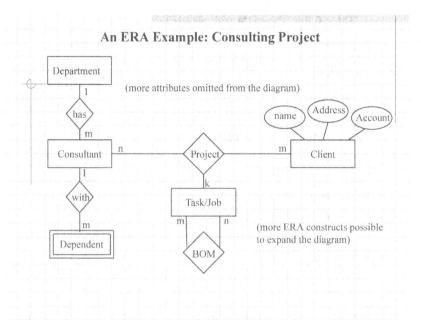

Figure 6.4: An entity-relationship-attribute model for database design.

Compared to the data normalization concepts, the one-to-many relationship evidently implies a FD from the many side (Consultant) to the one side (Department), while the Weak Entity implies a fixed mapping ($\rightarrow \rightarrow$) from the owner to the member. The many-to-many, or plural relationship implies a composite PK whose member key attributes come from the PK of the entities and/or relationships that participate in it. In contrast, an entity is expected to have a singular PK, although this is not required. It should be evident that an ERA model helps guide data normalization; but by the same token, it should be abundantly clear, too, that the ERA convention per se does not guarantee to always yield entities and relationships that are automatically normalized, without going through FD analysis. Moreover, even though one can envision doing ERA modeling in a DFD-style top-down manner, such a practice does not come automatically, though. One needs some useful methodology to guide the effort.

Table 6.3:   The BOM table — a bill-of-materials sample.

Part-super (the immediate assembly)	Part-sub (the immediate component)	Quantity required (called for in BOM)
P1002–320	P1002–311	3
P1002–320	P1001–286	1
P1002–320	P1004–099	5
P1002–311	P1004–099	2
P1002–311	P2980–758	6
P1004–099	P1004–032	5
P1004–099	P2981–344	4
P2980–758	P2981–344	12
P2980–758	P1004–099	7

The BOM relationship in Figure 6.4 deserves special attention. Table 6.3 shows a classical BOM for parts. We use it to illustrate the concept since the recursive structure of parts assembling into products is well-known.

The complete BOM structure requires a Part table in addition to Table 6.3. The Part table, comparable to Task in Figure 6.4, will contain the detailed part data, including the top-level parts which we customarily call products. The Part entity plays two roles in the BOM: the immediate assembly and the immediate component. All three data items — Part No., Part-Super, and Part-Sub — are defined on the same domain to signify that they are equivalent. A BOM is a self-to-self plural relationship, not a fixed tree, because the decomposition has variable levels and those levels can mix, or network — such as the case of the super- and sub-categories in the e-commerce scenario. A BOM can be extremely complex, just think a modern jetliner; and yet its semantic representation (and relational implementation) can be so simple. This is ERA modeling at its best. To recover the BOM for the table, however, is anything but trivial. It has been established in the field (see, e.g., Date, 2004) that no single session of SQL can accomplish the job because there is no definitive number to the end of the decomposition.

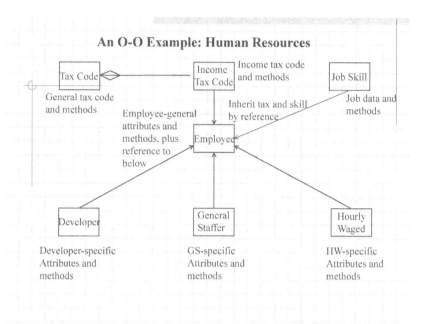

Figure 6.5: An object-oriented model for database design.

The logic requires dedicated programming to augment SQL. The Task structure in Figure 6.4 is inspired by the manufacturing practice, Part, since it is possible for consulting firms and construction companies to define services (tasks and jobs) in a similar manner.

The baseline concepts of the O-O model are illustrated in Figure 6.5. This self-explanatory model shows that the personal income tax object is part of the general object representing the general tax code, while the employee object inherits information contents (attributes and methods) from the income tax object and the job skill object — i.e., it has the same information contents as these two objects but without duplicating them. It merely refers to them by virtue of the declaration of inheritance. In a similar way, the three specialization objects at the bottom of the diagram represent the specific information contents pertaining to the specialization, so the employee object does not have to contain them but refer to them.

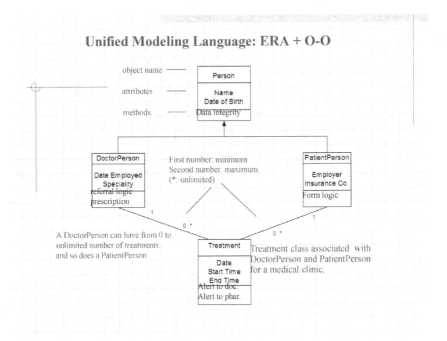

Figure 6.6:   The Unified Modeling Language at a quick glance.

The need for a graphical representation of the O-O paradigm has inspired the Unified Modeling Language (UML), as illustrated in Figure 6.6. In a nutshell, the UML combines the ERA features with those of O-O. For example, one may consider the bottom part of the model in Figure 6.6 as one of ERA and the top part an O-O. The figure is otherwise self-evident. The popularity of the UML is a testament that both ERA and O-O are required in semantic modeling. This book further suggests that the concept of processes (beyond the notion of methods which are encapsulated within the objects) is needed, too. Between ERA and O-O, one may find the former more widely applied outside of the field of software engineering per se.

In general, the O-O method is a generalization of the network database model originated at the dawn of database technology for, especially, engineering database design. It is a direct outcome of the advancement in CAD, CIM, and concurrent engineering (see Section 1.4 of Chapter 1). At the time, objects were envisioned to be directly saved, managed, and processed as such, and therefore replace relations to be the construct of the databases. The vision called for O-O to be the unifying paradigm for both software engineering (application program design) and database design (O-O DBMS). However, the ensuing development converged to a different fate: The field does see O-O dominating in software engineering, but it also sees this concept largely absorbed into the relational technology at the data management level. In other words, objects may be corresponded (build time definition) to views which will materialize (constructed) from relational databases when being called into use (run-time data manipulation). This is why an object is customarily considered an encapsulation.

It should be pointed out that the inheritance relationship, regardless of how one calls it, generalization or specialization, is comparable to the relational concepts of FK and fixed association, or the Weak Entity of the ERA method. For instance, the structure of the general information for the employee vs. the specific information for the three classes of employees is equivalent to a general employee relation with FKs to three relations that represent these three specializations. Either way, the notion of data normalization to avoid duplicates that cause inconsistency is the same. The big picture here is, therefore, that all three paradigms of database design — relational, ERA, and O-O — are comparable at the root level of data normalization to consolidate enterprise data resources. Furthermore, all three paradigms need a methodology to guide the development of information resources, before they can apply themselves to analyze these resources. In other words, the methods of process modeling can be useful here.

Based on this realization, and the proven use of DFD (data stores) to drive relational design, this book presents TSER to illustrate how a particular method may be developed to connect process modeling with semantic modeling to help determine information resources and accomplish data normalization.

6.3 The Two-Stage Entity-Relationship (TSER) Method: A Little Help to Semantic Modeling

The TSER method adds to the previous methods instead of replacing them. The method formally separates the broad semantic concepts from that of data normalization, and then connects these two sets in a structural way so that they are amenable to algorithmic mapping. The semantic concepts of the first stage include processes and high-level objects, entities, and relationships. These concepts will be employed to model for an IS without considering data normalization (or, the rules of data management), which is the task of the second stage. The normalization concepts, for data consolidation, refine the previous ERA constructs to make them strictly enforce the normal forms, especially the BCNF. Finally, the rules of FD and processing logics help map the semantic constructs to those of the normalization. Thus, the TSER method may be coupled with DFD and other similar process models to transition their results to relational database design; or applied independently (standalone) to perform the complete IS design job from a master plan. In any case, the O-O paradigm may be incorporated directly in the semantic modeling — i.e., the Objects may be defined directly as some Subjects.

An overview of the TSER constructs is provided in Figure 6.7. The first Semantic Modeling stage uses Subject and Context; while the second Normalization stage uses Entity, Plural Relationship (PR), Referential Relationship (FR), and Mandatory Relationship (MR). One can see the clear correspondence between the TSER concepts and those of process modeling, semantic modeling, and data normalization. In a way, Subject has two possible applications: a unification of the nouns (e.g., data store, data flow, and external entity) in process modeling (e.g., the DFD method), and an Object. Both may be mixed, as long as the leaf-level Subjects are fleshed out with FDs. The intra-Subject rules are comparable directly to the methods of Objects, while Contexts, or grouping of inter-Subject rules, correspond to processes (of the DFD). From the perspective of database design, it does not make sense for Contexts to connect directly with other Contexts. As for Subjects, direct connections among them, unless in

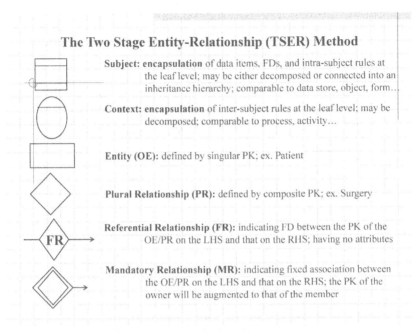

The Two Stage Entity-Relationship (TSER) Method

Subject: encapsulation of data items, FDs, and intra-subject rules at the leaf level; may be either decomposed or connected into an inheritance hierarchy; comparable to data store, object, form...

Context: encapsulation of inter-subject rules at the leaf level; may be decomposed; comparable to process, activity...

Entity (OE): defined by singular PK; ex. Patient

Plural Relationship (PR): defined by composite PK; ex. Surgery

Referential Relationship (FR): indicating FD between the PK of the OE/PR on the LHS and that on the RHS; having no attributes

Mandatory Relationship (MR): indicating fixed association between the OE/PR on the LHS and that on the RHS; the PK of the owner will be augmented to that of the member

Figure 6.7: The TSER modeling constructs.

an inheritance hierarchy, do not make sense, either. In any case, the stage of semantic modeling provides broad perspective to data normalization and adds contextual knowledge to data.

The hospital scenario of Section 6.1 may be represented in TSER as two Subjects (representing the two application tables/views) at the first stage, and one consolidated normalized ERA model at the second stage. Figure 6.8 abstracts the Hospital relations based on the FDs formulated; and helps illustrate the revised ERA constructs of TSER.

Because the revised ERA constructs adhere to normal form requirements (BCNF), they give rise directly to relational design. Each Entity and PR represents a relation, while FR and MR represent integrity control rules. There are eight relations indicated in the figure, including one for Date, which is unary or containing just one field, the data item Date. Unary relations are useful for further integrity control, such as defining the valid, operational dates allowed. However, they may be omitted from implementation, on the grounds

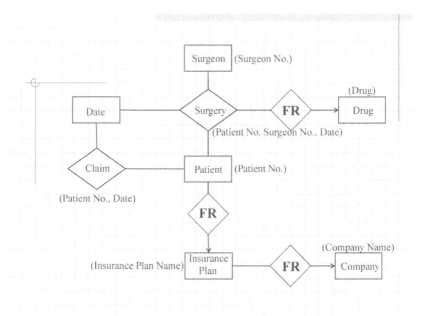

Figure 6.8:   The TSER representation of the hospital database.

that they are already included in the relations (PRs) in which they participate; such as the case with Date in Surgery and Claim. There are three FKs (three FRs) indicated, but no fixed association (MR).

The e-commerce scenario is modeled in TSER as shown in Figures 6.9 and 6.10. The semantic modeling stage is mainly an effort of information organization; i.e., document the three perspectives of data analysis in a structured way that facilitates the ensuing global normalization endeavor. At first glance, the semantic data model may appear to be only marginally helpful in this rather straightforward design exercise, since it does not add much to the FD analysis we have already performed. However, the organization itself, or the structured approach that TSER adds to the FD analysis, could be valuable especially when these perspectives themselves were unknown to the FD formulation at the beginning of the design. The organization helps global cross-referencing, too, as well as document processing logics.

The Semantic Modeling Stage: Subject and Context

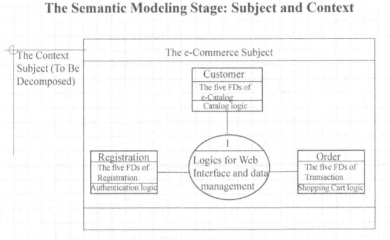

Please note that the decomposition is hierarchical; however, for clearer presentation, this figure shows the decomposed sub-model inside the context subject.

Figure 6.9: The TSER semantic model for the e-commerce scenario.

The three Subjects in Figure 6.9 are consolidated globally into the normalized ERA model shown in Figure 6.10.

As for the Hospital scenario, the model indicates directly a full relational design: twelve (BCNF) relations (eight Entities and four PRs); three FKs (three FRs); and two fixed associations (two MRs). One unary relation is included in the twelve. Again, the PK for a PR is always composite, made of the PKs of the participating Entities and/or PRs in it. In contrast, the PK of an Entity is always singular, made of only one key attribute.

The following shows a simple *TSER modeling methodology for logical database design*:

- **Step 0:** Obtain an IS master plan and/or a process model.

The Normalization Stage: Entity, PR, FR, and MR

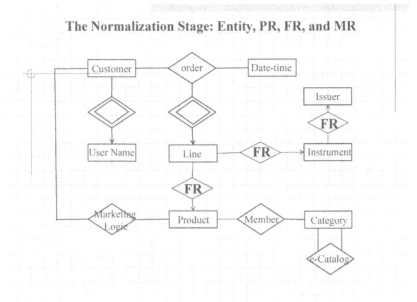

Figure 6.10:   The TSER normalized ERA model for the e-commerce scenario.

- **Step 1:** Perform Semantic Modeling to obtain Subjects and Contexts, using any appropriate methods available, including:

  The O-O alternative: Recognize Objects as Subjects, and add Contexts, if any.

  The DFD alternative: Recognize data stores (and data flows and external entities) as Subjects, and processes as Contexts, if appropriate.

  The TSER-independent alternative: Recognize the information *forms* (workflows, records, input/output to processes, etc.) and similar natural groupings of data in the Information Resources class of IS elements as Subjects. Add Contexts as appropriate.

- **Step 2:** Perform Normalized ERA modeling and define the full relational model.
- **Step 3:** Define the conceptual schema from the relational model.
- **Step 4:** Define the external schemas from Subjects and Contexts.

The AircraftExchange.com Scenario: Suppose a corporate jet-liner maker was collaborating with a leading operation services provider specialized in the mid- to long-range corporate jets market, to hyper-network their information resources and customer bases in an innovative marketing strategy. They envisioned to build an IS that connects to the FAA public databases, the industry's published data (models, etc.), the provider's proprietary marketing data, and the maker's production databases, so that they can monitor the movement (buy and sell, and repairs and upgrades) of *individual* aircraft in the market. (Note that all aircraft are identified in the U.S. by a unique N-number, and they have to register their ownership with the FAA once their proprietors change. The FAA publishes such data weekly, among other things, in disciplined digital files.) The IS will publish marketing newsletters featuring individual aircraft to subscribers, in digital format. The publication system uses Access running on PCs in the business office, which draws data from the main enterprise database, in a manner shown in the first class of Figure 5.2. The new venture also envisions expanding its services to cover aircraft brokers and pilots, to become a one-stop aircraft exchange for the market. As such, the IS must be embedded into the societal cyber-infrastructure.

The TSER model of Figure 6.11 shows the vision. The shaded part of the model represents the current scope of the information resources, and the white constructs represent the future expansions. This model will be revisited in the next chapter.

6.4 The Metadatabase Model: Its Conceptual Schema and Population with TSER Models

An important reason for standardizing the semantic modeling concepts, as TSER does, is to allow consolidation of information resources — pulling together heterogeneous models in a community to make hyper-networking of databases feasible — i.e., to implement the metadata principle for systems of IS (see Section 5.4 of Chapter 5). Again, the information collaboration model discussed there involves the Metadatabase. The Metadatabase presented employs a TSER-based conceptual schema to define the domain of concepts used in

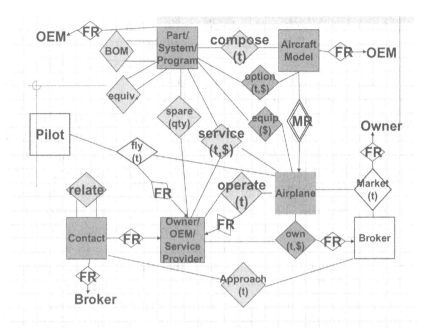

Figure 6.11: The TSER model for the AircraftExchange scenario.

the information models that it contains. Therefore, the conceptual schema of the Metadatabase represents in effect the ontology of data modeling for the information collaboration model.

The ontology must work if the Metadatabase design is to work for heterogeneous user groups. Two reasons that the ontology should work in many cases: First, the TSER method embraces ERA, O-O, and DFD (and similar process modeling methods such as SADT, including methods derived from them), which cover a significant range of IS practices (e.g., UML and IDEF-based modeling). And second, algorithmic mapping between TSER and these traditional concepts has been proven to be feasible in the literature (e.g., Hsu *et al.*, 1993). This book now elaborates on the Metadatabase design.

The original conceptual schema of the Metadatabase (Hsu *et al.*, 1991) is shown in Figure 6.12, which is focused on representing multiple data models and rule-based models. A few minor revisions have been suggested, and an extension of it for representing analytic

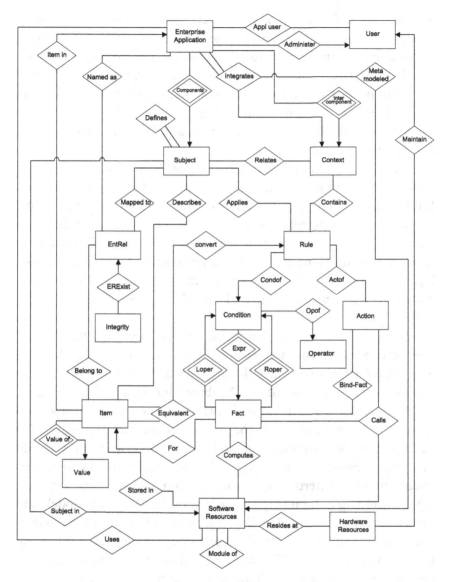

Figure 6.12: The conceptual schema (ontology) of the Metadatabase.

models has also been proposed. However, for our purpose, the original design is sufficient to illustrate the general feasibility of connecting information resources by virtue of metadata. The metadata types are based on the TSER concepts. Each icon in the figure represents either a table of metadata or a particular type of integrity control rule. The meta-tables are categorized into four inter-related groups: Users-Applications, Database Models, Contextual Knowledge, and Software and Hardware Resources.

The Database Models group is comprised of metadata types that define application data models for enterprises. They include Subject, Entity-Relationship, and Data Item. The meta-relationship Define supports recursive Subjects, showing the super-sub hierarchy between Subjects in a BOM-style structure. The Contextual Knowledge is structured in terms of the metadata types Rule, Condition, Action, Operator, and Fact. These types constitute a Rulebase Model as a particular representation method for Rules (Bouziane and Hsu, 1997).

The Condition and Action metadata types represent the declaration of conditions and actions for the predicates of rules, both of which are further substantiated with Operator and Fact. Fact is corresponded to Data Items of the Database Models, and therefore integrates Database Models with Contextual Knowledge. These two groups are further linked, on the one direction, with the aggregated definition of Users-Applications, and on the other, with Software and Hardware Resources. The User-Application group is defined to represent multiple enterprises, application families, and user interface types (including natural language input) of the Database Models and their Contextual Knowledge. The Software and Hardware Resources group represents the particular computing platforms, networking middleware, and other IT solutions involved in the implementation design of the databases and knowledge systems.

The Equivalent meta-relationship cross-references data items from one application data model to their equivalents in others. Together with the conversion routines represented in Software and Hardware Resources, they achieve data semantics reconciliation for the community. This part of the Metadatabase model is also recognized to be a core set of metadata that a distributed Metadatabase design can use to install in local sites and facilitate peer-to-peer data reconciliation and collaboration (Hsu *et al.*, 2006). This conceptual schema defines the meta-tables of the Metadatabase, which in turn is implemented and processed as a standard relational database.

Application information models are "saved" into the Metadatabase by first reverse-representing their constructs (e.g., the object types) into the neutral TSER constructs, and then entering this neutral representation (e.g., the metadata) into the corresponding meta-tables in the Metadatabase. Thus, an information model will have a number of entries in a number of meta-tables in the Metadatabase representing it. New information models are added to the community in the same way, using the neutral method TSER. This process extends to the modification of existing models represented in the Metadatabase, too. This conversion process is amenable to using a CASE tool, while the insertion and updating processes are just ordinary relational operations. Thus, the Metadatabase does not need to shut down during the insertion and update. In this sense, the Metadatabase, implemented as a relational database, provides an *open and scalable common schema* to the community.

The Metadatabase Model allows for a distributed design to support peer-to-peer information collaboration, as mentioned in Section 5.4 of Chapter 5. Again, the Equivalent meta-table can be the core for such designs. In general, the distribution design will center on creating a minimum Metadatabase to reside at participating sites and facilitate collaboration (information sharing and exchange) among them. In fact, any site that supports a thin database (e.g., a system on a chip) can meet the requirements of the participation. This low threshold includes some of the advanced wireless sensor system and RFID (radio frequency identification) tags in the class of possible participants for information collaboration (see Chapter 8). The global Equivalent meta-table is the only necessary element of any minimum Metadatabase design. It is also possible to decompose the Software and Hardware Resources meta-tables of Figure 6.12 and include them in the Local Metadatabase to support the implemented IT solutions.

Needless to say, the TSER ontology is the limitation of the Metadatabase design. Regardless of how open and scalable it is conceptually, it still requires reverse-engineering, which thereby restricts its applicability and performance. Better methods are possible in the future — and this is precisely the point that this book makes here, and the purpose for introducing this particular design. The generic concepts promise to have broad implications.

To conclude, this book observes that the field has available sufficient results to support large-scale consolidation of information resources, and to make them work as one. Thus, pursuing the hyper-networking of information resources to renovate IS is both feasible and enlightening. We recognize this promise in the concluding principle of this chapter:

The Overlap-Modeling Principle of Data Management for Systems of IS: *Develop open and scalable repository of community metadata, distributed or not, to identify overlaps and inter-operations among independent information resources; and focus the global data management tasks on controlling these overlaps by using the community metadata.*

This is a continuation of the previous metadata principle presented at the end of Chapter 5. In fact, the query of the community information resources requires such metadata, too. That is, in order to hyper-network people and information resources, the IS needs to expose the underlying data models as metadata to the users of database query languages. The next chapter discusses the logic and facility of relational database query.

Chapter 7

Techniques of Database Processing: From SQL for Single Databases to Extensions of SQL for Global Query of Independent Databases

Just as the single database model has been extended to support the connection of multiple independent databases (see Chapter 5), the de facto industry standard of relational query system, ANSI SQL (Structured Query Language), has been incorporated in many extensions to allow global query of massively distributed databases on the Web. The marvelous fact is that these extensions, undertaken over the past decades, tend to be consistent in basic ideas despite their vibrantly different mechanisms; and the query logic remains simple. This is elegance at its best, and a tribute to the SQL. This chapter presents the core logic of database query. It starts with the relational algebra and calculus, which are the mathematic foundations of SQL, and moves gradually to the data definition (DDL) part and the data manipulation (DML) part of SQL. Both parts are illustrated with ample examples. A good feature of SQL is its relative ease to be embedded in a programming environment, which gives it considerable openness and scalability in the relational technology-dominated database world. Open sources such as PHP, Perl, Java, and XML, as well as the C family, have all supported SQL. Thus, the field has plenty of proposals to use SQL, with rather straightforward extensions, for interchanging queries among Internet databases. One such example is XQUERY, which wraps SQL in XML to swap queries between individual Web databases. However, extensions that allow users to globally query multiple databases as if they were one are rare, since this class of global query requires global connection of information resources at the database level (Chapter 5). This chapter offers some design ideas of global query at its conclusion.

7.1 Relational Algebra and Calculus

A data model not only represents and organizes information resources, but also operates on them to fulfill the missions of a database. For the relational model, the representation of data is achieved by the definition of relations, as discussed in Section 6.1 of Chapter 6; but the operation of relations is accomplished expressly by relational algebra and calculus. In general, a dedicated database language has two integral parts: the data definition language (DDL) that creates the database objects, and the data manipulation language (DML) that processes them. For the relational model, the ANSI SQL (Structured Query Language) is *the* language, which creates database schemas according to the definition of relations, and manipulates tables and views according to relational algebra and calculus.

7.1.1 Relational Algebra

Seven core operators constitute relational algebra: Union, Difference (or Minus), Selection, Projection, Cartesian product, Join (on condition, natural, outer, etc.), and Division. These operators always work on relations — either a single relation or multiple relations — and yield only relations as the output. Even when the output is in effect a single data item, the single data item is considered a relation that consists of only one row and one column, rather than a singular (a data item by itself). In this sense, relational operators are set-based and ought to be interpreted as such; they work on the whole set rather than on the individual elements of the set. They can be mixed to form algebraic expressions, as ordinary algebraic operators can.

We use the two relations below to show how they work:

Relation A	
A.ID	A.Name
310265	Park
435011	Williams
867943	Schneider

Relation B	
B.ID	B.Name
435011	Williams
885219	Salvado

Union (∪): Vertical concatenation of two *homogeneous* tables (relations that have the same definition — i.e., of the same meaning and structure), with duplicates removed from the result.

Example: A ∪ B

A.ID	A.Name
310265	Park
435011	Williams
867943	Schneider
885219	Salvado

Intersect (∩): A new relation made of the common rows of two *homogeneous* tables.

Example: A ∩ B

435011	Williams

Difference (or Except/Minus) (−): Removal of the common rows between two *homogeneous* tables from the first table. Unlike union, this operation is directional.

Example: A–B

A.ID	A.Name
310265	Park
867943	Schneider

Example: B–A

B.ID	B.Name
885219	Salvado

Selection (σ): Outputting the rows from the designated table that satisfy the selection condition.

Example: $\sigma_{\text{A.Name} = \text{'Park'}}$ **(A)**

310265	Park

Projection (π): Outputting the designated columns from the designated table. Either the name (heading) of the column or its order (e.g., 1, 2...) may be used as the designation. The order in which the columns appear in the designation determines that of the resulting new table.

Example: $\pi_{\text{B.ID}}$ **(B)**

435011
885219

Note that replacing B.ID by 1 will yield the same result. On the other hand, $\pi_{2,1}$ **(B)** will yield re-ordering of table B; i.e., the column of B.Name will appear as the first column, followed by B.ID. Selection and projection are the only two operators that work on single tables, one at a time. All others involve two tables, immediately.

Cartesian Product (×): Horizontal concatenation by pairwise joining of rows from any two tables. If these two tables are (m, n) and (l, k) in size, respectively, then the result is a table of (m × n) rows and (1 + k) columns. This is by far the most powerful and costly relational operation. If the joining does not make sense, then the results will not, either.

Example: A × B

A.ID	A.Name	B.ID	B.Name
310265	Park	435011	Williams
310265	Park	885219	Salvado
435011	Williams	435011	Williams
435011	Williams	885219	Salvado
867943	Schneider	435011	Williams
867943	Schneider	885219	Salvado

Clearly, the operation is directional, i.e., A × B is not the same as B × A, in that these two results will have different ordering of columns; although their sizes are identical.

Join (∞): Refinement of Cartesian product with selection conditions. This operation will conceptually perform Cartesian product on the two tables designated, then apply selection operation on the result according to the join conditions, and finally remove duplicates. There are basically three types of join conditions: outer join, conditional join, and natural join. Outer join is comparable to Cartesian product. Conditional join will specify conditions for the final selection operation. And natural join uses only one type of condition — that of the two tables having some common attributes that share the same values. Usually, the natural join is the default type for the join operation.

Example: A ∞ B on θ, with θ indicating the condition. If θ = A.ID <= B.ID, then the resulting table will contain all rows in the above A × B table except the fifth one of Schneider and Williams. Conversely, if the condition is A.ID > B.ID, then only the fifth row will be included in the result. The natural join, where θ is replaced by A.Name = B.Name, will yield the following result, which contains only one row:

435011	Williams	435011

All the above seven relational operators may be used directly in SQL expressions.

Division (÷): Reversal of Cartesian product, or partial uncoupling of local data in the first table by referencing to the second table. This operation is complicated because of the or-clause. The partial uncoupling seeks to identify from the first table a group of attribute values that is associated with another group of attribute values identified in the second table. The first table must have more columns than the second, and the two groups of columns must be disjoint.

Example: $(A \times B) \; / \; A = B$

Example: $D \div E = F$

Relation D

101	SPA	071011	50
298	EPA	062911	90
455	DRC	053112	40
298	EPA	121511	76
332	SPA	020312	69

Relation E

062911	90
121511	76

Relation F

298	EPA

Finally, this book introduces the notion of *query optimization*. This concept is concerned with the cost of the relational expression required to answer a query; and the cost is determined primarily by the size of the Cartesian product involved. For example, $A \times B$ involves $3 \times 2 = 6$ pairing operations, and $6 \times 4 = 24$ cells of storage. For the natural join example shown above, one can let the join operator perform the selection operation on $A \times B$; or, alternatively, one can pre-process both tables by performing selection to them to single out Williams, *if* one knows that the join condition will work on Williams. In this latter case, the Cartesian product is performed on two (1×1) tables, requiring only one pairing and $1 \times 4 = 4$ cells of space.

Of course, usually one does not know what exact matches exist there, and that's precisely why one wants to do query in the first place. However, this logic does hold in the general sense, where a sequence of relational operations will be performed. Here, one should pre-process the tables to reduce their sizes as much as possible, before joining them. In particular, say, a relational expression is to find out the rows that satisfy some conditions from the results of a natural join of two tables, and then output only one field of the selected rows. One can do the join first, followed by the selection, and conclude with the projection. The join will involve the full sizes of these two tables in this case. A better way is to pre-select and even pre-project both tables before joining them.

The Principle of Query Optimization: *Minimize the number and size of the source tables against which the query will be performed. For relational algebraic expressions, this means performing selection and projection on individual tables to minimize their sizes before joining them. When query with automatic optimization capability (e.g., SQL), the user still needs to apply human knowledge to reduce the scope of search (number of tables) before formulating the query conditions.*

Please note that ANSI SQL expressions are built from relational algebraic expressions. That is, the SQL syntax (see the next sections) may be considered as some higher level synthesis of relational algebraic operations. Thus, SQL performs mandatory query optimization at this relational algebraic level, automatically, after it interprets the SQL expressions for computer processing. However, relational algebra level of query optimization is not the end of the story for users. The automatic query optimization works within the set of source tables specified in the SQL expressions by the user. The minimization of the scope itself is still the user's job.

EXERCISES (Referring to the Supplier table, Part table, and Supply table shown below; whose ideas are inspired by Date (2004), with some new columns and completely new data)

1. Write a relational algebraic expression to find all suppliers (names) from Taipei.
2. Similarly, find the materials of all parts heavier than 20.
3. Get all parts (P# and names) that have had a supply quantity (one time) of 300 or more.

4. Get suppliers (names) who supplied part "P437."
5. Get the cost of every part that supplier Siemens supplied in a quantity of 200 or more.
6. Can you find the best relational algebraic expression (with the least pairing operations and space requirement) and the worst (the most operations and space) for the query in Question 5? What are the best and worst numbers?

Supplier Table

Supplier ID	Supplier Name	City	Certified Tier
S1	Troy Tools	Troy	1
S2	Precision Bearings	Buffalo	3
S3	Siemens	Stuttgart	1
S4	Gold Star	Seoul	2
S5	Evergreen	Taipei	2

Part Table

Part ID	Part Name	Material	Weight	Unit Cost
P129	Bearing	Steel	12	23
P437	Axis	Alloy	35	110
P273	Housing	Iron	132	95

Supply Table

Supplier ID	Part ID	Date	Quantity Supplied
S1	P273	09112012	45
S2	P129	07282012	350
S3	P437	04122012	210
S4	P437	01302012	50
S3	P273	11212011	35
S2	P437	09122011	400
S3	P129	07112011	1100

ANSWERS

1. $\pi_{name}\ \sigma_{city\ =\ \text{'Taipei'}}$ (Supplier)

2. $\pi_{material}\ \sigma_{weight\ >\ 20}$ (Part)

3. $\pi_{Part\ ID,Name}\ \sigma_{Quantity\ >=\ 300}$ (Part ∞ Supply on Part ID)

4. $\pi_{Part\ ID,Name}\ (\sigma_{Part\ ID\ =\ \text{'P437'}}$ (Supply) ∞ Part on Part ID)

5. $\pi_{Cost}\ \sigma_{Supplier.Name\ =\ \text{'Siemens'}\ and\ Quantity\ >=\ 200}$ ((Part ∞ Supply on Part ID) ∞ Supplier on Supplier ID)

   The assumption here is that the user only knows the supplier name, not its supplier ID.

6. The relational algebraic expression given above is the worst possible answer. It requires $5 \times 3 \times 7 = 105$ operations, and $105 \times 13 = 1365$ cells of storage. The best possible answer is as follows:

   $(\pi_{Cost,\ Part\ ID}$ (Part) $\infty\ \pi_{Supplier\ ID,\ Part\ ID}\ \sigma_{Quantity\ >=\ 200}$ (Supply) on Part ID) $\infty\ (\pi_{Supplier\ ID}\ \sigma_{Supplier.Name\ =\ \text{'Siemens'}}$ (Supplier) on Supplier ID).

The number of operations is $1 \times 3 \times 4 = 12$, with $12 \times 5 = 60$ cells. Of course, if the supplier ID is known to the user, then this information can be used in selection to further reduce the size of the Supply table before joining; and the numbers would be $1 \times 3 \times 2 = 6$ operations, and $6 \times 5 = 30$ cells. (Or, the Supplier table can be dropped from the joining since it is no longer needed.) This answer illustrates the query optimization principle for relational algebra. However, is query optimization frivolous given today's computing power?

Please note the magnitude of reduction in percentage. With today's superior computer technology, one would think, so what? It would take at most seconds to process any query with or without optimization. This is true, but only to an extent. Think of a moderate business case for the e-commerce scenario of Section 6.1 of Chapter 6, where the username table has 10,000 rows; the order-line table 50,000 rows; and the product-category mixing table 1,000 rows — wouldn't this be a humble business with only 50,000 overall purchases of individual products for 10,000 total usernames registered interested in 1,000 combinations of product and e-catalog categories? However, this humble example would require $10,000 \times 50,000 \times 1,000 = 500,000,000,000$ or 500 billion operations if these three tables were to be joined fully. Moreover, if each row takes up 100 bytes, then the space requirement is 50 Giga-bytes CPU (RAMs). This join operation could easily break even a common workstation. What if the e-commerce has more usernames or purchase lines; or the query needs to join more tables?

In industry, it is well-known that complex BOMs, such as one for a large turbine power generator, could require many computer hours to build from the parts database which may contain millions of parts. In a similar way, factory scheduling IS could take one or two full days to produce a full production schedule for, say, a modern jet engine. Think about the scale of contemporary social networking databases or the Web search engine databases. The potential size of join operations could be mind-boggling. Again, query optimization is not only a relational algebraic matter which may be automated, but more importantly it is a human design matter that needs to continuously renovate itself.

7.1.2 *Relational Calculus*

Unlike relational algebra, which is navigational, relational calculus is the first order logic, which is non-navigational. It uses logical expressions of predicates to indicate the request for processing of relations. These expressions are formulated by using four main classes of operators: *Booleans*, including "and" ($\wedge$), "or" ($\vee$), "not" ($\sim$); *qualifiers*, such as "there exists" ($\exists$), "For every" ($\forall$), etc.; *set theoretic*, e.g., "belonging to" ($\in$), "contained in" ($\cap$), "such that" ($\ni$), etc.; and the ordinary *comparison* operators =, $\neq$, <, and >.

The relational calculus expression below is equivalent to the next two relational algebraic expressions that follow it:

$$\{c | (\ni b) \ (G(a,b) \wedge H(b,c))\}$$
$$1. \ \pi_C(\sigma_{A=a}(G \infty H)) \text{ with } G(A,B), H(B,C)$$
$$2. \ \pi_C(\pi_B(\sigma_{A=a}(G)) \infty H)$$

The relational calculus expression explicitly indicates all values involved (the instances of the tables). In particular, the expression shows the value (a) required for column A of relation G, while "A=a" is a selection condition in the relational algebraic expressions. Natural join on the common attribute B is assumed by default.

The industry standard for relational languages is the ANSI SQL (Structured Query Language), which is pronounced "sequel" after its predecessor, the SEQEUL language of the IBM. This book illustrates the DDL and DML of SQL in the next two sections, respectively.

7.2 The DDL of ANSI SQL: Define the Conceptual Schema

The mission for the DDL part of SQL is plain to define: create relations according to the (normalized) design. Therefore, the baseline facility of the language is the Create Table expression, with clauses to define data items (format, domain, etc.), PK, FK(s), and controls. The controls supported include user access and security measures — what data items may be read or written by what users under what conditions; intra-table data integrity rules such as non-null, non-duplicate, and indexed for designated data items (e.g., alternate key); and inter-table cascading rules when data values get changed or deleted. Triggers (alerts) may also be defined upon the change of values to designated data items. We illustrate the DDL with a partial script of database creation for the AircraftExchange.com scenario in Section 6.3 of Chapter 6.

The AircraftExchange.com Scenario — a partial SQL script for database creation

(Beginning of the partial script)

```
CREATE TABLE Entity     (EntityName text,
                Person-or-Corporate text,
                Type text,
                Local Address text,
                City text,
                State text,
                Country text,
                Zip text,
```

```
                    Base text,
                    CellPhone text,
                    BusinessPhone text,
                    HomePhone text,
                    Fax text,
                    email text,
                    URL text,
                    Symbol text,
                    IndustrialRating text,
                    UserStatus text,
                    Remark text,

                    PRIMARY KEY (EntityName),
                    CHECK (Person-or-corporate = 'person'
or Person-or-Corporate = 'corporate'),
                    CHECK (Type = 'owner' or Type =
'prospect' or Type = 'Dealer' or Type = 'OEM-Aircraft'
or Type = 'Supplier' or Type = 'MRO-Vendor' or Type =
'Operator' or Type = 'Financial Institution' or Type =
'Lease Holder'),
                    CHECK (UserStatus = 'subscriber' or
UserStatus = 'user' or UserStatus = 'non-user'));

CREATE TABLE AircraftModel (AircraftModel text,
                    Class text,
                    AircraftGroup text,
                    YearModelStarted integer,
                    YearModelEnded integer,
                    Diagrams text,
                    IndustrialRating text,
                    Manufacturer text,
                    BasePrice integer,
                    TotalMade integer,
                    Remark text,

                    PRIMARY KEY (AircraftModel),
                    FOREIGN KEY (Manufacturer) REFERENCES
Entity on UPDATE CASCADE,
                    CHECK (Class = 'small' or Class =
'medium' or Class = 'large' or Class = 'ultra long
range'));
```

```
CREATE TABLE Airplane    (AircraftModel text,
                Serial# text,
                YearManufactured integer,
                InServiceDate date,
                CofAdate date,
                AirframeHours integer,
                TotalLandings integer,
                MonthlyHours real,
                Images text,
                CustomFloorPlans text,
                Range-miles integer,
                SafetyRating text,
                Report text,
                AircraftNote text,

                PRIMARY KEY (AircraftModel, Serial#),
                FOREIGN KEY (AircraftModel) REFERENCES
AircraftModel on UPDATE CASCADE,
                CHECK (MonthlyHours <= AirFrameTime));

CREATE TABLE Item (ItemID text,
                ItemName text,
                Pictures text,
                Supplier text,
                MeanTimeBetweenFailures integer,
                MTBFUnit text,
                IntervalBetweenInspections integer,
                IBIUnit text,
                IndustrialRating text,
                Remark text,

                PRIMARY KEY (ItemID),
                FOREIGN KEY (Supplier) REFERENCES
Entity on UPDATE CASCADE,
                CHECK (MTBFUnit = 'hours' or MTBFUnit =
'months' or MTBFUnit = 'landings'),
                CHECK (IBIUnit = 'hours' or IBIUnit =
'months' or IBIUnit = 'landings'));

CREATE TABLE Contact    (ContactName text,
                email text,
```

```
                    CellPhone text,
                    BusinessPhone text,
                    HomePhone text,
                    HomeAddress text,
                    City text,
                    State text,
                    Country text,
                    Zip text,
                    Non-BrokerEmployer text,
                    BrokerEmployer text,
                    Title text,
                    JobDescription text,
                    DateOfBirth date,
                    URL text,
                    IndustrialRating text,
                    Remark text,

                    PRIMARY KEY (ContactName),
                    FOREIGN KEY (BrokerEmployer)
REFERENCES Broker on UPDATE CASCADE,
                    FOREIGN KEY (Non-BrokerEmployer)
REFERENCES Entity on UPDATE CASCADE);

CREATE TABLE Broker      (BrokerName text,
                    email text,
                    CellPhone text,
                    BusinessPhone text,
                    HomePhone text,
                    LocalAddress text,
                    City text,
                    State text,
                    Country text,
                    Zip text,
                    Representative text,
                    Title text,
                    URL text,
                    IndustrialRating text,
                    UserStatus text,
                    Remark text,
```

```
            PRIMARY KEY (BrokerName),
            CHECK (UserStatus = 'full privilege'
or UserStatus = 'subscriber' or UserStatus = 'user' or
UserStatus = 'non-user'));

CREATE TABLE Pilot        (ATPRating text,
            PilotName text,
            email text,
            CellPhone text,
            BusinessPhone text,
            HomePhone text,
            Local Address text,
            City text,
            State text,
            Country text,
            Zip text,
            Credential text,
            IndustrialRating text,
            Remark text,

            PRIMARY KEY (ATPRating));

CREATE TABLE Own   (Owner text,
            AircraftModel text,
            Serial# text,
            AcquisitionDate date,
            Own-Financed-Lease text,
            PurchasePrice integer,
            Share% real,
            LienHolder text,
            LeaseHolder text,
            Broker text,

            PRIMARY KEY (Owner, AircraftModel,
Serial#, AcquisitionDate),
            FOREIGN KEY (Owner) REFERENCES Entity
on UPDATE CASCADE,
            FOREIGN KEY (AircraftModel, Serial#)
REFERENCES Airplane on UPDATE CASCADE on DELETE CASCADE,
            FOREIGN KEY (Broker) REFERENCES Broker
```

```
on UPDATE CASCADE,
            FOREIGN KEY (LienHolder) REFERENCES
Entity on UPDATE CASCADE,
            FOREIGN KEY (LeaseHolder) REFERENCES
Entity on UPDATE CASCADE);
CREATE TABLE Equip       (AircraftModel text,
            Serial# text,
            Equipment text,
            UnitCost integer,
            Quantity integer,
            LastInspection date,
            LastService integer,
            Unit text,
            PRIMARY KEY (AircraftModel, Serial#,
Equipment),
            FOREIGN KEY (AircraftModel, Serial#)
REFERENCES Airplane,
            FOREIGN KEY (Equipment) REFERENCES
Item on UPDATE CASCADE,
            CHECK (Unit = `hours' or Unit =
`months' or Unit = `landings'));
CREATE TABLE Option      (AircraftModel text,
            Equipment text,
            FirstOfferDate date,
            EndDate date,
            UnitPrice integer,
            Quantity integer,
            FleetTotal integer,
            FleetRatio% real,
            MarketTotal integer,
            MarketRatio% real,
            IndustrialRating text,
            Remark text,
            PRIMARY KEY (AircraftModel, Equipment,
FirstOfferDate),
            FOREIGN KEY (AircraftModel) REFERENCES
AircraftModel,
            FOREIGN KEY (Equipment) REFERENCES
Item on UPDATE CASCADE);
```

```
CREATE TABLE Compose    (AircraftModel text,
                Equipment text,
                FirstListDate date,
                Quantity integer,
                IndustrialRating text,
                Remark text,

                PRIMARY KEY (AircraftModel, Equipment,
FirstListDate),
                FOREIGN KEY (AircraftModel) REFERENCES
AircraftModel,
                FOREIGN KEY (Equipment) REFERENCES
Item on UPDATE CASCADE);

CREATE TABLE Service    (AircraftModel text,
                Serial# text,
                Equipment text,
                ServiceProvider text,
                ServiceDate date,
                ServiceType text,
                LeadTime integer,
                DownTime integer,
                TotalCost integer,
                Quantity integer,
                Evaluation text,
                Remark text,

                PRIMARY KEY (AircraftModel, Serial#,
Equipment, ServiceProvider, ServiceDate),
                FOREIGN KEY (AircraftModel, Serial#)
REFERENCES Airplane,
                FOREIGN KEY (Equipment) REFERENCES
Item on UPDATE CASCADE,
                FOREIGN KEY (ServiceProvider)
REFERENCES Entity on UPDATE CASCADE,
                CHECK (ServiceType = 'inspection' or
ServiceType = 'repair' or ServiceType = 'replacement'
or ServiceType = 'upgrade'));

CREATE TABLE Spare       (PartNumber text,
```

```
                ServiceProvider text,
                ShelfTimeAllowed text,
                TimeOnShelf text,
                Price integer,
                Quantity integer,
                Remark text,

                PRIMARY KEY (PartNumber,
ServiceProvider),
                FOREIGN KEY (PartNumber) REFERENCES
Item on UPDATE CASCADE,
                FOREIGN KEY (ServiceProvider)
REFERENCES Entity on UPDATE CASCADE);

CREATE TABLE BOM   (Part text,
                NextLevelPart text,
                Quantity integer,
                Remark text,

                PRIMARY KEY (Part, NextLevelPart),
                FOREIGN KEY (Part) REFERENCES Item on
UPDATE CASCADE ON DELETE CASCADE,
                FOREIGN KEY (NextLevelPart) REFERENCES
Item on UPDATE CASCADE ON DELETE CASCADE);

CREATE TABLE Equivalent (PartName text,
                EquivalentPartName text,
                Remark text,

                PRIMARY KEY (PartName,
EquivalentPartName),
                FOREIGN KEY (PartName) REFERENCES Item
on UPDATE CASCADE ON DELETE CASCADE,
                FOREIGN KEY (EquivalentPartName)
REFERENCES Item on UPDATE CASCADE ON DELETE CASCADE);

CREATE TABLE Operate    (AircraftModel text,
                Serial# text,
                ServiceProvider text,
                ContractDate date,
                ContractType text,
                ContractTo text,
```

```
                Evaluation text,
                Remark text,
                PRIMARY KEY (AircraftModel, Serial#,
ServiceProvider, ContractDate),
                FOREIGN KEY (AircraftModel, Serial#)
REFERENCES Airplane,
                FOREIGN KEY (ServiceProvider)
REFERENCES Entity on UPDATE CASCADE,
                FOREIGN KEY (ContractTo) REFERENCES
Entity on UPDATE CASCADE,
                CHECK (ContractType = 'operation' or
ContractType = 'insurance'));

CREATE TABLE Market      (AircraftModel text,
                Serial# text,
                Broker text,
                EntryDate date,
                EntryType text,
                Status text,
                AskingPrice integer,
                FinalPrice integer,
                Prospect text,
                Value text,
                EvaluationReport text,
                Remark text,

                PRIMARY KEY (AircraftModel, Serial#,
Broker, EntryDate),
                FOREIGN KEY (AircraftModel, Serial#)
REFERENCES Airplane,
                FOREIGN KEY (Broker) REFERENCES Broker
on UPDATE CASCADE,
                FOREIGN KEY (Prospect) REFERENCES
Entity on UPDATE CASCADE,
                CHECK (EntryType = 'valuation' or
EntryType = 'new listing' or EntryType = 'evaluation'
or EntryType = 'other update'),
                CHECK (Status = 'for sale' or Status
= 'deal pending' or Status = 'sold' or Status =
'possibility for sale' or Status = 'not on market'));
```

```
CREATE TABLE Approach   (Broker text,
                Contact text,
                LogDate date,
                LogType text,
                Report text,
                Status text,
                Evaluation text,
                Remark text,

                PRIMARY KEY (Broker, Contact, LogDate),
                FOREIGN KEY (Broker) REFERENCES Broker
on UPDATE CASCADE,
                FOREIGN KEY (Contact) REFERENCES
Contact on UPDATE CASCADE,
                CHECK (LogType = 'email' or LogType =
'phone' or LogType = 'meeting' or LogType = 'other'),
                CHECK (Status = 'closed' or Status =
'open' or Status = 'action pending' or Status =
'other'));

CREATE TABLE Relate     (Contact text,
                RelatedContact text,
                RelationType text,
                Remark text,

                PRIMARY KEY (Contact, RelatedContact),
                FOREIGN KEY (Contact) REFERENCES
Contact on UPDATE CASCADE on DELETE CASCADE,
                FOREIGN KEY (RelatedContact)
REFERENCES Contact on UPDATE CASCADE on DELETE
CASCADE,
                CHECK (RelationType = 'senior to the
related' or RelationType = 'work for the related' or
RelationType = 'peer' or RelationType = 'friend' or
RelationType = 'relative'));

CREATE TABLE Fly  (ATPRating text,
                AircraftModel text,
                Serial# text,
                StartDate date,
```

```
            EndDate date,
            Operator text,
            EmploymentType text,
            Evaluation text,
            Remark text,

            PRIMARY KEY (ATPRating, AircraftModel,
Serial#, StartDate),
            FOREIGN KEY (ATPRating) REFERENCES
Pilot on UPDATE CASCADE,
            FOREIGN KEY (AircraftModel, Serial#)
REFERENCES Airplane,
            FOREIGN KEY (Operator) REFERENCES
Entity on UPDATE CASCADE,
            CHECK (EmploymentType = 'regular' or
EmploymentType = 'charter' or EmploymentType =
'other'));
```
(End of the Script)

Please note that the above script is for illustration purposes only. It may contain syntax idiosyncrasies that do not conform to the particular SQL facility at a particular DBMS. In any case, the script is incomplete and may not be implemented directly. The logic of the script corresponds to the TSER design shown in Figure 6.11. The logic is, nonetheless, accurate.

The DDL script is self-explanatory. It creates entity tables (tables pertaining to entities) first so that ensuing relationship tables can correctly refer to them in the FK clauses. In each Create Table expression, data items are defined before anything else, and followed by PK, FK(s), and integrity rules. Intra-table domain and check on values can go with the data items concerned; but inter-table ones need to go with FK. CHECK is a built-in alert/trigger based on data values.

The undoing of creating a table is Drop Table. It may come in handy at the database creation stage especially when one has already wrongly entered data into a table. The Delete Table command only removes a table's definition from the schema, but the content of the table remains. (In contrast, the Delete command in the next section only removes rows from a table.) The creation of views will follow the creation of the tables from which the views are defined. A view may be defined by simply including the select data items which have already been defined elsewhere in the base tables in a Create View expression. However, a more flexible way is to Define Views from manipulating the tables (and other views) by using the DML. Thus, this chapter defers its discussion until the next section.

7.3 The DML of ANSI SQL: The Embodiment and Embellishment of Relational Algebra and Relational Calculus

A DML needs to perform the four basic types of database operations: retrieval, insertion, updating, and deleting. It also needs to support views, user interface including GUI and report generation, and application software programs. Finally, it needs to provide productivity facility to batch process data input and output, among other things. All these operations tend to be straightforward and can be performed in an almost "touch button" fashion — except *random retrieval*. This is the hardcore of the SQL logic, or for that matter, the spirit to any query language. Therefore, we concentrate our discussion on the formation of ad hoc queries.

The Search: random retrieval of on-demand information

The core of the DML part of SQL is the Select clause:

*Select list of data items separated by comma **From** list of tables separated by comma **Where** list of search conditions joined by "and" and/or "or".*

Please note that the keyword Select here is really comparable to the Projection operator of relational algebra, not the Selection operator. The From clause identifies the source tables of search. When more than one table is identified, the relational algebraic (natural) Join operation is implied. Thus, the Where clause contains the join conditions, such as the matching of common attributes from the joining tables, as well as the relational algebraic Selection conditions, if any. A very powerful feature of SQL is the provision to nest SQL expressions in the Where clause as search conditions. For example, if one wishes to join two tables, then one can modify the two tables with their own SQL expressions, where the first SQL uses the second as a qualifier (search condition) and embeds it in its Where clause. The result is still a single SQL expression, but with sub-expressions nested in it.

EXERCISES (Refer to the Supplier table, Part table, and Supply table of Section 7.1)

1. Can you script an SQL expression to find all suppliers (all attributes) from Taipei?
2. Similarly, please write an SQL expression to find the materials of parts heavier than 20.
3. Get all parts (P# and names) that have had a supply quantity (one time) of 300 or more.
4. Get suppliers (names) who supplied part "P437."
5. Get the cost of every part that supplier Siemens supplied in a quantity of 200 or more.
6. Can you craft a nested SQL expression in the spirit of the optimal sequence of relational algebraic operations for the query in Question 5?
7. Since each sub-query contains just one table or less than three tables, does this mean that the SQL expression will not need to join tables, or at least, join fewer tables?
8. Does the nesting make any difference since SQL performs automatic query optimization?

The SQL expressions for the first six questions are shown below:

1. **Select***
   From Supplier
   Where city = 'Taipei';

2. **Select** Material
    From Part
    Where Weight > 20;

3. **Select** Part.Part_ID, Name
    From Part, Supply
    Where Part.Part_ID = Supply.Part_ID and Quantity_Supplied
    >= 300;

4. **Select** Name
    From Supplier
    Where Supplier_ID in (**Select** Supplier_ID **From** Supply **Where**
    Part_ID = 'P437');

5. **Select** Cost
    From Supplier, Part, Supply
    Where Supplier_Name = 'Siemens' and Quantity_Supplied >=
    200 and Part.Part_ID = Supply.Part_ID and Supplier.Supplier_
    ID = Supply.Supplier_ID;

6. **Select** Cost
    From Part
    Where Part_ID in
        (**Select** Part_ID
        From Supply
        Where Quantity_Supplied >= 200 and Supplier_ID in
            (**Select** Supplier_ID
            From Supplier
            Where Supplier_Name = 'Siemens'));

A somewhat counter-intuitive fact is that the nested SQL expressions do not change a bit in terms of the actual database operations involved. Nesting is only a matter of style, which may be significant, however, in certain complex cases where only a divide-and-conquer logic can do the job — such as when the conditions need to be formed online in steps as some set of data (an example is given later). However, nesting or not, when a query references multiple tables, then exactly all these tables must be joined globally one way or another, since it is the only way to establish the global view for the correct cross-reference. The nested SQL expressions do suggest reduction of tables before joining them. It is only that this reduction, or technical optimization, is always performed by SQL regardless of the style of the query expressions. That is, the SQL expressions in answers 5 and 6 will yield exactly the same answers and the same performance, since underlying them will be the same database operations that perform them.

We now show some useful techniques of SQL formulation:

1. Join a table with itself:
   Query: Get suppliers who are located in the same city in pairs.
   Logic: Perform natural join on City with City.
   SQL expression:

   > **Select** FIRST.Supplier_ID, SECOND.Supplier_ID
   > **From** Supplier FIRST, Supplier SECOND
   > **Where** FIRST.City = SECOND.City AND FIRST.
   > Supplier_ID < SECOND.Supplier_ID;

   The From clause creates two aliases (images) for the Supplier table, so as to be able to use them as if they are two different, regular tables in the SQL expression to match pairs. Note that the last predicate will exclude permutations and give unique pairs. This technique is useful for, e.g., making matches such as the meeting schedules for athletes or teams.

2. Search by exclusion:
   Query: Find all suppliers who do not supply (have not supplied) Part P129.
   Logic: Identify empty sets (null answer) for suppliers who have supplied P129.
   SQL expression:

   > **Select***
   > **From** Supplier
   > **Where** NOT EXISTS
   > (**Select** Supplier_ID
   > **From** Supply
   > **Where** Supplier_ID = Supplier.Supplier_ID
   > AND Part_ID = 'P129');

Not Exists means empty set. The inner Select will be checked against each Supplier_ID from the Supplier table and return a set that contains the Supplier_ID if the value P129 is found to be associated with it in any row. Otherwise, an empty set will return. It is this empty set answer that satisfies the search condition. Thus, the Supplier_ID against which the inner Select performed will be outputted. Please note that Not Exists is a very important search technique since often we do not know all the conditions that our target meets, but we do know what it does not. Or, it may be easier sometimes to enumerate the negatives rather than the positives.

3. Relational Division:

    Query: Find the supplier names who have supplied all parts.

    Logic: Divide Supply by the set of all parts; i.e., identify the suppliers who are associated with the set of all parts in the Supply table. This means to define the set of all parts from run-time search of the Part table and compare it to the set of parts supplied by each supplier. The "no-difference" suppliers are the answer.

    SQL expression:

    Select Supplier_Name
    From Supplier S
    Where NOT EXISTS ((**Select** P.Part_ID
                    From Part P)
                    Except
                    (**Select** SP.Part_ID
                    From Supply SP
                    Where SP.Supplier_ID =
                    S.Supplier_ID));

The inner search includes two SQL expressions and one relational algebraic operator: Except, which is Difference. The first inner SQL expression establishes the set of all parts at this moment, and the second SQL finds the set of parts that a particular supplier has supplied. This inner search is performed for each supplier in the outer SQL from the Supplier table. The Except operation will return an empty set if these two sets of results from the inner search are identical — see Section 7.1. And an empty set is precisely what the Not Exists condition wants to see. Thus, the supplier for which an empty set is returned from the inner search will be outputted.

It is worthwhile to note that one may not know *all* the parts that the Part table contains; or at least, one may not be able to easily put them all in the SQL expression. Just consider a non-trivial business where the part types can number in thousands. Other relational algebraic operators may be used in SQL expressions, too. For example, Union will come in handy to join the same type of results from different searches on different sources (SQL expressions). These searches may otherwise be performed as independent, separate queries.

4. Pro Forma processing of data in the query (count, sum, avg, min, max):
    Query: Find the individual supplies whose quantity is larger than 200, for parts whose total supply have exceeded 300, and list the maximum quantity supplied for each part, and the date for the maximum supply.
    Logic: Determine the grouping and statistics online for the search.
    The SQL expression:
    Select Part_ID, Date, MAX(Quantity_Supplied)
    From Supply
    Where Quantity_Supplied > 200
    Grouped By Part_ID
    Having SUM (Quantity_Supplied) > 300
    Order By 3, Part_ID, DESC;

Note that the keywords Grouped-By and Having work as a pair. Either one of them may be implicit (hidden): only Grouped-By (sorting) or only Having (proper) need to appear. All attributes used in these operators must appear in SELECT. The number "3" in Order-By means the third field of the result table. Thus, the output will include the three fields that the attribute list in Select indicates, in that order; and the resultant table will be sorted first by the maximum quantity and then by Part ID, in descending values.

SQL has two versions of implementation: embedded (in programs for batch processing) and interactive (for online users). The former is used by programs and the latter by humans, obviously. Both versions work exactly the same. However, for humans, the interactive online query environment does offer a unique advantage to overcome some inherently hard searches: divide and conquer. That is, one may plan a sequence of SQL searches to gradually gather information and arrive at the final answer. If a single Select expression is too hard to formulate, or even impossible, then one can try a sequence of single Select expressions. Finally, this book wishes to reiterate the importance of human intelligence in query optimization. Just like doing interactive queries, where one can adjust the search logic according to the run-time intermittent results obtained, one can minimize the scope of search to alleviate the burden of automatic query optimization, too. An analogy is Internet search: If one knows that only a few top universities can offer qualified doctoral programs in certain advanced scientific areas, then one could limit the search to these likely suspects, instead of searching every university.

Views: external schemas

Views may be defined by using Select expressions. A common template is the following:

Create/Define View view-name as Select list of data items From table(s) Where condition for inclusion.

In general, SQL allows a view name to appear where a relation name is allowed. The only caution is about changing data values in a view: the view must be a subset of a relation to be permissible for inserting, deleting, and updating data in it. Inserting data into a view that comes from more than one table, for example, could easily result in erroneous and inconsistent data values in these tables especially when a field in the view appears commonly in multiple tables. There is no automatic mapping of a value to multiple common fields whose semantics may not be identical. The rule of thumb is that one ought to assure correct cascading of any data that are shared by multiple tables. This means that insertion, updates, and deletion should be performed at the level of base tables for any shared data.

Insertion: interactive, batch, and transfer

Inserting data into a relational database is to insert them into the appropriate tables, one at a time. Entity tables (with a singular PK) must be populated before relationship tables (with a plural PK) in order to make the FKs (of the latter) work — i.e., one must first insert the data (in one table) to which an FK (in another table) refers such that no violation of the integrity rule would result. If the order is reversed, then the DBMS would typically issue a warning and reject the inserted data. The insertion operation is performed row by row.

The baseline, interactive **insertion** template is of this form:

Insert into table-name Values () where the parentheses include rows of data values as scripted according to the format of data items in the order in which they appear in the definition of the table, separated by semi-colon between rows.

A sample insertion for the Supplier table may be this: Insert into Supplier Values ('S10', 'Albany Works', 'Albany', '3'; 'S11', 'Danube Manufacturing', 'Budapest', '2'). Thus, one may word-process a script for the Insert expression, including a large number of such rows in the Value clause, and then input the script file as an external source that SQL reads. The data entry job may become alleviated once some tables have been populated. One may use Select expressions to transfer data from tables that have already been populated to tables that have not:

Insert into table-name Select-From-Where as usual and as appropriate.

- Example: **Insert into** Placeholder_Supplier (Supplier_ID, City) **Select** Supplier_ID, City **From** Supplier **Where** Certified_Tier = '3';

Batch inputting could be straightforward if one prepares the source input files to follow the format of the target base tables; then one can **Copy** the files into the tables. However, the details may vary from one DBMS to another. To batch populated tables from combining different files, or to split a file to feed different tables, one may want to **Copy** the input files to placeholder tables first, and then use Select expressions to transfer data from these tables into the target ones.

Updates: replacement of existing data

The basic template for performing updates is this:

Update table-name Set equation(s) for updating field(s) Where conditions for identifying the values (rows) of the field(s) to change. The Select expression may be used in Set and Where.

- Example 1: **Update** Part **Set** Weight = Weight * 454/1000;

The above example represents a wholesale change of the unit of weight in the Part table from pound to kilogram. The Where clause is always optional, or "as needed"; as is the case with the Select expression. The next three examples show additional features and templates:

- Example 2: **Update** Supplier **Set** City = 'Schenectady', Certified_ Tier = '2' **Where** Supplier_ID = 'S1';
- Example 3: **Update** Supply **Set** Quantity_Supplied = (**Select** Quantity_Supplied **From** Placeholder_Supply **Where** Placeholder_ Supply.Supplier_ID = 'S2' and Date = '02192012') **Where** Supplier_ID = 'S2' and Date = '02192012';
- Example 4: **Update** Part **Set** Cost = **Case When** Cost > 100 **Then** Cost = Cost + 5 **When** Cost > 50 and Cost <= 100 **Then** Cost + 3 **Else** Cost + 1 **End;**

Delete: removing all tuples or just a proper subset of them from a table

Similar to Update, Delete can be really simple or really complex. We show a few examples to illustrate the point. The basic template is:

Delete from table-name Where conditions for selecting the rows from the table to delete. The Where clause holds all the complexity and may use the Select expression.

- Example 1: **Delete from** Supply **Where** Date = '02192012';
- Example 2: **Delete from** Supply;

Without the Where clause, as in Example 2, the Delete command will remove all tuples from the table. However, the table definition remains in the schema.

- Example 3: **Delete from** Supply **Where** 'Troy Tools' = (**Select** Supplier_Name **From** Supplier **Where** Supplier.Supplier_ID = Supply.Supplier_ID);

Please note that Example 3 requires explicitly a join between Supply and Supplier on Supplier_ID. It removes from the Supply table all supplies by Troy Tools.

As a final reminder, all data changes must be carefully controlled in order to maintain data integrity of the database. To the extent possible, the need for such changes should be anticipated at the time the database is designed, and then incorporated into the conceptual schema using the provisions by the DBMS. The DDL of Section 7.2 shows some of the built-in controls that go with tables. The checking and cascading rules, for example, will be activated upon the insertion and/or updating of the data items specified in them.

7.4 Global Query: Movement Towards Natural Language Search Commands on the Web

The ANSI SQL technology has accomplished an absolutely crucial task required of global query, which is the ability to randomly retrieve on-demand information resources across multiple databases or even across the Web; that is, it provides a de facto common facility for databases everywhere. Thus, any IS that wishes to hyper-network information resources with other IS can start with SQL and improvise to design additional capabilities around it. But of course, it is better that ANSI SQL be extended to provide the additional capabilities and minimize the need for improvising. This book recognizes two categories of high value extension: freer syntax and global query.

SQL was lauded as a "near natural" language for database query at the time of its introduction. It certainly is if compared to programming scripts written in, e.g., FORTRAN, Java, and the C family of languages. However, one would be hard pressed to consider the SQL examples in the above sections near natural if one considers how much technical knowledge is required of the user to use the language correctly, not to mention the anti-natural restrictions imposed on the syntax. The first and foremost anti-natural limitation is perhaps the requirement of using precise technical terms (as defined in the database schemas) in the SQL expressions. The users must know exactly what data are defined as what fields of what tables, and adhere to their formats. This precise technical knowledge (e.g., Part_ID, P#, PartNo... are synonyms) is a hindrance to any natural user, who would refer to data by natural meaning only (e.g., part). Although the SQL linguistic structure mimics the English language, it is far from being as flexible as the latter.

These limitations stem, of course, from the need to sort out ambiguity. Users must use only the terms that SQL knows (by design or by user definition), and use them only in the precise way that SQL can interpret. These terms are not insurmountable when the users are sophisticated in databases and the scope of search is confined to single databases. However, as more databases are inter-operated for enterprises and extended enterprises (see Chapter 5), and more (strategic) non-technical end users are drawn in the IS community, the tolerance for such limitations wears thin, quickly. A case in point is Internet search, which has become pervasive for all people. The users only need to provide a few keywords chosen by them as they see fit. Regardless of how often one may criticize the imprecision of such search results, no one seems to be willing to trade ease of use for precision and advocating for SQL-style search languages.

In fact, Internet search engines might arguably represent the state-of-the-art for global query of massive numbers of open and scalable information resources on the Internet, using natural language. These search engines make ambiguity a commodity rather than an absolute evil: They trade precision for ease of use, and substitute inclusiveness for accuracy. The users (almost) always get what they want, along with a lot more that they do not want. It is up to the users to learn and improve on their search terms, by trial and error. The problem, of course, is that these search engines work only for homepages, and do not apply to databases.

The IBM Deep Blue supercomputer, with its recent triumph at the TV game show of Jeopardy (Winter Season 2010–2011), exemplifies the other extreme of natural language query: achieving both precision and flexibility at the expense of openness and scalability. The Deep Blue beat national champions in this completely natural language game (two wins and one tie) and proved its correctness. However, it is unclear how far this technology can be generalized to support ordinary database queries at business-affordable cost and development cycle time.

This book recognizes the Google class of Web search as the low end of open and scalable global query. Google employs a data warehouse style of architecture (see Figure 5.2) to achieve its goals, rather than performing real-time inter-operation of multiple Web sites. The XQUERY class technology represents the high end of database global query on the Internet at the present time, where SQL-style queries are wrapped in XML templates for interchange among Web sites. The users need to know exactly the semantics of each local database in order to use XQUERY correctly. These predicates are too severe for general case global database query. The field needs to do better. It needs to provide easiness of making queries and the capability of global query. Indeed, the ability to easily query databases anywhere on the Web is key to hyper-networking people and information resources and forming systems of IS.

In between search engines and IBM Deep Blue on the one hand (natural language), and XQUERY and company on the other (global query), this book presents an alternative approach to enhancing SQL and removing some of the limitations mentioned above without compromising accuracy. The idea is to use metadata to help query formation: putting the data models online to assist the users formulating queries (*model-assisted query*). A particular design is introduced below as an example, which employs the Metadatabase model developed in Section 6.4 of Chapter 6 as an online knowledge base to assist users, and thereby facilitates their global query of multiple databases in an SQL style.

The first design method of this approach is to augment SQL with metadata in a design called the Metadatabase Query Language (MQL) — see Cheung and Hsu (1996). With this design, the user will browse the Metadatabase in a GUI environment, using any combination of abstractions offered in Figure 6.12, including Applications, Subjects, Contexts, ERA, relations, and the like, to navigate. Constructs will be picked along the way and put into an MQL expression by the system. Necessary mappings between them and reconciliation of ambiguities will be accomplished by the Metadatabase before the MQL expression is converted into SQL expressions, which are to be processed at participant (local) databases by the respective DBMSs. Results will be assembled back at the Metadatabase for the user, too.

Consider this example: Part_ID, P#, and PartNo are three separate PKs representing respectively three different Part tables in three relational databases, and the Equivalence meta-table has established that they are all equivalent to Part along with required format conversion routines in between them. Then, the user may use Part, or any one of them, to form an MQL query to globally assemble parts data from all three DBMSs, without having to know about Part_ID, P#, and PartNo, nor even the very fact that these data are stored in three separate databases. Thus, MQL is a step towards removing the limitation on having to know the precise technical definitions of all relations involved. Although technical knowledge is still required, the requirement is nonetheless reduced to the level of global models, rather than local relations, where the users may start with high-level concepts such as Applications and Subjects.

The next design method augments the Metadatabase with user words and other usage data — see Boonjing and Hsu (2006); it provides a natural language replacement of the MQL where the linguistic syntax is completely relaxed. Instead of formulating queries precisely in terms of unambiguously defined terms and syntax, the users may now craft user words and put them in any form they wish. To make this possible, the design substitutes automatic, internal semantic search for syntax, by using an open dictionary of user words and history data (with learning capability) that is linked to the Metadatabase to provide contextual knowledge for interpretation. The free form query is ultimately reduced to an internal MQL and the rest of the processing is similar to that of the MQL.

The third design method, discussed before in Section 5.4 of Chapter 5, is developed in, e.g., Levermore *et al.* (2010). In essence, it extends the MQL results into exMQL for information collaboration on the Internet. Section 5.4 covered the basic concepts and the overall architecture of the global query design, but left the justification of the design ideas for this section. The central element of global query for information collaboration is a Query Database, which is designed to implement exMQL and process the information requests and offers for matching. The Query Database uses a dedicated version of the Metadatabase for this purpose. The main changes are found in the SYSTEM, QUERY, and VIEW meta-entities, which replace the APPLICATION, SUBJECT, and ENTREL meta-entities in the original version. Figure 7.1 presents the dedicated design for the Query Database.

The main changes are summarized below. The SYSTEM meta-entity identifies the enterprise databases that are currently participating in global query, and accordingly the export databases that represent them. A unique identifier defines each export database, which is determined at design-time when the local data model is integrated into the Metadatabase. The QUERY meta-entity identifies the queries submitted by the export database. Each query submitted to the Global Blackboard is associated with a unique identifier that is assigned at run-time, along with a timestamp. The related COMPONENTS meta-MR associates queries with a particular export database and upholds existence and dependency integrity. The VIEW meta-entity is an alias for the QUERY meta-entity, analogous to the traditional definition of a database view. It is important to note that there cannot be multiple instances of unique identifiers in the Query Database. The ITEM meta-entity remains unchanged from its original definition (Hsu *et al.*, 1991), and represents the data items specified in each query. The BELONG TO meta-PR associates data items to a specific VIEW, while DESCRIBES specifies the data items that

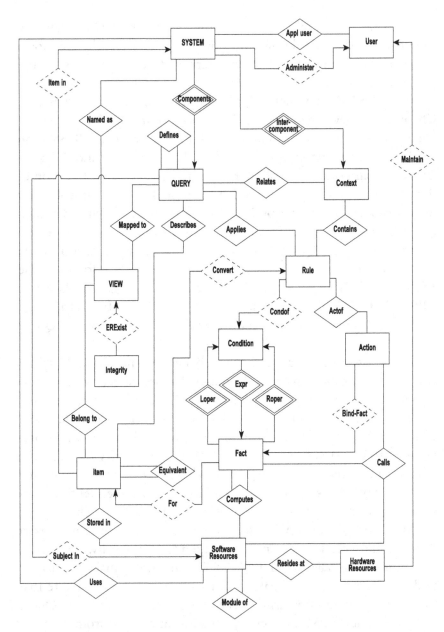

Figure 7.1:   The conceptual schema for Query Database.

belong to each QUERY. The detailed design, including the syntax of exMQL and how this language works, is provided in Levermore *et al.* (2010) and Hsu *et al.* (2007).

The above Metadatabase examples are presented as an experimental reference point. This book includes these ideas to illustrate the big picture: It is desirable as well as feasible to enhance SQL with rich metadata and thereby achieve the ideals of hyper-networking people and information resources available in the society. The current de facto standard, ANSI SQL, needs extensions on linguistic flexibility to make it more suitable for random search of single databases by end users. This need becomes an absolute must for global query where people try to conduct similar random search of information resources from multiple independent databases. Rich metadata as shown in the Metadatabase could help. Information collaboration on the Web represents the high end of such global query. The key to such extensions may be the provision of online semantics and logics to support the users and to reconcile conflicts among databases. Information models provide such semantics. This observation illustrates, again, the IS design principle about embedded assistance, discussed in Section 3.4 of Chapter 3. In this big picture, we present the design principle for global query below:

The Design Principle for Global Database Query: *It is expected that successful global query languages will employ ANSI SQL as a basis for local database processing, and incorporate user views and semantic information models to assist users expressing their requests in linguistically free forms, to support hyper-networking of information resources among themselves.*

With this principle proposed, this book has completed the development of a design science for innovative IS, from setting up visions to global query. The next chapter moves up to the big picture of IS, again, to illustrate the strategic planning of IS for innovation in a particular case: renovating a regional economy by instrumentation of a highway corridor.

Chapter 8

A Strategic Planning Case: Innovation by Hyper-Networking Humans and Physical Environment to Improve a Regional Economy

Chapters 1–3 presented a conceptual framework for developing IS visions of innovation from hyper-networking people and resources. This chapter illustrates how the framework might work in actual economic innovation projects, and shows that the scope of IS resources can include physical environment. The particular goal is improvement of the regional economy, and the innovation is the instrumentation of ground infrastructure (highways). The conceptual framework is applied to develop innovative strategies (*a master plan*) for a system of IS that possibly "digitizes" the I-87 Northway Corridor in upstate New York between Albany, NY and the US-Canada border. This exercise highlights IS as an agent of innovation and expands the conventional societal IS resources to incorporate the instrumented corridor for hyper-networking. Benefits are identified, such as opportunities for trip safety, tourism, highway administration, value-added services, and new service industries. The broad significance is that the master plan represents a new paradigm of hyper-networking physical infrastructure and cyber-infrastructure for a knowledge economy. To bring the technical nature of this new paradigm to the fore, the *Subject–Environment–Enterprise Interaction* model is presented, which calls for integration of multi-modal data (data from RFID, wireless sensor networks, and enterprise databases) to make the environment a part of the IS to assist the life cycle tasks for people and enterprises. This chapter also presents specific value propositions and assesses the feasibility of the master plan. Both technical and managerial strategies for its implementation are discussed.

8.1 Value Propositions for Hyper-Networking People, Enterprises, and the Northway Corridor: An IS Master Plan for Instrumentation of Infrastructure

This chapter opens with a basic observation: the scope of societal cyber-infrastructure may include the physical environment, or the digitized environment. This observation leads to the notion of innovation by convergence of physical space and cyber-space. We ask: what is the technical nature of instrumentation of the environment and the systems of IS that incorporate this instrumentation? What is Schumpeter's gale of creative destruction in this case (see Chapter 1)? Strictly speaking, the innovation here is more about construction than destruction. In fact, digitizing physical objects and the environment is not exactly new. Many industrial practices have mounted digital devices on factory equipment, structures, vehicles, vessels, and aircraft to achieve computerized control. Scientific research has also routinely used digital devices for monitoring animals, environment, and tsunamis and earthquakes, to name a few. The military offers some of the most comprehensive instrumentation of the environment, such as surveillance and positioning. The newness of the ideas in this chapter, however, is to hyper-network the instrumented physical systems and environment with conventional cyber-space to spawn innovation. The technical challenges are, therefore, how can we connect the new classes of IS elements with the old, and hyper-network them for innovative value creation?

In a general sense, all economic activities arguably need to interact with the environment. Industrial network flows are a case in point. Transportation systems require real-time data on real-time traffic conditions on streets and highways in order to really control their performance. Logistics in global supply chains also needs to take into account the real-time conditions of ongoing freights in transit since they represent the true availability and requirements of resources — in fact, they may be considered the "supply and demand on the move". Tourism enterprises, in a similar way, have to integrate real-time conditions of the environment into their operation. However, in the past, the environment tended to be treated as something to cope with but not to integrate with. A basic reason for this is that we cannot acquire real-time control data on it.

In the past, all such network flows tended to ignore the environment dimension — or, more precisely, they contented themselves with relying on additional resources (e.g., inventories or backups, and facilitating arrangements) to cope with uncertainties from the environment. The situation is changing. Now, with digital connections, using for example sensors and RFID (radio frequency identification) tags/chips, the environment becomes measurable and can be monitored, on a real-time and online basis. Hence, civil infrastructure is being increasingly instrumented, and incorporated in network flows such as intelligent transportation systems (e.g., smart buses, toll collections, fast lane controls). Network flows, in turn, are being incorporated into supply chain management. The question is how much farther can and should we continue to expand and extend along this line for all genres of economic activities? For simplicity of discussion, we use the term *instrumentation of the environment* to refer to the general idea of adding digital devices and systems to the environment and connecting them to the other digital connections of the world, in order to monitor the condition of the environment. We also refer to the instrumentation as creating *a DCS layer for the environment*.

From the perspective of IS visions (Chapter 1), the question is, what characterizes the conceptual nature of instrumentation and how does it bring about innovation to the economy? This book recognizes the significance of instrumentation to be its ability to hyper-network traditional economic activities by virtue of the new DCS layer. The new IS vision is, therefore, to enable hyper-networking. It follows that the strategic planning of IS for innovation will feature the connection of IS elements from all parties involved, especially the DCS layer of the environment and the conventional systems of IS.

This chapter first develops an instrumentation design for a particular domain, civil infrastructure or network flows. It then analyzes how instrumentation may spawn new value propositions. The DCS layer for this domain involves, conceptually, three dimensions: infrastructure, individual subjects of movement, and planning and control of the movement. Digitization of the infrastructure provides real-time data to facilitate its operation (new value propositions), while digitally connecting its subjects to the infrastructure allows for tailored services and support to particular subjects (new value propositions). Connection of both to enterprise information systems enables adaptive control for applications (e.g., logistics) at a global optimization level (see, e.g., Lei *et al.* (2006) for an example of global optimization of production, inventory, and logistics) — which also represents new value propositions.

The literature is full of results providing planning/routing, real-time monitoring, and trip support for each of the three dimensions, but this chapter focuses on their integration using the DCS layer. A metaphor for the integration is an adaptive control panel administering an automated "material handling system" on network flows. In this metaphor, the IS is the nervous system of the integrated whole, to hyper-network all IS elements in support of the person-centered and task-centered control panel. The civil infrastructure therefore becomes "controllable" in a way comparable to factory conveyors and automated guided vehicles.

This book presents the following statement as the highest level description of the intellectual nature of the instrumentation design. It is the technical summary of the master plan for the envisioned IS:

The Subject–Environment–Enterprise (SEE) Interaction Model
Mission: *To help the (regional) economy.*
General approach: *Build a DCS layer for the environment concerned; then develop an IS to incorporate the DCS layer and connect the people and organizations involved in the mission; finally, seek new value propositions by hyper-networking the people, organizations, and the SEE IS information resources.*
The instrumentation for intelligent network flows: *Use mobile system-on-a-chip devices (e.g., RFID), stationary systems (e.g., wireless sensor network), and multi-modal data fusion to build the DCS layer.*

The baggage handling systems at some airports (e.g., the Hong Kong International Airport and the Incheon International Airport of Korea) offer a metaphoric reference point for the SEE concept. They attach an RFID label to every piece of luggage and move them through material handling systems equipped with networks of sensors interacting with the RFID labels. A control panel displays the status of the system, down to the level of individual pieces of luggage, and directs their individual movement on the conveyers to different dispatching points. In the SEE model, network flows can be compared to conveyers in this metaphor, and the subjects would be the pieces of baggage. The SEE IS performs adaptive control on dispatching directives back to the subjects and back to the network flows, to enable them to adjust.

We now analyze for innovation by instrumentation of the environment. To be specific, this chapter focuses on intelligent network flows and recognizes the life cycle tasks that people and organizations perform on highways and related infrastructure, such as global supply chains (logistics), intelligent transportation systems, and tourism. What new value propositions may arise from the instrumentation? One way to analyze for opportunities is to identify the limitations due to the previous inability to hyper-network with the environment. As a quick review, we consider the Just-in-Time (JIT) production system as a starting point.

The JIT system tends to have a weak link in the case of freights on highways. This can be monitored by using, e.g., a GPS or global positioning system, but cannot previously be adaptively optimized — such as rerouting them automatically according to the real-time conditions on the roads. In general, if intra-factory material handling systems are a benchmark of performance, then inter-factory network flows fail to provide similar success. The latter lacks the following: reliable information on the real-time conditions of the highways, sufficient journey support for the individual subjects on the move (e.g., drivers, vehicles, and cargos), and integration of these real-time data with enterprise information systems (e.g., logistics, production and inventory, and infrastructure operation). These limitations all represent opportunities for improvement, by innovation on connections to the network flows.

The SEE Interaction model, when implemented, promises to facilitate the operation of the infrastructure and provision of customized journey support to the users of the infrastructure. The former can be seen in the case of highways, where the transit authority can use, e.g., global (fleet) data from all highways to better manage any particular ones. The latter is reflected in such possibilities as building usage history and thereby profiling individual needs. When it is connected to enterprise databases along the global supply chain, this new capacity further becomes an enabler for adaptive control of network flows at a global level.

More broadly, we apply the results of Chapter 2 to develop specific visions for hyper-networking by employing the new connections of the DCS layer. This chapter formulates three progressive levels of possible integration of life cycle tasks for people and organizations on the intelligent network flows. The first level is the *infrastructure life cycle tasks* from the authority's perspective (i.e., infrastructure project initiation and planning, engineering design, construction, on-demand and scheduled maintenance, transportation management, inspection, and renovation). The second level is the *user journey life cycle tasks* from the subjects' perspective (e.g., the scheduling, routing, moving, monitoring, and receiving of cargos for freight users; other life cycles similarly exist for other classes of users). And the third level is the *logistics control process life cycle tasks* (e.g., demand, supply, monitoring, adaptive control, and integration of logistics for enterprise processes at both ends of the journey). Together, they define the basic classes of value propositions and determine the requirements of the SEE IS. Three classes of technical capabilities are derived from the DCS analysis: *message generation and acquisition, transmission*, and *processing/storage*.

- **Value Propositions and Requirements for Infrastructure Operations:** *acquisition and integration of data and knowledge used in the infrastructure authority (e.g., New York State Department of Transportation) to better develop the Smart Highways and better run the transportation management centers.*

This class of values improves the performance of (public sector) Corridor administration and helps put the taxpayers' money to better use. Broadly speaking, the DCS layer should help the infrastructure monitor its own health and usage, and thereby automatically acquire vital data to streamline the authority's operations. Specific possibilities include the following:

— environment assessment data and usage patterns by location for project initiation and planning; usage and maintenance data for engineering design;
— 24/7 real-time and historic traffic data for construction and work zone management;
— road conditions surveillance and reports for on-demand and regular maintenance;
— non-destructing, non-intrusive data collection and evaluation for inspection;
— work zone monitoring, 24/7 traffic surveillance, incident reports, and computer sign/signal systems for project control and transportation management centers; and
— integration of these data for renovation of the intelligent network flows.

In a sense, the DCS layer should facilitate its own planning, design, construction, maintenance, inspection, control, and renovation to help the authority's mission. The DCS layer could be likened to a map that "talks", in the sense that each locality on the map spells out what it demands and what it "sees", in the way of data and knowledge for its development and operation. Therefore, the locality-identified messages become an agent of integration for the whole life cycle of operations, since tasks are traceable to these localities. At present, data collection and task integration are difficult to achieve, resulting in high transaction costs and long cycle times for infrastructure maintenance and development.

For instance, a State Department of Transportation may use different information systems to maintain environmental impact assessments, geographical data (land, bodies of water, etc.), initiation plans, design files, construction contracts, maintenance reports, inspection records, and other mandated data for the operation of its projects. In addition, the Traffic Management Centers (TMCs) bring in their own computerized signs, signals, video cameras, and even Web-based systems. A DCS layer could provide location-based messages on a 24/7 basis to facilitate or supplement these systems. Even the vehicles on the highways could, when equipped with proper sensors on board, serve as probes for the network flows to automatically generate these location-based data. An integrated life-cycle operation promises to be easier to provide seamless support to users. TMCs would become an immediate beneficiary of the new capability, since they could use the integrated, 24/7 messages to better coordinate with emergency services, schedule routine maintenance, and direct the help trucks and other rapid response systems.

- **Value Propositions and Requirements for Infrastructure Users:** *integration of journey information and driver decision support to achieve Smart/Safe Driver and Smart Public Transportation, as well as Smart Freight, for the general public.*

The second class of values may lead to new value-added services which may be provided by the public sector authority or by private businesses where users pay the service fees. Highway users include local commuters, tourists, and truckers. They all have similar wishes: information and assistance to enable them to achieve zero-accident safety in all weather conditions, one-call/one-stop assistance to personal needs, and 24/7 decision support throughout the journey. Of these wishes, the decision support requirements are dependent on the nature of the tasks and journeys, and need to be fleshed out from the perspective of the life cycle tasks for each genre of users.

Safety is the first concern of all users. Safety is determined by road conditions, the interaction of the vehicle and the road, and the user's ability to negotiate the road and the traffic. The DCS layer should help in providing the users with real-time information about the road conditions, and facilitate automatic delivery, assimilation, and enactment of such information. That is, the DCS layer can interact directly with the vehicles as well as with the users, through information integration among global positioning systems, driver information support systems (such as On-Star), user's hand-held wireless devices, and the like. When vehicles are equipped with on-board computers, they can interact directly with the road sensors and other DCS layer devices/systems; the vehicles can even function as mobile sensors to feed road conditions to the DCS layer. The data may go to rapid response teams and help trucks on the provider side, or into the control and maneuvering of vehicles on the user side (trip guidance of the vehicles). The DCS layer can also complement highways that embed guiding cables, magnetic strips, or other systems to help control the vehicle and help manage the traffic on-demand. This is hyper-networking of the instrumentation with subjects and organizations at its best.

Personal assistance (value-added services) extends beyond safety to include all the services that a user requires. The very nature of the assistance can be described as an e-commerce portal for on-the-road travel with real-time transactions. The information-transaction portals connect the users to all kinds of service providers including hospitals, lodging, and local attractions. Physical service-telecommunications-computing stations on the highway extend today's service stations and provide a portal for travelers who may not already have the capability and so need this connections facility. The personal assistance capability can be part of the IS control facility and promises to open up new opportunities for value-added services.

Tourism, business travel, and freight illustrate the notion of **24/7 decision support for the journey.** This class goes beyond personal assistance and into business assistance, whose nature depends on why the user is making a journey on the highways — i.e., the genre of the user. The life cycle of a journey starts with its planning, followed by execution and adjustment, and completes with the business mission accomplished (or failed). The DCS layer should give the user access to his/her home base IS to conduct these tasks on the road. For industrial truckers, the unique tasks are business communications and freight monitoring. Thus, new value propositions and requirements may arise from enabling the notion of a *warehouse on the move.* The warehouse here is, of course, the truck, whose cargo on-board is the stock in the warehouse. The vision here involves ubiquitous and pervasive connection of company networks and freights to perform online computing, not just locating the trucks by GPS and calling the drivers by cell phone. One example is handling hazardous materials. The trucker needs on-demand information throughout the life cycle of the journey to monitor the situation, handle exceptions, and, most acutely, control damages should a problem occur.

*   **Value Propositions and Requirements for Logistic Processes and Control Activities:** *integration of logistic processes and enterprise databases to achieve adaptive optimization of routing and scheduling, just-in-time supply, and reduction of logistics cost and cycle time.*

The third class of values may indicate a new business space for the service industry. At minimum, the possibilities may lead to a new level of global supply chain management. The notion of a moving warehouse is discussed above from the truckers' perspective (the subjects). It is also an innovation for the extended enterprise of global supply chain. The new capability stems from making the network flows a part of distributed production. Recall that a factory typically uses automated guided vehicles or other material handling systems to connect the various workshops and workstations within it. The SEE-enabled JIT conceptualizes highways and railroads as the material handling systems among factories and enterprises. It "internalizes" public infrastructure for extended enterprise processes — i.e., enterprises can rely on public infrastructure to deliver JIT supply for their processes as if it were their private material handling system to connect the supply chain. Thus, business assistance by the DCS layer simply completes the picture: It includes the "warehouse on the move" in the life cycle of logistics for the extended enterprise, to connect cargos in transit to the enterprise processes in the global supply/demand chain that use them.

A SEE IS will achieve the different levels of integration envisioned in the above analysis. The essence is, again, the hyper-networking of conventional IS elements with those of the DCS layer. The DCS layer provides messages, transmits messages, and processes and stores messages to enable innovative services by the IS. The DCS layer is a common asset to the society, so enterprises can build their own custom processes on it to overcome the weak link in many economic activities: the environment (in this case, the open highways).

One needs to analyze the technical nature of the DCS layer and establish the feasibility of such an innovation first. The next sections focus on investigating the feasibility. A conceptual prototype design is employed to help substantiate the investigation.

8.2 The Technical Nature of the SEE Interaction Model for the Northway Corridor

We start with a scenario modeled after a recent example of intelligent network flows: the I-87 Multimodal Study (Parsons, 2003). Suppose the SEE interaction model is proposed to an authority to build a DCS layer for the Northway Corridor (I-87 between Albany, NY and the US-Canada border), as an agent for improving the regional economy. Some public sector authority would own and administer the DCS layer as a public domain asset, and enterprises can collaborate with highway authorities to use the public data for their own logistics control. This way, each enterprise's logistics control becomes a (concurrent) user of the DCS layer. This concept is similar to the societal cyber-infrastructure depicted in Figure 5.7.

Figure 8.1 depicts the baseline vision for an instrumented Corridor. The DCS layer consists of RFID systems, which are mounted on vehicles and along the highways, and wireless sensor networks embedded into the civil infrastructure in the Corridor. The value propositions discussed in the previous section pertain to this scenario, too. Figure 8.2 illustrates how the DCS layer spawns innovation by synthesizing these new value propositions around the common DCS layer. Although Figure 8.2 depicts only three main categories of innovation, others can be envisioned and supported by the same common facility.

On this basis, we provide a reality check on the scenario. (More reality checks are available from Hsu and Wallace, 2007.) It turns out that the scenario also demonstrates the general feasibility of the SEE interaction model. Both RFID and wireless sensor networks

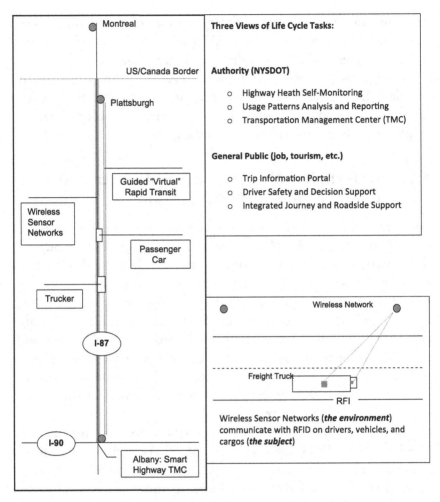

Figure 8.1:   A DCS layer for the infrastructure of the SEE interaction model.

technology have been widely employed for environment monitoring (e.g., seismic study, animal habitats, and military applications), intelligent transportation systems (e.g., vehicle tags, rider smart cards, and rush-hour traffic control), and inventory management (e.g., item tags). They have been proven to be capable of serving as real-time data collectors, processors, and even dispatchers for enterprise information systems. As the technology continues to improve, we expect each

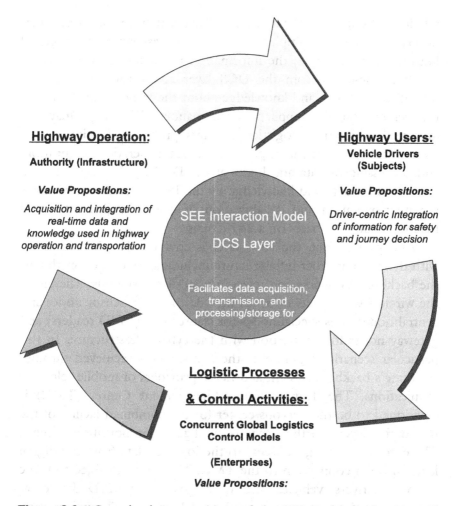

Highway Operation:

Authority (Infrastructure)

Value Propositions:

Acquisition and integration of real-time data and knowledge used in highway operation and transportation

Highway Users:

Vehicle Drivers
(Subjects)

Value Propositions:

Driver-centric Integration of information for safety and journey decision

SEE Interaction Model

DCS Layer

Facilitates data acquisition, transmission, and processing/storage for

Logistic Processes

& Control Activities:

Concurrent Global Logistics
Control Models

(Enterprises)

Value Propositions:

Figure 8.2: General value propositions of the SEE model for instrumented infrastructure.

RFID tag and wireless sensor node to continue to shrink in size while expanding in computing power, to become, e.g., a PC on a chip. The problem of adequate energy supply may remain a limiting factor, but solar photosynthesis technology seems to promise to alleviate it.

The value propositions require integration of multi-modal data that uses different time frames (from real-time data streams to persistent relations of enterprise databases), and hyper-networking of information resources from multiple sites. Using business assistance for global logistics as an example, the information resources involved include real-time messages from the DCS layer about the movement of freight, and all data and knowledge about the freight and the use of the freight from the suppliers and demanders. The scope may also include the shipping or logistics providers' processes. The integration has two categories of challenges: the physical generation, acquisition, and processing of data and logics at the DCS layer; and the logical integration of data and knowledge by the IS. The technical nature is the inter-operation and collaboration of massively distributed and heterogeneous databases on a 24/7 basis.

As a public asset, the DCS layer is envisioned to be integrated with the existing cyber-infrastructure including, among other things, the backbone networks and telecommunications systems. Therefore, the wireless sensor networks will include the usual sensor nodes and central nodes, plus special nodes for transceivers (RFID readers) and gateway nodes for connection with the cyber-infrastructure. In this particular scenario, Figure 8.1, the connection is achieved through the State's backbone system and tier 1 providers of mobile telecommunications. The Transportation Management Center (TMC) is envisioned to be the nervous center for the combined facility of the new digital layer and the previous intelligent transportation systems. The enterprises will gain access to the logistics data from the digital layer through connection to the TMC. The moving subjects on the highway (drivers, vehicles, and/or cargos) carry RFID devices as required by the particular control models in use. The information feed from the RFID devices to the DCS layer will pass through the TMC to reach the logistics control models, with the TMC directing drivers through the usual channels of telecommunications. Drivers also gain journey support from the TMC, and possibly even directly from the DCS layer. In the latter design, the wireless sensor networks could trigger commands directed at the appropriate RFID devices, TMC signs, or driver support portals.

The knowledge side involves mainly the adaptive control logics for subjects (e.g., safety and journey decision support), infrastructure (e.g., operation), enterprise processes (routing, scheduling, and production and inventory planning), and global logistics. At the high end, the IS needs to connect the real-time freight information processing to the Enterprise Resources Planning systems, production and inventory control systems, shop floor-level manufacturing execution systems, and warehousing and delivery scheduling throughout the supply chain. As discussed in Chapter 5, the database industry has provided sufficient results to allow for the development of custom solutions for the job. Furthermore, information models could be determined for standard classes of data from RFID and wireless sensor networks, and they could be incorporated into standard database facilities (see Chapter 5). Then, some inter-operation protocols, including parsers, could use the information models to complete the cycle of information feed. This is an information model-centric solution approach (see below).

The technical elements required are available today, except for the common standards of inter-operation among wireless sensor networks, RFID systems, and enterprise databases. Of these, the lack of international standards for RFID systems is a major inhibitor to global implementation of the SEE model. At present, a number of national authorities are exerting considerable influence on the regulation of and standard development for RFID. They include USA/FCC; Canada/DOC; EU/ERO, CEPT, ETSI, etc.; Japan/MPHPT; China/MII; Australia/AUMA; and Singapore/IDA. International standards groups are also being organized under the auspices of the ISO and United Nations, in addition to industrial consortia (e.g., EPCglobe). For the purpose of this book, we leave the international standards out of the investigation and simply note that the currently available technology has already permitted some significant implementation of the SEE vision.

The next section elaborates on an information model-centric master plan for a possible SEE IS. The analysis focuses on information integration: the connection of wireless sensor networks with existing operation processes of the infrastructure; the interaction of RFID systems with the sensors; and the fusion of sensor data with enterprise databases. That is, the integration design is essentially a methodology for data fusion among these multiple sources. It builds on existing cyber-infrastructure, which is capable of transferring data between wireless sensor networks and enterprise databases and between RFID and enterprise databases.

8.3 A Conceptual Master Plan for SEE Information Integration: A Roadmap

This chapter presents the conceptual outlines below, and then proceeds to elaborate on the requirements for multi-modal data fusion in the plan and justify their feasibility. The *master plan* is as follows:

1. Adopt the SEE Interaction model as the overarching guiding concept. Vest the ownership with the public sector and embed the IS in societal civil- and cyber-infrastructure.
2. Confirm and consolidate the value propositions discussed in Section 8.1 to improve regional economy by assisting local environs (enhancing safety and the efficiency of the Corridor); providing value-added services, e.g., safety, tourism, and logistics; and creating new businesses such as global logistics providers.
3. Determine the infrastructure requirements, both technical and managerial, and thereby identify the core stakeholders for the baseline DCS layer as shown in Figure 8.1.
4. Develop strategies for acquiring the stakeholders' collaboration; better yet, involve them in some joint effort to satisfy the requirements determined above.
5. Formalize the overall information requirements of the Northway Corridor IS: first, organize the general requirements as concerned in the value propositions and the DCS layer of Sections 8.1 and 8.2; next, map them to the current databases and other IS elements in use; lastly, identify their information models and other semantic designs.
6. Recognize possible data transfer regimes and technology choices for the interaction of RFID devices and wireless sensor networks, such as using the sensor nodes as the RFID transceivers, or incorporating RFID readers into the purview of central nodes.

7. Identify the possible paths of information feeds from the DCS layer to the databases (e.g., going through the TMC and/or other authorities as the intermediaries).

8. Determine the possible types of information models and technology that the system will use to represent and process the multi-modal data (data feeds between the DCS layer, the databases, and the freight driver/controller), respectively; and then determine the logistics control measures and applications.

9. Define such requirements as protocols, procedures, and/or parsers for transcribing the data feeds between the information models determined above. Tools such as XML may be used to interact with the authority that feeds the DCS data to the databases.

10. Determine the possible approaches to fusing the multi-modal data. For example, use a common repository to consolidate the RFID data model (subjects), the DCS data model (infrastructure), and the database model (enterprises), and provide the analytics required for assisting the users to synthesize semantics and logically integrate the data.

11. Pursue a legislation mandate to start a Corridor authority and create the envisioned SEE IS in a phased project (see Section 8.4). Design the IS as a system-of-IS embedded in societal cyber-infrastructure to minimize the cost and maximize the usage.

The technical feasibility of the SEE model hinges on data fusion; that is, the interaction between RFID and wireless sensor networks, and the feeding of DCS layer data into the logistic databases. Some reference model is needed to achieve the integration; which may be some open and scalable common schema for the common data resources, or a loose global dictionary, or anything in between. Theoretically speaking, the notion of a common schema is a generalization of the three-schema database model shown in Figure 5.1. This task may be daunting and will in any case require some ontology to give it a definitive scope and stable structure. However, Section 6.4 of Chapter 6 shows that alternatives are possible if certain conditions are satisfied.

Consider the Metadatabase-based design (Hsu *et al.*, 2007; Hsu and Wallace, 2007; see also Figure 5.6) as a case in point. In this approach, a Proxy/Export Database Server could be created for each participant of the Corridor community (e.g., a gate node of wireless sensor networks and an enterprise database) to serve as the Local Site for it. The Local Sites will register themselves and create TSER representations of their Export Databases as new metadata entries to the Metadatabase. This process is amenable to using an automated computer-aided software engineering tool. Updates could be handled in a similar process. Using Efficient Computing, a thin, minimum Metadatabase might be implemented on sensors and RFID chips. For instance, the global Equivalent meta-table could reside at the sensor nodes, at the transceivers, and at the transponders, to facilitate data transfer between them. It is also possible to include the Software and Hardware Resources meta-tables in the Local Sites and thereby support the sensors and RFID chips.

The rest of the data fusion task involves computation at the DCS layer for generating (acquiring) messages, transmitting messages, and processing and storing messages. We look beyond the standard technology such as wired or wireless telecommunications, GPS and other satellite-based technology, and Internet services to examine new chip-based technology and systems. The goal is to garner their potential for seamless inter-operation between the DCS layer and the other IS elements.

- *Message Generation/Acquisition: Wireless Sensor Networks and Beyond*

At the core of the message generation (data acquisition) technology is chip-based wireless sensor networks. This class of technology and systems has been proven in numerous science and military applications. A wireless sensor network typically consists of a central node with significant computing capacity and a large number of sensor nodes whose computing power tends to be limited by the capacity of its battery. The chip on a sensor node performs data collection, on-board storage, and wireless transmission to the central node, which could be further connected to enterprise information systems. The content of the chip is programmable and can be updated from commands issued at the central node. Sensor nodes are rapidly becoming a full-fledged computing processor as the industry moves to realize the vision of a PC on a chip, and enhance power supply by solar technology. It is entirely likely that sensor networks in the near future will have a database and an operating system on board to function as a self-contained autonomous information system capable of activating RFID devices and collaborating directly with enterprise databases.

A large number of wireless sensor networks can be deployed along major highways and their significant limbs. Their purposes (and hence their control logic and configuration) are simply to *monitor the environment,* including weather and road conditions, and to *monitor the users and interact with their activities.* While the former can be performed by the sensor networks alone, the latter would need enhancement by *collaborating with appropriate RFID devices.* The collaboration is the innovation brought about by the SEE model. With the interaction with RFID devices, the digitized infrastructure promises to not only monitor and direct the general traffic, but also interact with particular freights, vehicles, and cargos. The interaction could then be further extended to enterprise databases to support intelligent network flows. The specific design of the complete system is a function of the requirements determined.

- *Message Transmission and Inter-Operation: Chip-Based RFID*

At present, infrastructure users already use a number of different mobile technologies (e.g., radio, camera, and GPS) for communication while working with it. The SEE model goes further to digitize the entire infrastructure and incorporate it into the purview of user enterprises such as tourism and intelligent network flows. From the perspective of the subjects, the objective is to acquire automatic and non-intrusive interaction with the infrastructure to satisfy their particular needs during particular journeys. Therefore, the subjects need to be "digitized," too, beyond the usual means of radio, GPS, and Internet services, which are non-ubiquitous and/or non-integrative with the infrastructure. The active RFID technology meets this need by constantly and proactively *reporting themselves* to the infrastructure.

The current RFID specification is primarily an extended bar-code embodied in a tiny, inexpensive (a few cents) chip. The RFID chip typically goes into a label-like transponder attached to the commodity to transmit the identifier on activation through radio to a remote transceiver. However, chip-based RFID does not have to limit its information content to that of a bar-code. The chip could store an entire smart card or even a thin computer on it and transmit it over radio frequency with current technology. Advanced RFID devices already serve to embed pre-coded information into products such as engines, vehicles, packages, container, and much more to help their operation and maintenance. For example, utilities companies have mounted RFID chips to their meters to allow remote meter reading, and intelligent transportation systems used RFID technology at rapid transit stations and highway toll collection booths. The big picture is that more is coming.

The SEE model expects RFID chips to store and transmit data about, for instance, the whole history of a cargo, a truck, and a driver; while it continues to miniaturize. Compared to wireless sensor networks, an RFID device does not generate (new) data, but only transmits pre-loaded data upon activation by a reader. Technically, the only thing that really separates these two classes of technology is that sensors need an operating system on board the chip but the RFID does not. Therefore, RFID chips may be accommodated as a special class of sensor nodes to facilitate their inter-operation. The design would have to depend on the RFID standards, of course. The authorities of infrastructure may become de facto promoters of some standards if they proactively set certain RFID requirements in their implementation design for the DCS layer.

- *Message Processing/Storage: Data Fusion of Messages and Enterprise Databases*

The vision of an office and a warehouse on the move involves data fusion at the enterprise database level as well as the wireless sensor networks and RFID level. Consider, for example, the needs of an international logistics company. The global logistics control process involves databases at distributed facilities, and it also needs to connect to the distributed client databases, in order to coordinate the supply chain. The newness of the SEE model is its extended connection with the infrastructure: the data acquired by the wireless sensor networks from the environment and by the RFID chips from the users and user activities. The traditional part of information integration is discussed in Chapter 5, leaving only the specific issues of inter-operating sensor network and RFID data with enterprise databases for further discussion.

The minimum data fusion required here is to connect the messages obtained from sensor networks and RFID chips with the data originated from enterprise databases. Custom design, or improvising, is always possible. However, some general protocols would help. A core element of the protocol is expected to be common metadata that all sources subscribe to for the processing of messages and enterprise data. In this sense, if the Northway Corridor master plan can develop some conceptual design for such metadata, it may help define a model for the industry. From the information integration perspective, it would be most interesting if the database information collaboration technology (Section 5.3 of Chapter 5) can extend to sensor networks and RFID chips, with some thin reference model stored on board a sensor node and a transponder. There is nothing theoretical to prevent this vision from being realized, when sufficient storage and computing become available from the emerging chip technology for these devices.

To conclude, the SEE model may be implemented with two classes of technology for the moving Subjects: regular (current) RFID chips and (future) full-PC capable RFID nodes. In either case, the RFID devices possess database capability at the system (e.g., transceiver) level. It is only the individual Subjects that may or may not possess such capabilities depending on the availability of technology. In any case, Subjects connect themselves to enterprise databases through digitized Infrastructure, and all three classes — Subjects, infrastructure, and enterprise databases — are represented in a reference model which may be distributed. All IS elements use the common societal cyber-infrastructure for data communication, along with embedded analytics support. Hsu and Wallace (2007) provide some empirical evidence which verifies the feasibility of data transmission and processing as envisioned.

8.4   Progressive Applications and Benefits: A Public Domain Perspective

We now review the managerial (organizational) feasibility of the SEE model, which depends clearly on the cost and benefit perceived. The cost side is essentially technology-driven, while the benefit side is value-dependent. This chapter has evaluated above the benefits according to the basic IS values discussed in Chapters 1–3; i.e., reduction of transaction cost and cycle time for personal and organizational tasks. The whole vision may appear less overwhelming if the master plan is implemented in phases, to minimize the initial cost required. Thus, an approach of **progressive strategies** is presented next.

Strategy I (Conservative): Digitize the Corridor as improvement of driver safety and highway administration. That is, build a minimum DCS layer on tax money using standard technology. This strategy will seek to liberally deploy wireless sensor networks on highways and mount RFID on vehicles. Otherwise, it relies on current designs to do minimum data fusion. The scope of multi-modal data will be limited to the central nodes and gateways of sensor networks, the transceivers of the RFID systems, and the regular enterprise databases. In this case, a moving Subject is represented only by the RFID mounted, and each complete sensor network and RFID system is treated as an enterprise data source. The central sites of these networks and systems will be augmented with an information collaborator of certain design to handle messages (see Section 8.3) and perform integration — these collaborators are the proxies of the IS to hold the otherwise independent components together as a whole system. The new development required will primarily be these collaborators. In fact, most sensor networks and RFID systems already manage their data resources as databases. They only need a new global model in this vision to treat them as enterprise-level data resources and integrate them with the traditional enterprise databases. Strategy I can be implemented without much new development, and will be capable of feeding real-time data sources as enterprise data into enterprise databases.

Strategy II (Moderate): Pay for the Corridor with new value-added services. That is, use new revenues to build a DCS layer with extended capability to support minimum hyper-networking. The assumption here is that sensor nodes and transceivers are widely distributed, and each possesses a light database, such as the TinyDB technology for sensor nodes and the transceiver nodes. This technology is suitable for toll booths of the EZ-PASS technology. The full vision of moving Subjects (database-equipped RFID chips) will be supported. This strategy may be implemented with two new designs: First, implement an information collaborator at the central sites and consider each complete network or system as an enterprise data source (participant) in the collaboration. Second, also create global query capability for each data source and link them together at a global query server. For each wireless sensor network and a complete RFID system, some Local Reference Model will be created to represent the data models of the sensor nodes and the distributed transceivers, which would most likely be homogeneous within each network or system. The Local Reference Model will also include the on-board analytics (e.g., data-triggered rules and instructions) at the distributed nodes that use these local data. This way, the central nodes can perform queries against the distributed light databases and update the analytics according to the global conditions. These new facilities provide the hyper-networking capability to distributed nodes within the purview of each Local Reference Model. They also inter-operate with enterprise databases to enable system-to-system hyper-networking.

Strategy III (Aggressive): Promote the full vision of the SEE model as tools of economic innovation (e.g., tourism and new service businesses for logistics and global supply chain). Build a full DCS layer to pursue maximum hyper-networking capability for the systems of IS and thereby support new human value networks. This strategy assumes that the capability of "system-on-a-chip" exists for sensor nodes, distributed transceivers, and RFID chips. It further assumes that the system design includes a PC-class database component on the chip, along with the usual communication capabilities. Finally, the strategy also assumes that industrial standards exist to allow the RFID chips to function as mobile sensor nodes, and the sensor nodes as transceivers. Therefore, the class of full Subjects (database-equipped

RFID chips) is fully supported to hyper-network with others, as well as with enterprise information resources. This strategy has the flexibility to consider each sensor node, each distributed transceiver, and even each RFID chip as an independent data source for any virtual enterprise on the SEE model. The Local Reference Model architecture may be scaled down to the level of individual chips. Obviously, there can be a number of different combinations of possibilities and assumptions.

In summary, Strategy I requires only the common RFID and wireless sensor network technology, but does not support full digital connection for individual Subjects with two-way interaction capabilities. Strategy III requires new results on technology and system design, but offers full digital connection at the individual level. Strategy II is in the middle of these two. Phased implementation accompanies phased acquisition of benefits.

Next, we review below the potential benefits to the public, as part of the feasibility study — why the public may be willing to develop such a DCS layer as a public asset. The review further elaborates the previous value propositions (see Section 8.1) and concentrates on the reduction of transaction cost and cycle time for people and organizations.

- *Benefits to the Use of Infrastructure: safety and intelligent traffic control*

The layer of wireless sensor networks can provide *stored sensor data* to facilitate the infrastructure while authorities conduct the infrastructure life cycle tasks, as discussed in Section 8.1. The primary benefits are the reduction of transaction cost and cycle time for certain data acquisition tasks. In addition, the DCS layer can also provide *real-time sensor data feeds* to improve traffic control systems and enhance safety, such as by yielding accurate real-time guidance to drivers. New variable programmable text signs could also be added to each ramp, on each bridge, and at all locations of high risks of incidents, using these sensor data. Further connection with GPS and geographic information systems can expand the guidance into proactive assistance to drivers and help manage traffic in all weather, all road conditions, and all seasons. The connections also promise to support on-demand maintenance and other infrastructure operations by the authorities.

- *Benefits to Infrastructure Users: personal journey assistance and freight tracking*

When Subjects of the SEE model are digitized as well, with RFID and vehicle-embedded wireless computing devices, they can interact with the instrumented infrastructure to reduce personal transaction cost and cycle time. Consider, in particular, *customized roadside services.* Sensor nodes on highways could serve as transceivers to bring about proactive, ubiquitous support to the drivers. Current public-assistance systems (e.g., 911) do not have built-in data concerning the particular vehicles, drivers, and cargos that they try to assist or handle; while private services (e.g., On-Star) do not have connection to TMC and other public authorities to acquire real-time conditions on the infra-structure. Moreover, all such systems require the users to take actions (e.g., call) to activate the services, even though radio communications may not work in all areas under all weather conditions. The proposed RFID system will store information on the person/cargo/vehicle, and the sensor networks will provide real-time conditions. Connecting these two will fill in the gaps and accomplish the objective of proactive journey assistance, such as sending emergency services to the driver if the sensor networks detect any incidents. The SEE model may enable new genres of value-added service providers for the service economy.

The same technology and systems can monitor *hazardous mate-rials* on freights. From the public safety perspective, it makes sense to require RFID chips of cargos and vehicles. In the event of incidents, the response teams can act quickly on the data about the hazardous materials, the vehicles, and the origins and destinations, as well as the precise locations of the incidents.

- *Benefits to Business: tourism, logistic services, and public security*

When the sensor network data and RFID information are fused with enterprise databases, the infrastructure would become "controllable" in the response to changes, and hence quicken the response time and accuracy. The vision of office on the move and warehouse on the move, as discussed above, means new opportunities for business: people and companies can provide this capability as well as use it for their own purpose. The moving office and warehouse capability, in turn, promises to enhance the area economy (e.g., tourism) by attracting more people and organizations to this area as well as by making the current economy perform better.

For logistics control, as an example, previous systems rely on using GPS and radio communications to adjust routing, which lack reliable information about the choices (e.g., the conditions of all alternate routes at the time) to really make an optimal decision. The SEE model provides such information to drivers and logistic controllers. Besides, the model also makes it possible to connect logistics to production planning and control across the supply chain, and thereby reduce the transaction cost and cycle time of the whole extended enterprise.

The SEE model can be further extended to connect to public sector databases such as transportation management, national security control, and law enforcement. When this happens, the public and the logistics industry can request help faster and obtain pinpoint assistance easier. Law enforcement officers also can quickly assemble real-time comprehensive information on drivers/passengers, vehicles, and cargos, which means that they can better conduct *security checks* on cargos and vehicles at roadside and border crossings. The federally mandated Commercial Vehicle Information Systems and Networks (CVISN) program in the U.S. is a harbinger to the extended vision by the SEE model.

- *Benefits to Intelligent Transportation*

Looking further into the future, one can see an interesting class of possibilities arising from connecting the DCS layer with the emerging automatic vehicle guidance technology. At present, vehicle guidance technology tends to rely on such designs as laying embedded guidance cables on the designated lanes of highways to direct vehicle movement; or using on-board sensing and computing systems to interact with control systems mounted on roads to adjust the movement. The DCS layer represents a new capability for control. It may help define virtual vehicle guidance lanes and virtual divides of highways, such as designating the fast lanes for fee-paying vehicles from the regular users. The fast lanes could be designated adaptively according to the real-time road conditions, and some virtual rapid transit on the highways (consisting of such lanes) may result. Violations could be detected by the DCS layer, too.

The SEE model helps substantiate some general concepts of hyper-networking and shows how the IS principles of Chapters 1–3 guide the development of new visions for instrumentation of the environment. In addition, it applies the design concepts of Chapters 4–7 to provide some implementation designs for the vision. All these results constitute a master plan for a possible SEE IS envisioned for the Northway Corridor. The multi-modal data fusion design also extends the scope of IS elements to include the instrumentation IT, especially the RFID and wireless sensor networks technology. As such, this chapter provides a review, substantiation, and extension for the materials covered in the previous chapters.

On this note, this book proceeds to its conclusion.

Chapter 9

Information Systems and Knowledge Economy: Review of Select Student Projects, Preview of New Microeconomic Production Functions, and A Case for Optimism

A few reflections conclude this book. If knowledge drives the ongoing economic trends (Solow, 2000), then information systems incubate the knowledge and carry these trends. If hyper-networking of people using IS to cocreate values is a reasonable description of the world, then the world is indeed on the verge of major change. No one knows what hyper-networking holds for humankind: worldwide turmoil and clashes of civilizations, or global renaissance and fulfillment of personal promises? Nevertheless, one can elect to look at what humans have done right and extrapolate the positive trends of the world to a more pleasant future. This book submits that hyper-networking by IS is at least consistent with cultivating serendipity, equality, and sustainability at the grassroots; and hence points to a prolific plausible future. This concluding chapter has three main themes. The first is a quick review of select student projects from the author's classrooms to assist the readers in finding exercises. The second presents an economic worldview of how the notion of systems of IS may help describe the unfolding knowledge economy. It postulates on person-centered hyper-networking, and extends to organization-centered and society-centered hyper-networking for economic innovation. The third theme formalizes the notion of innovation by hyper-networking in terms of a new class of microeconomic production functions, where the DCS model provides a multiplier to production factors and technological innovation. The new production function helps characterize how hyper-networking IS (collaboration in value creation) may help propel a knowledge economy.

9.1 Student Projects: Real-World Information Systems Developed in the Classroom

Much of the materials in this book have been used in classrooms as well as tested in real-world consulting and research projects. A number of undergraduate upper-class students, graduate students and working professionals in management and engineering curricula have applied the materials to real-world IS problems, as their class term projects, senior capstone design projects, or master thesis/projects. All these projects have developed IS designs from vision to implementation, and have proved their technical feasibility with laboratory prototyping. Some of them have led to actual employment of the IS ideas so designed in the target enterprise. We provide below a brief overview of some of the representative student projects, where the parentheses include the student names and their degree programs at the time of the project. All proprietary data have been suppressed from the description.

Conversion of Wing Testing Data from Spreadsheets to Access Database to Allow for Hyper-Networking (Megan Gallagher, Senior)

This undergraduate IS independent study project conducted a field study at an aircraft wing manufacturer which subcontracts from major defense original equipment manufacturers (OEM). The company conducts tests and maintains the testing data throughout the manufacturing process at the factory. At the time of the project, the company stored the testing data in Excel; and the IS vision was to convert the data into Access database and make it accessible by select users from the Internet. The conversion was needed because the Excel files had become unwieldy for auditing and maintenance; and also because the company wanted more engineers and managers with different interests to have access to the testing data. The connection to the Web was added to the company's original wish list due to the realization that both the OEMs and the defense supervisors would appreciate such capability for them to review the testing data. All in all, hyper-networking of testing data and stakeholders was recognized as a high-priority goal and assigned strategic significance. The IS project involved database design (featuring a BOM-style table to help organize testing); embedded analytics for data inputting and outputting (for integrity and security controls); and VBA applications for Web access. Forms and programs for batch processing of data conversion from Excel to Access were developed, too. Microsoft SharePoint and Groove were employed to develop the Web connections to the Access database.

Life Cycle Integration by IS for Non-Profit Veggie Sales to Area Seniors (D. Grove, J. Watts, S.-M. Bae, J. Pringle, and K. Chadha, Senior)

This is an undergraduate engineering capstone design project. A non-profit organization buys vegetables and fruits from local farmers and sells them to inner-city senior housing complexes, via veggie trucks and lighter mobile carts. Since the profit margins are thin and the reliance on volunteers is high, the organization needs a low-cost IS to help them better plan, manage, and deliver. In particular, they need to coordinate with farmers in prices and supplies (e.g., donation of surpluses to the organization); improve point-of-sale transactions (speed, accurate accounting, and debts/IOUs collection); and schedule staff for inventory and delivery (heavily dependent on volunteers). The organization also needs all kinds of supporting data to substantiate their reports and grand proposals to their funding agencies and donors. Thus, the IS vision developed sought to integrate all these life cycle tasks with a turn-key solution based on a Microsoft inventory software. The reasons of selection are relatively low cost and reasonable ease to acquire technical support and maintenance. The package provides a bar-code based point-of-sale module to go with its inventory management functionality. The team also designed custom extensions to supplement the commercial software, especially the query and reporting logics, Web homepages, and online connections to farmers (e.g., product code). However, the bulk of the team's effort was devoted to the analysis of the organization's "as is" processes and information requirements; and the design of the "to be" system, including all pro forma data management procedures, forms, and operational "cookbooks". The organization reported over 50% of overall improvement on operations during the first few months of the initial implementation of the IS.

Embedding a Horse Supplements Business in the Web with B2C and B2B Capability (J. Farkas, Senior)

This is a term project for an undergraduate IS class. The author of the project, who had little prior exposure to IS before the class, developed a complete IS design for a family-run horse supplements business, which encompassed both the B2C end (customers) and the B2B end (suppliers) of the value chain. The value chain of raising a thoroughbred involves many business providers who are mostly families that have been in the business for generations. The services of horse supplements are part of the chain. The industry enjoys significant government support (e.g., the Basic Nutrients USA). A working prototype implemented the design using societal cyber-infrastructure, including open source software, which was tested in actual business use. The main IS components included an Access database (the supplements, stakeholders, shipments, etc.) and its Web presence (homepages and connections). Analytics were developed in VBA using open source results available on the Internet. Although the analysis part of the IS project was straightforward, its planning and design were inspirational. The main point was to hyper-network family businesses and public resources along the value chain. The value of embedment in societal cyber-infrastructure was plainly demonstrated in the fact that the IS prototype was low in cost, easy to maintain, and ready to hyper-network. The project chose Microsoft technologies for reason of lower initial learning curves; both the student and the other stakeholders were more familiar with Access and Office than with MySQL and, say, PHP or Perl. However, the choice of technologies can change if necessary.

Connecting a College Fraternity House Operational IS with Other Web-Based IS Operations *(A. Beece and K. Krolik, Senior)*

A "system of IS" design is found in this otherwise standard term project for an undergraduate IS class. Two fraternity house officers and operatives designed a renovation for the fraternity's food ordering process, by connecting its internal IS to the Web sites of the wholesalers from which it purchases (e.g., the Sam's Club). The result would be a seemingly seamless integration where the members could indicate their preferred food supplies directly on the wholesaler's homepages, while the fraternity IS could feed these orders into its own database for storage and processing. This level of integration goes beyond the usual connection (linking) to a Website and requires getting under the skin of the Websites to gain operational-level connections. A switchboard design that connects to the open code of the homepages at the Web site accomplishes this integration. The idea is generalizable, and the significance is that any IS should be able to use some IS elements of other Web-based IS as part of its own operational components. Conversely, any Web-based IS (e.g., the Sam's Club) that wishes to connect to external users (e.g., customer sites) should also design the IS elements in a way that enables the external IS to incorporate them, as shown in this project. Thus, the innovative idea here is really the extended scope of IS — i.e., an embedment design for the vision of system of IS.

Integrating Multiple Streams of Customer Service Data to Determine Uniform Performance Measures *(R. Chang, working professional graduate)*

The author of this term project, which was required for a graduate database course, worked at the time for a major heavy equipment manufacturer which provided multiple channels to help its customers diagnose their problems with the products. These channels included a live call center which was outsourced offshore, and some other US-based operations such as self-service at a customer service Website and SMS text messaging. The company needed to benchmark these operations and assess its performance in terms of customer satisfaction and cost efficiency, especially since it was putting customer support under the same strategic purview as e-business. That is, both of them were considered a part of the corporate IS. The first order of business for the project was to figure out a strategy for integrating these multiple data streams and build a panorama view of a customer's experience with these services. This problem stemmed from the fact that the call center technology was self-contained (e.g., interactive voice response program, analytics, and fixed reporting capabilities) and incompatible with the other data streams and e-business systems. The strategy conceived would adopt the data warehouse approach illustrated in Figure 5.2. It called for transcribing (using parsers, etc.) operational data from multiple channels into a consolidated database in the back-end — the data warehouse — for panorama analysis. The design also included the ability to take XML data feeds from third party vendors. The moral of the story conveyed by this project is the prowess of the data warehouse concept as design logic.

Facilitating Compliances and Change Control at a Major Pharmaceuticals (M. Ranjitkar, working professional graduate)

The basic objective of this graduate-level database term project was rather straightforward: the IS/IT department of the pharmaceuticals needed an online change control system to better maintain its compliance to FDA regulation 21CFR-11. The company had hundreds of users who could request changes to regulated data and other IS resources that need to be validated for compliance with federal regulations. In addition, the changes could take place in many sites, functions, and processes throughout the enterprise, and the requests could be made at many application programs. Requests for change had to come from local users, while they must be subjected to global control to assure compliance. The workflow of change approval could take up to 1–2 weeks to complete, and the process lacked the ability to automatically enforce control procedures. It also needed to have the ability to capture the global change history (company-wide overview and cross-references/analyses). Besides, users were prone to making numerous mistakes in the process. The successful solution needed to consider two dimensions — managerial mandate and user buy-in — and combining both led to a facilitation design. The technical core of the solution was a common database of change requests and approvals, in a manner typical of workflow integration. The database provided site-specific implementations (in a distributed design) which were inter-linked through a secure corporate network. Therefore, the IS Compliance Group could exert global online control with rapid turn-around time, while the local users continued to enjoy autonomy in the way of owning their particular applications. The moral is that mandate alone will not guarantee smooth compliance; only user buy-in can really remove errors. Thus, IS design has to facilitate the users, not just enforce the instructions.

Promoting World Peace by Hyper-Networking People via Synchronized Meditation (J. DiPierro and A. Singhal, graduate)

We include this graduate-level IS term project here to recognize the students' initiative and innovative effort for hyper-networking people towards a common worthy cause. They conceived the notion of helping people meditate and coordinating the meditations as a positive way to show solidarity among people towards some common themes at appointed times. For instance, one might post a request to the Internet community to meditate for someone's cure from a cancer, for a victory at the World Cup, or for peaceful resolution of a geo-political conflict. A Web site could help promote this practice by facilitating the requests, such as coordinating events and providing background music and other support. The students believed that when people of diverse origins and locations routinely meditate together to common calls, then a common sense of bonding may develop and thereby contribute to world harmony. They put their idea to work and developed a Web site for their belief. The IS components were standard: a database of registrants, music library (e.g., soothing tunes and religious chants), and events; calendars and scheduling tools; a Web presence with request forms and embedded analytics; and the like. They parked the Web site at a minimum-cost ISP, but lacked any ability to advertise it. The site did not seem to last too long as the initial effort failed to gather many members. Still, we fondly remember the project as a reminder of what youthful minds like to do.

9.2 The Economic Innovation by Hyper-Networking IS

The first three chapters of this book established the connectionist definition of IS and characterized its intellectual nature to be hyper-networking of people and resources for innovative value creation. What economic values has the new IS/IT — or, the new hyper-networking by IS/IT — brought to the society? This book has recognized e-commerce to be the economic gains due to hyper-networking by IS/IT. Some of the gains stemmed from creation of new economic activities, and others from net improvement over the previous ones (see Section 2.2 of Chapter 2). These e-commerce activities substantiate what and how hyper-networking by IS has contributed to the economy. The next question is, what next?

This book contemplates on the answer by extrapolating the hyper-networking trends observed, based on plausible value-drivers: would new "value to person", "value to organization", and "value to society" be created if the hyper-networking deepens and broadens? That is, we review how hyper-networking (enabled by IS) might contribute to *person-centered innovation, organization-centered innovation,* and *society-centered innovation* on economic activities. These three perspectives of innovation are, of course, synergistic to each other. We focus on person-centered innovation, and then derive the other innovations from it.

The notion of person-centered innovation was first discussed in Hsu and Pant (2000) and then elaborated in Hsu (2009). The basic point is that if businesses exist to serve people's life cycle needs, then the progress of IS promises to open whole new industries to further promote this basic mission. For example, to extrapolate considering e-commerce alone, one might see new business designs thriving from providing the whole Web to a person in the way s/he requires, such as some new "concierge" portal to personalize the access to resources and services available on the Web. In particular, hyper-networking providers would make such portals work by connecting Web enterprises and resources for people. This e-commerce view reflects a deep conviction that the Web should be personalized as if it were designed and created expressly for each person. This *person-alization* might extend to the general economy beyond e-commerce.

Consider the notion of a concierge service industry that provides personalization of the economy to people using systems of IS (embedded in the societal cyber-infrastructure and connected to the physical environment). Future waves of knowledge economies just might feature new genres of businesses that provide all kinds of personalization services to improve the traditional economic activities for the populace. New hyper-networking industries would also enable people and organizations to collaborate by virtue of personalized ubiquitous assistance that allows them to employ and deploy economic resources and activities in a way consistent to personal and societal synergism. This is the *person-centered innovation of a knowledge economy.*

"Person" in this notion refers to both the individual end-customers and the knowledge workers in enterprises, as they are just two different roles of the same people. This common definition of end-customer and knowledge worker also connects person-centered innovation and organization-centered innovation, and makes these two perspectives mutually supportive. Enterprises would be expected to use mass personalization to achieve economies of scale for the personalization services, as they do with mass customization of physical products. As such, individuals are placed at the center of the economy: they hyper-network with various enterprises as well as with various other persons, by virtue of the systems of IS. These hyper-networking activities either add to the economy as new activities (e.g., new service industries), as did the e-commerce providers and social networking sites, or enlarge the economy by enhancing the conventional activities (e.g., the progress from computer to iPhone/iPad and cloud computing services). Therefore, person-centered innovation is a justification for why hyper-networking promises to uplift microeconomic production functions of the society.

Figure 9.1 exhibits such a person-centered view of a knowledge economy that features hyper-networking. Intuitively speaking, this view depicts the economic structure as a hyper-networking architecture evolved into being by the force (value) of connecting an individual

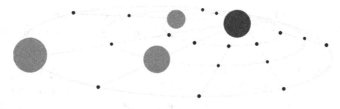

Personal Wizard Architecture

Figure 9.1: Person-centered innovation of knowledge economy.

(the base orb at the center of the figure) with any other individuals (not shown in the figure) through layers of connectors (the surrounding orbs in the figure) throughout the economy. Individuals in this view are considered capable of functioning as mainstream providers of services and resources for all kinds of economic activities, enabled by enterprises that function as connectors.

For example, television networks would be connectors that provide on-demand programming of contents provided by individuals as well as independent studios to subscribing viewers of Smart TV, iPhone/ iPad, etc. Similar connectors may match educational courses and e-learning seminars offered by experts and schools to any other individuals as students. A common business model for such connectors may be "e-Bay for Service/Knowledge". Furthermore, manufacturing, consulting, agriculture, and even (renewable) energy production may also feature open co-ops of massively distributed independent shops, professionals, and household-based providers, as well as large-scale firms.

More formally, the Personal Wizard Architecture symbolizes the hyper-networked world as seen by an individual through the (embedded) personalization services afforded to him/her. All economic activities in the world are interpreted in terms of their roles in the personalization: digitization provider, connection provider, utilities provider, IS elements provider (open sources and technology), hyper-networking provider, application provider (products and services), and the like; plus personalization provider. Of course, the actual world is the aggregation of such personalization for all people. Different levels of enterprising can result from different levels of aggregation of persons, organizations, and resources in the common world. One might use the notion of meta-enterprises to describe the aggregation of personalization, virtual firms, and extended enterprises.

In the figure, the central node is the person in command, and all other nodes are enterprises providing services to the person. One might interpret enterprises on the inner-most concentric orbits to be providers of digitization, digital connections, Internet utilities, resources, personalized societal cyber-infrastructure, and hyper-networking. Those on the outer orbits may be providers of products, traditional services, and applications. In between could be various types of meta-enterprises enabled from configuring the other enterprises — such as on-demand business/service industries. When people are sufficiently empowered, person-based enterprising may become a massive genre of meta-enterprises. As an illustration, individual knowledge workers may not only work from home, they may proactively franchise themselves as independent consultants to form virtual, extended firms. At present, the society has already instituted many supports such as personal potable pensions (e.g., 401k and IRA), insurance, and infrastructure (e.g., location-free phone number) to incubate personal enterprising. We expect to see more such practices as such institutions continue to expand.

The logic of person-centered innovation also describes the innovation for organizations. For example, an enterprise might conceive itself at the center of its own virtual "Enterprise Wizard Architecture", and thereby command the economy to serve it throughout its many demand chains and supply chains. However, all enterprise wizard architectures would ultimately lead to people when following the demand chain to end-customers, and the supply chain to knowledge workers. Both of them converge at the end, and characterize a synergistic worldview for economic input (from the people) and output (to the people). When an economy pursues this synergism, then we have the O-I fusing paradigm that the next section discusses.

The society-centered innovation will encompass the above two views and consolidate their central nodes. The above two worlds of people and organizations converge in this societal view. The common denominator, however, is still people. For reason of brevity, we stop here. In theory, an economy can feature as many personal wizard architectures as it has people; and as many enterprise wizard architectures as there are organizations. Each of such architectures would be a virtual configuration of the societal cyber-infrastructure enabled by hyper-networking of the extended IS elements (see Section 3.4 of Chapter 3 and Section 5.4 of Chapter 5). Needless to say, they collectively (the output) represent the benefits of the scale of the societal cyber-infrastructure (the input).

The person-centered view is, of course, an ideal; but it describes very well some emerging trends on the Web. Prime examples include the convergence of social networking and e-commerce/e-business, and the combination and consolidation of business designs on the Web (see Section 2.2 of Chapter 2). They are consistent with the interpretation of the personal wizard architecture, especially personalization and person-centered businesses. All of the practices of attaching "my" and "i" to products and services, and all of the races to outdo "my" and "i" in labeling, attest to this point. In fact, if one considers the whole economy as a societal virtual enterprise (or as a system of IS), then top-down recursive decomposition would lead the whole economy to industries, enterprises, and people. The notion of personal wizard architectures may not be as outlandish as it sounds.

Please note that the Personal Wizard Architecture is more a viewpoint, an interpretation of the connected world than a design. It further elevates and generalizes the previous notion of iWeb discussed in the first three chapters. Thus, Figure 9.1 may be considered an illustration of the connectionist definition of IS, to shed light on all the principles and design methods developed. In this sense, human value networks are tangibly structured by hyper-networking enterprises, meta-enterprises, and connectors on societal cyber-infrastructure, with virtual personal manifestations. Using the term *networked design* to refer to all the design methods in the book, we submit that networked design belongs in the production function of knowledge economy. The next section reviews this perspective of microeconomics.

9.3 A New Mode of Production: The Hyper-Networking Innovation of a Knowledge Economy

Now, we move to the big picture: what is the role of IS in a knowledge economy? How does hyper-networking by IS contribute to the basic mode of production in our economy? The simplest answer, albeit the most abstract, may be that it fosters collaboration, or value cocreation (service), as a basic mode of production and thereby transforms the economy. The e-commerce of the past two decades is only the beginning.

This book recognizes the microeconomic notion of basic mode of production to be the anchor for the concluding analysis. We review the modes prior to the Industrial Revolution, during the Industrial Revolution, and post-Industrial Revolution; and contemplate on how does hyper-networking analytically characterize the third mode.

The analysis begins with this basic question: What does hyper-networking mean in terms of the utility theory and production functions of microeconomics (see, e.g., Becker, 1971; Friedman, 1976; and Solow, 2000)? At this point, we revert back to hyper-networking's more precise technical definition: digital connections scaling (DCS) — see the DCS principle of hyper-networking of Section 2.2 of Chapter 2. Clearly, it has to mean what DCS does, first, in the utility of the product (value to the customer); second, in the utility of providing the product (value to the maker/provider); and third, in the utility of applying DCS to making the product (value to production). On this basis, this book formulates the following simple conceptual representation of *microeconomic mode of production: E = O/I*, where E indicates economic efficiency, or the societal perspective of utility; O indicates the output, or the customer perspective of utility; and I indicates the input, or the provider perspective of utility. The particular way of yielding the *ratio of output to input (O/I)* represents the mode of production whose analytic nature is characterized by production functions.

Before the Industrial Revolution, utility to the customer was the driving force behind all economic activities that focused on people. A product was custom-made according to the utility that it was supposed to deliver to the customer; and the maker provided production as a service (value cocreation). The making of the product possessed many characteristics that people now attribute to service, such as being one-of-a-kind and even perishable — the production might never repeat for another customer and another product (e.g., building a noble carriage, a church, or a dam). We refer to this mode of production as the *Output Pulling Paradigm (O)*. In this O-Paradigm, pair-wise relationships constitute the economic connections in the production, i.e., the direct pairing between the provider and the customer. The science of scaling in this mode is the identification of the generic rules and possibility of pairing people.

Each pair has an individual ratio of output to input (O/I), and the performance of the economy under the historical O-Paradigm is basically the average of all such individual ratios. Back then, it was near impossible to connect pairs and scale up either side of the relationship in a manner that would change the production function. The pooling of pairs would not change the performance. A telling example is hair cutting. Even in today's world, having a thousand barbers concurrently cutting hair for a thousand customers at the same place and at the same time would not change the performance a bit, and would be identical to cutting hair at a thousand different places at different times. The way each hair cutting was done would remain the same, too. Companies like IBM could not exist in this paradigm. Consulting businesses could not exist in this paradigm, either. The notion that today's service industry operates in this truly customized O-Paradigm is nothing but a myth, since this paradigm does not scale while service industries must scale. By the same token, we see little need for IS in the O-Paradigm production.

Modern machinery made the pooling of input possible, and hence came the Industrial Revolution. The swordsmiths of the O-Paradigm could then use large-scale foundry and other related equipment to standardize production and transform their production functions, to scale up the forging of swords with disproportionally larger ratio of output to input (labor). The pooled production became so significant that the provider side dominated the customer-provider relationship, and value cocreation (e.g., making a 4-inch drill for a particular 4-inch hole) ceded to one-sided value creation. What resulted was a new mode of production that focused on products (e.g., a generic 4-inch drill), from which utility got alienated (e.g., the 4-inch hole) — we refer to this mode as the *Input Pushing Paradigm (I)*. Service, which continued to focus on utility, was separated from products in this I-Paradigm. Providing the products' utilities to the owners of the products became a new major genre of service. Examples include the new industries of transportation, insurance, and gasoline stations which provide the new economic activities that support the use, operation, and maintenance of aircraft, vessels, and vehicles.

The science of I-Paradigm features innovative technology to achieve the disproportional scaling between input and output; and this scaling characterizes the production functions of the new economic ratio (O/I) under this paradigm. The science also led to the optimal ways of connection for production factors: organizing them into a hierarchy of economic entities and activities, with the entity Firm residing at the core of economic institutions to minimize societal transaction costs. However, the scaling is limited to the provider side. The end-users of products are connected neither with other users, nor with the production and the maker. The science of service, therefore, was little affected by the new science and continued to follow the production functions of the O-Paradigm. This is why in today's world we still see barbers working their ancient trade in largely the same ancient way (except for the tools and gimmicks employed). We see craft production continuing to exist in corners of the economy where the pressure of scaling up does not apply. And we see the progress of enterprise IS attending mostly to scaling up for companies of the I-Paradigm, such as conglomerates which perfected themselves as a manufacturer. Time alone does not make the world post-Industrial Revolution, but new production functions do.

Innovations to the I-Paradigm came in the form of digital connections for people and resources, due to IT; which renovate the previous production functions. These new digital connections opened up a completely new world for scaling, in which the customer side can be pooled for production, too. Furthermore, production factors, including knowledge workers, can be connected with customers and hence make both sides amenable to being unified, again. The value cocreation pairs can now be scaled up in any configuration of O, I, and O-I aggregation to change the O/I ratio to their favor. In other words, the production functions can now incorporate digital connections scaling and thereby transform themselves. With this new capability, the world is afforded a new mode of production that fuses the O-Paradigm and I-Paradigm to reap benefits from both of them. This is referred to as the *Output-Input Fusion Paradigm (O-I)*. This O-I Paradigm is characterized by DCS, and IS is an integral part of its design science.

The O-I Paradigm scales individual customer-provider pairs of the O-Paradigm by connecting customers (output) for the same input; production factors and providers (input) for the same customer; and/or any input and output for any value proposition. Such connections constitute hyper-networking guided by the pursuit of utility. Therefore, service and product may reunite in this new mode of production, with higher production ratio (O/I). The barbers (or, oh, alas, hairdressers) and master masons may elect to continue their ancient trades in the ancient way, but they now also have the choice to join forces and pool talents as doctors and other healthcare providers do. At the least they can enjoy the benefits of marketing, professional improvement, and trade promotion due to DCS. Companies like IBM can excel as a hyper-networking provider to people and enterprises, and also as a manufacturer and a consulting business provider. Is e-commerce better described by the O-I paradigm than by any other way? Does the convergence of social networking and e-commerce fit precisely with the O-I fusion view?

In essence, the O-I fusion paradigm describes a *collaboration* mode of production, which this book recognizes as the defining characteristic of a knowledge economy. What new production functions might fully define it? The field is rich in results that define the O-Paradigm and the I-Paradigm — see Solow (2000) and Betancourt and Gautschi (1998). They provide microeconomic production functions, transformation functions, and taxonomy of economic activities to define the production ratio (O/I) at various levels of aggregation.

This book proposes a general model below for the O-I paradigm. The model describes a new class of production functions featuring collaboration by DCS between the demand chain (customer perspective) and the supply chain (provider perspective). (See Hsu, 2007; Hsu and Spohrer, 2009; and Hsu, 2009 for more analysis.) The general model prescribes the role of systems of IS in knowledge economies.

The Model of Production by Extended Firms (for collaboration across demand chain and supply chain, using DCS, or hyper-networking by IS):

- **Objective:** maximization of utility (U) and/or minimization of cost (E) across the demand chain and/or supply chain.
- **Decision Maker:** customers and providers of the value cocreation pair — with the output being either service or product (collaboration through digital connections).
- **Production Functions: f, g, h, and f^n, where:**

  $E = f(I, F, S, Z)$, the *total utility (U) or cost function (C)* of production where I: the institution; F: the non-digital, non-person production factors; and

  $S = g(D, K, P)$, the *scaling function* where D: the digital connections/societal cyber-infrastructure, including the instrumentation of the environment; K: the digital, knowledge production factors; and P: the individual end-customers and knowledge workers;

  $Z = h(A, R, M)$, the *exogenous constraining function* where A: the consumption activities; R: the restrictions on the selection of A; and M: the market price for A. (The Z function is modeled after Betancourt and Gautschi (1998)). We further define that the nature of constraints R defines goods vs. services.

  $E^n = f^n(I, F, S \mid Z)$ if $n = p$ (provider); or
  $E^n = f^n(I, S, Z \mid F)$ if $n = u$ (customer).

(E^n is *recursively expandable* along the demand chain and the supply chain.)

Two conspicuous elements distinguish the model from previous results in the field: S (the DCS function) and E^n (the collaboration functions for demand chain and supply chain). The basic logic of S is either addition (new express activities) or multiplication (enhancement to other activities). This model will result in particular production functions for particular industries if its general logic is specified. The E function needs specification for the definitive mapping forms of f, g, h, and f^n. The forms may be specified at different levels of detail, representing different levels of requirement on the configurations of the IS involved. The configuration will also determine how each of the sub-functions and factors (arguments in the functions) contributes to the objective function and how they interact amongst them. When sufficient specificity exists, these contributions and inter-relationships can be revealed by taking appropriate partial derivatives of these functions, as has customarily been done in the field. The complexity of the E function lies in its recursive form, which defines collaboration among firms — or, the production of the extended firms by *collaboration*. Analyzing the recursive expansion of the E function is mathematically tricky and requires more assumptions and qualifications.

If the E^n functions are ignored, then the analysis is relatively straightforward. The effects of DCS, for example, can be isolated and recognized from how the S function appears in the mathematical form of the E mapping. In a linear form, where S is associated with a coefficient, the DCS model will contribute proportionally to the outcome in a formula weighted by the coefficient (as relative to other terms in E). Therefore, the way to improve the outcome is to scale up, down, or transformationally the scaling function of S. If E is non-linear and involves the product of S and some other arguments, such as S impacting on I, P, and/or Z, then the contribution can be more pronounced as well as complicated, depending on the specific functional form. In any case, the contributions of DCS represent those of the IS, too.

The DCS function, S, embodies the employment and deployment of systems of IS. It may reflect how the IS elements and their hyper-networking are designed. As analyzed in Chapter 8, the DCS function may ultimately have to be evaluated on the basis of transaction cost and cycle time by exploring the specifics of life cycle tasks that incur transactions. With this class of tasks identified (in, e.g., a taxonomy of activities), the S function may be specified accordingly. For the Northway Corridor case of Chapter 8, a production function for the global supply chain industry might serve as a starting point for the development of the new function.

The recursive application of the E^n function will ultimately lead to people: the customers and knowledge workers. At this level, the production function will become homogenous in functional arguments with IS elements — i.e., the model of production by extended firms can be reduced (specified) to one of systems of IS that connect people with resources for innovation. At the level of people, supported by IS, all economic activities may be unified and described by a uniform family of production functions. This logic shows that the specifications of person-centered innovation, organization-centered innovation, and society-centered innovation should be able to be derived from this family of production functions.

The above two sections represent only some possibilities of future development to grow knowledge economies, of course. However, they nevertheless show our conviction on the significance of IS for the future knowledge economy. Now, this book concludes, as follows.

9.4 A Look at the Bright Side

This book reviews the past to look forward into the future. Thus, we must consider where its outlooks may lead us. Does the worldview of person-centered innovation, organization-centered innovation, and society-centered innovation make sense? If it does, then two implications follow. First, the continuing progress of knowledge economies might indeed be driven by these three classes of innovation. Second, such innovations might bring about other profound changes to the world. And the world will have IS to thank (or blame).

A design science for IS is developed, featuring the networked design. Its overarching concept is simple and its development straightforward. The intellectual nature of IS is recognized to be the hyper-networking of people and resources to create values, on a potentially global scale. From value creation comes three basic worldviews: value to person, value to organization, and value to society. From hyper-networking comes the DCS model as the means to expand value and innovation. From innovation comes collaboration in the three worldviews, and therein comes the pursuit of systems of IS and embedment of them in the societal cyber-infrastructure, to optimize sustainability. The design science is, therefore, concerned with the principles, methods, and techniques of hyper-networking on *people, resources, connection,* and *innovation.*

Two sets of results constitute this book. The basic set is a pointed synthesis of the standard IS methods and techniques developed in the field over the past decades; which happen to be concerned primarily with *resources* and IS engineering. This set is useful to any student of IS for any purpose of study. The second set of results adds *people* to the *connection* for *innovation,* and presents new IS principles and visions for the emerging connected world. This second set reflects the integration of classic IS theory with the new results from network science and service science that affect IS. This book has strived to calibrate these principles and visions on empirical evidence in the field as well as on contemporary research. However, they are inevitably subject to predicament: this book may have overstated them or been overly optimistic in some of their premises. For example, the notion of a global knowledge economy may be illusionary for humankind in the longer term. In any case, we have worked hard to assure the IS principles' practical relevancy as well as their theoretical consistency.

This conclusion highlights the three concepts of IS design: the connectionist definition of IS; hyper-networking of people and resources; and (societal cyber-infrastructure-embedded) systems of IS. We submit that even if these three concepts have been overstated in one way or another, they still promise to shed unique light on IS and on innovation by IS.

Many factors can render the basic premises of the new IS design science of this book naïve and inappropriate. However, if we must speculate on the future, we would rather be wrong speculating positively than be right speculating into defeatism. That is, we elect to recognize the bright side and look forward to new innovations in IS, of IS, and by IS: hyper-networking through IS to pursue sustainable economic growth and a more open, liberal, and equitable society for humankind. At the minimum, hyper-networking reduces the distance between persons and enhances collaboration; and hence this approach has the promise of flattening the institutionalized elitism in society. In a similar way, it is consistent with promoting civil awareness and participation, both of which are required for progression towards a more sustainable civilization. Dangers such as cyber-security and loss of privacy are, of course, clear and present; however, we would rather work on the progressive side and believe that humanity will correct itself and the larger good will prevail.

The field has realized the value of IS for traditional business and industry. This book wishes to help extend the value further and farther.

Bibliography

Adams, J., *Risk*, 2nd ed., Routledge, London, UK, 2000.

Akyildiz, F., W. Su, Y. Sankarasubramaniam, and E. Cayirci, "Wireless Sensor Networks: A Survey," *Computer Networks*, vol. 38, 2002, pp. 393–422.

Alderson, D. L. and J. C. Doyle, "Contrasting Views of Complexity and Their Implications in Network-Centric Infrastructures," *IEEE Transactions on Systems, Man, and Cybernetics Part A*, vol. 40, no. 4, 2010, pp. 839–852.

Alter, S., *Decision Support Systems: Current Practices and Continuing Challenges*, Addison Wesley, Reading, MA, 1980.

———, *The Work System Method: Connecting People, Processes, and IT for Business Results*, Work Systems Press, Larkspur, CA, 2006.

———, "Service System Fundamentals: Work System, Value Chain, and Life Cycle," *IBM Systems Journal*, vol. 47, no. 1, 2008, pp. 71–85.

———, *Information Systems: The Foundation of e-Business*, 2nd ed., Prentice Hall, Upper Saddle River, NJ, 2002.

Amaral, L. A. N., A. Scala, M. Barthelemy, and H. E. Stanley, "Classes of small-world networks," *Proceedings of the National Academy of Sciences*, vol. 97, no. 21, 2000, pp. 11149–11152.

Anderson, J., A. Narus, and W. van Rossum, "Customer Value Propositions in Business Markets," *Harvard Business Review*, March 2006, pp. 91–99.

Argote, L., *Organizational Learning: Creating, Retaining and Transferring Knowledge*, Springer, New York, NY, 2005.

Atre, S., *Data Base: Structured Techniques for Design, Performance, and Management*, John Wiley and Sons, New York, NY, 1980.

Babin, G. and C. Hsu, "Decomposition of Knowledge for Concurrent Processing," *IEEE Transactions on Knowledge and Data Engineering*, vol. 8, no. 5, 1996, pp. 758–772.

Baker, A., "A Survey of Factory Control Algorithms That Can Be Implemented in a Multi-Agent Hierarchy: Dispatching, Scheduling, and Pull," *Journal of Manufacturing Systems*, vol. 17, no. 4, 1998, pp. 297–320.

Barabasi, A. L. and R. Albert, "Emergence of scaling in random networks," *Science*, vol. 286, no. 5439, 1999, pp. 509–512.

Batini, C., M. Lenzerini, and S. B. Navathe, "A Comparative Analysis of Methodologies for Database Schema Integration," *ACM Computing Surveys*, vol. 18, 1986, pp. 323–364.

Bayardo Jr., R. J., W. Bohrer, R. Brice, A. Cichocki *et al.*, "InfoSleuth: Agent-Based Semantic Integration of Information in Open and Dynamic Environments," *ACM SIGMOD International Conference on Management of Data*, Tucson, Arizona, 1997.

Becker, G. S., *Economic Theory*, Alfred A. Knopf, New York, NY, 1971.

———, *The Economic Approach to Human Behavior*, 2nd ed., University of Chicago Press, Chicago, IL, 1990.

Beinhocker, E. D., *The Origin of Wealth: Evolution, Complexity, and the Radical Remaking of Economics*, Harvard Business School Press, Cambridge, MA, 2006.

Bennett, S. G., C. Gee, R. Laird, A. T. Manes, R. Schneider, L. Shuster, A. Tost, and C. Venable, *SOA Governance*, Prentice Hall, Upper Saddle River, NJ, 2011.

Berger, P. L. and T. Luckmann, *The Social Construction of Reality: A Treatise in the Sociology of Knowledge*, Anchor, New York, NY, 1967.

Betancourt, R. and D. A. Gautschi, "Distribution Services and Economic Power in a Channel," *Journal of Retailing*, vol. 74, no. 1, 1998, pp. 37–60.

Beynon-Davies, P., L. Bonde, D. McPhee, and C. B. Jones, "A Collaborative Schema Integration System," Computer-Supported Cooperative Work: *The Journal of Collaborative Computing*, vol. 6, no. 1, 1997, pp. 1–18.

Bitner, M. and S. Brown, "The Evolution and Discovery of Services Science in Business Schools," *Communications of the ACM*, July, 2006, pp. 73–78.

Blass, T., *The Man Who Shocked the World: the Life and Legacy of Stanley Milgram*, Basic Books, New York, NY, 2004.

Boisot, M. H., *Knowledge Assets: Securing Competitive Advantage in the Information Economy*, Oxford University Press, Oxford, UK, 2002.

Bonabeau, E., "Agent-Based Modeling: Methods and Techniques for Simulating Human Systems," *Proceedings of the National Academy of Sciences*, vol. 99 Suppl. 3, 2001, pp. 7280–7287.

Boonjing, V. and C. Hsu, "A Feasible Approach to Natural Language Database Query," *International Journal of Artificial Intelligence Tools*, vol. 15, no. 2, 2006, pp. 323–330.

Bouziane, M. and C. Hsu, "A Rulebase Management System Using Conceptual Modeling," *J. Artificial Intelligence Tools*, vol. 6, no. 1, 1997, pp. 37–61.

Bowen, P., R. O'Farrell, and F. Rohde, "Analysis of Competing Data Structures: Does Ontological Clarity Produce Better End User Query Performance," *J. Association for Information Systems*, vol. 7, no. 8, Article 22, 2006.

Bradley, S. P., J. A. Hausman, and R. L. Nolan (eds.), *Globalization, Technology, and Competition: The Fusion of Computers and Telecommunications in the 1990s*, Harvard Business Press, Boston, MA, 1993.

Braumandl, R., M. Keidl, A. Kemper, D. Kossmann, A. Kreutz, S. Seltzsam, and K. Stocker, "ObjectGlobe: Ubiquitous Query Processing on the Internet," *The VLDB Journal*, vol. 10, 2001, pp. 48–71.

Buchanan, M., *The Social Atom: Why the Rich Get Richer, the Cheaters Get Caught, and Your Neighbor Usually Looks Like You*, St. Martin's Press, New York, NY, 2007.

Burch, J. G., *Systems Analysis, Design, and Implementation*, Boyd and Fraser Publishing Co., Boston, MA, 1992.

Caldarelli, G., A. Capocci, P. D. L. De Los, and M. Munoz, "Scale-free Networks without Growth or Preferential Attachment: Good get Richer," *Physica A*, 2004, p. 338.

Carley, K., *Organizational Change and the Digital Economy: A Computational Organization Science Perspective*, MIT Press, Cambridge, MA, 1999.

Carothers, C. D., D. Bauer, and S. Pearce, "ROSS: A High-Performance, Low Memory, Modular Time Warp System," *Journal of Parallel and Distributed Systems*, 2002.

Chan, W. K. V. and C. Hsu, "Service Scaling on Hyper-Networks," *Service Science*, vol. 1, no. 1, 2009, pp. 17–31.

———, "How Hyper-Network Analysis Helps Understand Human Networks?" *Service Science*, vol. 2, no. 4, 2010, pp. 270–280.

———, "Humans Hyper-network to Cocreate Value," *IEEE Transactions on Systems, Man, and Cybernetics, Part A*, vol. 42, no. 4, 2012, pp. 802–813.

Charnes, A. and W. W. Cooper, *Management Models and Industrial Applications of Linear Programming*, Volumes 1 and 2, John Wiley and Sons, New York, NY, 1961.

———, W. L. Gorr, C. Hsu, and B. von Rabenau, "Emergency Government Interventions: Case Study of Natural Gas Shortages," *Management Science*, vol. 32, no. 10, 1986, pp. 1242–1258.

Chase, R. B., F. R. Jacobs, and N. J. Aquilano, *Operations Management for Competitive Advantage*, Instructor's Edition, 10th ed., McGraw-Hill Irwin, New York, NY, 2004.

Checkland, P. and S. Holwell, *Information, Systems, and Information Systems: Making Sense of the Field*, 2nd ed., Wiley, Chichester, UK, 2005.

Chen, P. P.-S., "The Entity-Relationship Model — Toward a Unified View of Data," *ACM Transactions on Database Systems*, vol. 1, no. 1, 1976, pp. 9–36.

Chen, Y.-D., S. A. Brown, P. J.-H. Hu, C.-C. King, and H. Chen, "Managing Emerging Infectious Diseases with Information Systems: Reconceptualizing Outbreak Management Through the Lens of Loose Coupling," *Information Systems Research*, published online before print July 26, 2011.

Cherbakov, L., G. Galambos, R. Harishanka, S. Kalyana, and G. Rackham, "Impact of Service Orientation at the Business Level," *Special Issue on Service-Oriented Architecture of IBM Systems Journal*, vol. 44, no. 4, 2005, pp. 653–668.

Chesbrough, H. and J. Spohrer, "A Research Manifesto for Services Science," *Communications of the ACM*, July, 2006.

Cheung, W. and C. Hsu, "The Model-Assisted Global Query System for Multiple Databases in Distributed Enterprises," *ACM Transactions on Information Systems*, vol. 14, no. 4, 1996, pp. 421–470.

Cho, J. and C. Hsu, "A Tool for Minimizing Update Errors in Workflow Applications: the CARD Model," *Computers and Industrial Engineering*, vol. 49, 2005, pp. 199–220.

Chung, F. and L. Y. Lu, "The average distances in random graphs with given expected degrees," *Proceedings of the National Academy of Sciences of the United States of America*, vol. 99, no. 25, 2002, pp. 15879–15882.

Cingil, I. and A. Dogac, "An Architecture for Supply Chain Integration and Automation on the Internet," *Distributed and Parallel Databases*, vol. 10, no. 1, 2001, pp. 59–102.

Clearwater, S. H. (ed.), *Market-Based Control: A Paradigm for Distributed Resource Allocation*, World Scientific Publishing, River Edge, NJ, 1996.

Coad, P. and E. Yourdon, *Object-Oriented Analysis*, 2nd ed., Yourdon Press, Englewood Cliffs, NJ, 1991.

Cohen, L. and A. Young, *Multisourcing: Moving Beyond Outsourcing to Achieve Growth and Agility*, Harvard Business School Press, Boston, MA, 2006.

Collins, J., C. Bilot, M. Gini, and B. Mobasher, "Decision Processes in Agent-Based Automated Contracting," *IEEE Internet Computing*, vol. 5, no. 2, 2001, pp. 61–72.

Date, C. J., *Introduction to Database Systems*, 8th ed., Pearson, Upper Saddle River, NJ, 2004.

Dausch, M. and C. Hsu, "Engineering Service Products: The Case of Mass-Customizing Service Agreements for Heavy Equipment Industry," *International Journal of Service Technology and Management*, vol. 7, no. 1, 2006, pp. 32–51.

Davenport, T. H., "The Coming Commoditization of Processes," *Harvard Business Review*, June 2005.

———— and J. D. Brooks, "Enterprise Systems and the supply chain," *Journal of Enterprise Information Management*, vol. 17, no. 1, 2004, pp. 8–19.

Davis, G. B. and M. H. Olson, *Management Information Systems: Conceptual Foundations, Structure, and Development*, McGraw-Hill, New York, NY, 1974.

Davis, M. M. and J. Heineke, *Operations Management: Integrating Manufacturing and Services*, 5th ed., McGraw-Hill Irwin, Boston, MA, 2005.

De, P. and C. Hsu, "Adaptive Information Systems Control: a Reliability-based Approach," *Journal of Management Information Systems*, vol. III, no. 2, 1986.

DeLone, W. H. and E. R. McLean, "Measuring e-Commerce Success: Applying the DeLone & McLean Information Systems Success Model," *International Journal of e-Commerce*, vol. 9, no. 1, 2004, pp. 31–47.

Demers, A., G. F. List, W. A. Wallace, E. Lee, and J. Wojtowicz, "Probes as Path Seekers," Transportation Research Record: *Journal of the Transportation Research Board*, No. 1944, TRB, National Research Council, Washington, DC, 2006, pp. 107–114.

Dhar, V. and A. Dundararajan, "Information Technology in Business: A Blueprint for Education and Research," *Information Systems Research*, vol. 18, no. 2, 2007, pp. 125–141.

Dietrich, B. and T. Harrison, "Service Science: Serving the Services," *OR/MS Today*, June, 2006.

Dixit, K., *Lawlessness and Economics: Alternative Models of Governance*, Princeton University Press, Princeton, NJ, 2004.

Durkin, J., *Expert Systems: Design and Development*, Macmillan Publishing Co., New York, NY, 1994.

Elmasri, R. and S. Navathe, *Fundamentals of Database Systems*, 5th ed., Addison-Wesley, Reading, MA, 2007.

Erdős, P. and A. Rényi, "On the evolution of random graphs," *Magyar Tud. Akad. Mat. Kutató Int. Közl.*, vol. 5, 1960, pp. 17–61.

Erl, T., *Service-Oriented Architecture: Concepts, Technology, and Design*, Prentice Hall, Upper Saddle River, NJ, 2005.

Fagin, R., J. Ronald, Y. Halpern, Y. Moses, and M. Y. Vardi, *Reasoning About Knowledge*, MIT Press, Cambridge, MA, 2003.

Fefferman, N. H. and K. L. Ng, "How disease models in static networks can fail to approximate disease in dynamic networks," *Physical Review E*, vol. 76, no. 3, 2007, p. 031919.

Feldman, S. S. and T. A. Horan, "The Dynamics of Information Collaboration: A Case Study of Blended IT Value Propositions for Health Information Exchange in Disability Determination," *J. Association for Information Systems*, vol. 12, no. 2, Article 1, 2011.

Fitzsimmons, J. A. and M. J. Fitzsimmons, *Service Management: Operations, Strategy, Information Technology*, 6th ed., McGraw-Hill Irwin, New York, NY, 2007.

Fonseca, F. and J. Martin, "Learning The Differences Between Ontologies and Conceptual Schemas Through Ontology-Driven Information Systems," *J. Association for Information Systems*, vol. 8, no. 2, Article 4, 2007.

Friedman, M., *Price Theory*, Aldine Publishing Co., Chicago, IL, 1976.

Gallegos, F., D. R. Richardson, and A. F. Borthick, *Audit and Control of Information Systems*, South-Western Publishing Co., Cincinnati, OH, 1987.

Gane, C. and T. Sarson, *Structured Systems Analysis: Tools and Techniques*, Prentice Hall, Upper Saddle River, NJ, 1979.

Garcia-Molina, H., J. D. Ullman, and J. Widom, *Database Systems: The Complete Book*, Prentice Hall, Upper Saddle River, NJ, 2002.

Gebauer, J. and F. Schober, "Information System Flexibility and the Cost Efficiency of Business Processes," *J. Association for Information Systems*, vol. 7, no. 3, Article 8, 2006.

Glushko, R. and T. McGrath, *Document Engineering: Analyzing and Designing Documents for Business Informatics and Web Services*, MIT Press, Cambridge, MA, 2005.

———, J. Tenenbaum, and B. Meltzer, "An XML Framework for Agent-based E-Commerce," *Communications of the ACM*, vol. 42, no. 3, 1999, pp. 106–114.

Gotts, N. M., J. G. Polhill, and A. N. R. Law, "Agent-Based Simulation in the Study of Social Dilemmas," *The Artificial Intelligence Review*, vol. 19, no. 1, 2003, p. 3.

Gourdin, K. N., *Global Logistics Management: a Competitive Advantage for the 21st Century*, Blackwell Publishing, 2006.

Granados, N., A. Gupta, and R. Kauffman, "The Impact of IT on Market Information and Transparency: A Unified Theoretical Framework," *J. Association for Information Systems*, vol. 7, no. 3, 2006, pp. 148–178.

Granovetter, M. S., "The Strength of Weak Ties," *American Journal of Sociology*, vol. 78, 1973, pp. 1360–1380.

Grasman, S. E., "Dynamic Approach to Strategic and Operational Multimodal Routing Decisions," *International Journal of Logistics Systems and Management*, vol. 2, no. 1, 2006, pp. 96–106.

Gutek, B. A., *The Dynamics of Service: Reflections on the Changing Nature of Customer/Provider Interactions*, Jossey-Bass Publishers, San Francisco, CA, 1995.

Haas, L. M., M. A. Hernandez, H. Ho, L. Popa *et al.*, "Clio grows up: from research prototype to industrial tool," *Proceedings of the 2005 ACM SIGMOD International Conference on Management of Data*, Baltimore, Maryland, 2005, pp. 805–810.

Hales, D. and B. Edmonds, "Applying a Socially Inspired Technique (Tags) to Improve Cooperation in P2P Networks," *IEEE Transactions on Systems, Man, and Cybernetics, Part A*, vol. 35, no. 3, 2005, pp. 385–395.

Halevy, A. Y., "Answering queries using views: A survey," *The VLDB Journal*, vol. 10, no. 4, 2001, pp. 270–294.

———, Z. G. Ives, J. Madhavan, and P. Mork, "The Piazza Peer Data Management System," *IEEE Transactions on Knowledge and Data Engineering*, vol. 16, no. 7, 2004, pp. 787–798.

Hawryszkiewycz, I. T., *Database Analysis and Design*, Science Research Associates, Chicago, IL, 1984.

Hevner, A. R., S. T. March, J. Park, and S. Ram, "Design Science in Information Systems Research," *MIS Quarterly*, vol. 28, no. 1, 2004, pp. 75–105.

Hoffer, J. A., J. E. George, and J. S. Valacich, *Modern Systems Analysis and Design*, 6th ed., Addison Wesley, Reading, MA, 2011.

Hoffer, J. A., V. Ramesh, and H. Topi, *Modern Database Management*, 10th ed., Prentice Hall, Boston, MA, 2011.

Hsu, C., *Enterprise Integration and Modeling: the Metadatabase Approach*, Kluwer Scientific Publishers, Lowell, MA, 1996.

—— (ed.), *Service Enterprise Integration: an Enterprise Engineering Perspective*, Springer Science Publishers, Lowell, MA, 2007.

——, *Service Science: Design for Scaling and Transformation*, World Scientific and Imperial College Press, Singapore, 2009.

——, "Service Science and Network Science," *Service Science*, vol. 1, no. 2, editorial column, 2009, pp. i–iii.

——, "Hyper-Networking of Customers, Providers, and Resources Drives New Service Business Designs: e-Commerce and Beyond," *INFORMS Journal of Service Science*, vol. 3, no. 4, 2012, pp. 325–337.

——, "Structured Database System Analysis and Design Through Two-Stage Entity-Relationship Approach," *Proc. 4th International Conference on Entity-Relationship Approach*, IEEE Computer Society, Los Alamitos, CA, 1985, pp. 56–63.

—— and C. Skevington, "Integration of Data and Knowledge in Manufacturing Enterprise: A Conceptual Framework," *Journal of Manufacturing Systems*, vol. 6, no. 4, 1987, pp. 277–285.

——, A. Perry, M. Bouziane, and W. Cheung, "TSER: A Data Modeling System Using the Two-Stage Entity-Relationship Approach," *Proceedings of the 6th Entity-Relationship Approach Conference*, New York, NY, 1987, pp. 461–478.

——, M. Bouziane, L. Rattner, and L. Yee, "Information Resources Management in Heterogeneous Distributed Environments: A Metadatabase Approach," *IEEE Transactions on Software Engineering*, vol. 17, no. 6, 1991, pp. 604–625.

——, Y. Tao, M. Bouziane, and G. Babin, "Paradigm Translations in Integrating Manufacturing Information Using a Meta-Model," *Journal of Information Systems Engineering*, vol. 1, September, 1993, pp. 325–352.

——, "Manufacturing Information Systems," in R. C. Dorf and A. Kusiak (eds.), *The Handbook on Design, Manufacturing and Automation*, John Wiley and Sons, New York, NY, 1994, pp. 737–766.

——, J. Cho, L. Yee, and L. Rattner, "Core Information Model: A Practical Solution to Costly Integration Problems," *Computer and Industrial Engineering*, vol. 28, no. 3, 1995, pp. 523–544.

—— and S. Pant, *Innovative Planning for Electronic Commerce and Internet Enterprises: a Reference Model*, Kluwer Academic Publishers, Lowell, MA, 2000.

——, C. Carothers, and D. Levermore, "A Market Mechanism for Participatory Global Query: A First Step of Enterprise Resource Allocation," *Information Technology and Management*, vol. 7, no. 2, 2006, pp. 71–89.

——, D. Levermore, C. Carothers, and G. Babin, "Enterprises Collaboration: On-Demand Information Exchange Using Enterprise Databases, Sensor

Networks, and RFID Chips," *IEEE Transactions on Systems, Man, and Cybernetics, Part A*, vol. 37, no. 4, 2007, pp. 519–532.

————, "Models of Cyber-Infrastructure-Based Enterprises and Their Engineering," in C. Hsu (ed.), *Service Enterprise Integration: an Enterprise Engineering Perspective*, Springer Scientific Publishers, Boston, MA, 2007, pp. 209–243.

———— and J. Spohrer, "Improving Service Quality and Productivity: Exploring the Digital Connections Scaling Model," *International Journal of Service Technology and Management*, vol. 11, no. 3, 2009, pp. 272–292.

———— and W. A. Wallace, "Model Representation in Information Resources Management," in Y. Ijiri (ed.), *Creative and Innovative Approaches to the Science of Management*, Quorum Books, Westport, CT, 1993, pp. 135–158.

————, "An Industrial Network Flow Information Integration Model for Supply Chain Management and Intelligent Transportation," *Enterprise Information Systems*, vol. 1, no. 3, 2007, pp. 327–351.

Hugos, M. H., *Essentials of Supply Chain Management*, John Wiley and Sons, New York, NY, 2006.

Iansiti, M. and R. Levien, "Strategy as Ecology," *Harvard Business Review*, March 2004.

IfM and IBM, *Succeeding through Service Innovation: A Discussion Paper*, University of Cambridge Institute for Manufacturing, Cambridge, United Kingdom. ISBN: 978-1-902546-59-8, 2007.

Kalfoglou, Y. and M. Schorlemmer, "Ontology mapping: the state of the art," *The Knowledge Engineering Review*, vol. 18, no. 1, 2003, pp. 1–31.

Kauffman, S. A., *The Origins of Order: Self-Organization and Selection in Evolution*, Oxford University Press, Cambridge, UK, 1993.

Keen, P. G. W. and M. S. Scott Morton, *Decision Support Systems: an Organizational Perspective*, Addison-Wesley, Reading, MA, 1978.

Kelton, W. D., R. P. Sadowski, and D. T. Sturrock, *Simulation with Arena*, 4th ed., McGraw-Hill, New York, NY, 2007.

Kim, H., M. S. Fox, and A. Sengupta, "How To Build Enterprise Data Models To Achieve Compliance To Standards Or Regulatory Requirements (and share data)," *J. Association for Information Systems*, vol. 8, no. 2, Article 5, 2007.

Kim, W. (ed.), *Modern Database Systems*, Addison Wesley, Reading, MA, 1995.

———— and F. H. Lochovsky (eds.), *Object-Oriented Concepts, Databases, and Applications*, ACM Press, New York, NY, 1989.

King, J., "Sharing IS Secrets," *Computer World*, September 23, 1996.

Kleis, L., P. Chwelos, R. V. Ramirez, and I. Cockburn, "Information Technology and Intangible Output: The Impact of IT Investment on Innovation Productivity," *Information Systems Research*, published online before print April 8, 2011.

Koh, C. E., H. J. Kim, and E. Y. Kim, "The Impact of RFID in Retail Industry: Issues and Critical Success Factors," *Journal of Shopping Center Research*, vol. 25, November, 2006.

Kossmann, D., "The state-of-the-art in distributed query processing," *ACM Computing Surveys*, vol. 32, no. 4, 2000, pp. 422–469.

Krishnamurthy, A., "From Just-in-Time Manufacturing to On-Demand Services," in C. Hsu (ed.), *Service Enterprise Integration: an Enterprise System Engineering Perspective*, Springer Scientific Publishers, Norwell, MA, 2007, pp. 1–37.

Kroenke, D. M., *Experiencing MIS*, Prentice Hall, Upper Saddle River, NJ, 2010.

Kurbel, K. and L. Loutchko, "Towards Multi-Agent Electronic Marketplaces: what is there and what is missing?" *The Knowledge Engineering Review*, vol. 18, no. 1, 2003, pp. 33–46.

Lachman, R., J. L. Lachman, and E. C. Butterfield, *Cognitive Psychology and Information Processing*, Lawrence Erlbaum Associates, Publishers, Hillsdale, NJ, 1979.

Laudon, K. C. and J. P. Laudon, *Management Information Systems: Managing the Digital Firms*, 11th ed., Pearson, Upper Saddle River, NJ, 2010.

Lee, D.-J., J.-H. Ahn, and Y. Bang, "Managing Consumer Privacy Concerns in Personalization: A Strategic Analysis of Privacy Protection," *MIS Quarterly*, vol. 35, no. 2, 2011, pp. 423–444.

Lei, L., S.-G. Liu, A. Ruszczynski, and S.-J. Park, "On the integrated production, inventory, and distribution routing problem," *IIE Transactions*, vol. 38, no. 11, 2006, pp. 955–970.

Levermore, D. and C. Hsu, *Enterprise Collaboration: On-Demand Information Exchange for Extended Enterprises*, Springer Science Publishers, Lowell, MA, 2006.

———, G. Babin, and C. Hsu, "A New Design for Open and Scalable Connection of Independent Databases in Digital Enterprises," *Journal of the Association for Information Systems*, vol. 11, no. 7, 2010, pp. 367–395.

Levinson, M., *The Box: How the Shipping Container Made the World Smaller and the World Economy Bigger*, Princeton University Press, Princeton, NJ, 2006.

Litwin, W., L. Mark, and N. Roussopoulos, "Interoperability of Multiple Autonomous Databases," *ACM Computing Survey*, vol. 22, no. 3, 1990, pp. 267–293.

Lovelock, C., *Services Marketing: People, Technology, Strategy*, 6th ed., Prentice Hall, Upper Saddle River, NJ, 2007.

——— and E. Gummesson, "Whither service marketing? In search of a new paradigm and fresh perspectives," *Journal of Service Research*, vol. 7, no. 1, 2004, pp. 20–41.

Lusch, R. and S. Vargo (eds.), *The Service-Dominant Logic of Marketing: Dialog, Debate and Directions*, M. E. Sharpe, Armonk, New York, NY, 2006.

Madhavan, J. and A. Halevy, "Composing Mappings Among Data Sources," *29th VLDB Conference*, Berlin, Germany, 2003.

Maes, P., R. H. Guttman, and A. G. Moukas, "Agents That Buy and Sell," *Communications of the ACM*, vol. 42, no. 3, 1999, p. 81.

Maglio, P. P., J. Kreulen, S. Srinivasan, and J. Spohrer, "Service Systems, Service Scientists, SSME, and Innovation," *Communications of the ACM*, vol. 49, no. 7, 2006, pp. 81–85.

———, C. Kieliszewski, and J. Spohrer, *Handbook of Service Science*, Springer Publishers, New York, NY, 2010.

McCraw, T. K., *Prophet of Innovation*, Harvard University Press, Cambridge, MA, 2007.

McKenna, C. D., *The World's Newest Profession: Management Consulting in the Twentieth Century*, in Cambridge Studies in the Emergence of Global Enterprise series, Cambridge University Press, Cambridge, UK, 2006.

McKinnon, A. C., "A Review of European Truck Tolling Schemes and Assessment of Their Possible Impact on Logistics Systems," *International Journal of Logistics*, vol. 9, no. 3, 2006, pp. 191–205.

Melville, N. and M. McQuaid, "Generating Shareable Statistical Databases for Business Value: Multiple Imputation with Multimodal Perturbation," *Information Systems Research*, published online before print June 16, 2011.

Mena, E., V. Kashyap, A. Sheth, and A. Illarramendi, "OBSERVER: An Approach for Query Processing in Global Information Systems Based on Interoperation Across Pre-Existing Ontologies," *Distributed and Parallel Databases*, vol. 8, no. 2, 2000, pp. 223–271.

Mentzer, J. T., M. B. Myers, and T. P. Stank (eds.), *Handbook of Global Logistics and Supply Chain Management*, Sage Publishers, 2006.

Milgram, S., "The Small World Problem," *Psychology Today*, vol. 2, 1967, pp. 60–67.

Miller, R., L. Haas, and M. Hernandez, "Schema Mapping as Query Discovery," *26th VLDB Conference*, Cairo, Egypt, 2000.

Miller, J. H. and S. E. Page, *Complex Adaptive Systems: An Introduction to Computational Models of Social Life*, Princeton University Press, Princeton, NJ, 2007.

Moin, N. H. and S. Salhi, "Inventory Routing Problems: a Logistical Overview," *Journal of Operational Research Society*, advance online publication, August 2006, http://www.palgrave-journals.com.

Morris, J., *Rebirth Analysis for Sustainable Design: a theory, method, and tool*, unpublished doctoral dissertation, Engineering Science, Rensselaer Polytechnic Institute, Troy, NY 12180–3590, 2011.

Muglia, V. O. (ed.), *Enterprise Information Exchange: a roadmap for electronic data interchange for the manufacturing company*, Society of Manufacturing Engineers, Dearborn, MC, 1993.

Murphy, W., N. Pal, and I. Viniotis, "Summary of Position Papers," *Conference on Service Sciences, Management, and Engineering*, Palisades, NY, October 5–7, 2007, http://www.rendez.org/ssme-200610-digests.

Nayak, N., M. Linehan, A. Nigam, D. Marston, F. Wu, D. Boullery, L. White, P. Nandi, and J. Sanz, *Core Business Architecture for a Service-Oriented Enterprise*, IBM corp., Yorktown Heights, NY, 2007.

Newman, M. E. J., D. J. Watts, and S. H. Strogatz, "Random graph models of social networks," *Proceedings of the National Academy of Sciences of the United States of America*, vol. 99, 2002, pp. 2566–2572.

————, S. H. Strogatz, and D. J. Watts, "Random graphs with arbitrary degree distributions and their applications," *Physical Review E — Statistical, Nonlinear, and Soft Matter Physics*, vol. 64, no. 2, 2001, pp. 261181–261187.

————, "Scientific collaboration networks I: Network construction and fundamental results," *Physical Review E. Statistical Physics, Plasmas, Fluids, and Related Interdisciplinary Topics*, vol. 64, no. 1 II, 2001a, pp. 016131–1.

————, "Power Laws, Pareto Distributions and Zipf's Law," *Contemporary Physics*, vol. 46, 2005, pp. 323–350.

————, "Scientific collaboration networks II: Shortest paths, weighted networks, and centrality," *Physical Review E. Statistical Physics, Plasmas, Fluids, and Related Interdisciplinary Topics*, vol. 64, no. 1 II, 2001b, pp. 016132–1.

Nigam, A. and N. S. Caswell, "Business Artifacts: An approach to operational specification," *IBM Systems Journal*, vol. 42, no. 3, 2003.

Normann, R., *Reframing Business: When the Map Changes the Landscape*, John Wiley and Sons, New York, NY, 2001.

North, D. C., *Understanding the Process of Economic Change*, Princeton University Press, Princeton, NJ, 2005.

Oral, M., O. Kettani, and P. Lang, "A Methodology for Collective Evaluation and Selection of Industrial R&D Projects," *Management Science*, vol. 37, no. 7, 1991, pp. 871–885.

Ostrom, A., M. Bitner, S. Brown, K. Burkhard, M. Goul, V. Smith-Daniels, H. Demirkan, and E. Rabinovich, "Moving Forward and Making a Difference: Research Priorities for the Science of Service," *Journal of Service Research*, vol. 13, no. 1, 2010, pp. 4–36.

Palmisano, S. F., "The Globally Integrated Enterprise," *Foreign Affairs*, vol. 85, no. 3, 2006, pp. 127–136.

Peters, L., *Advanced Structured Analysis and Design*, Prentice-Hall, Englewood Cliffs, NJ, 1987.

Porter, M. E., *Competitive Strategy: Techniques for Analyzing Industries and Competitors*, Free Press, New York, NY, 1998a.

————, *Competitive Advantage: Creating and Sustaining Superior Performance*, Free Press, New York, NY, 1998b.

Prietula, M. J., K. M. Carley, and L. G. Gasser, *Simulating Organizations: Computational Models of Institutions and Groups*, AAAI Press/MIT Press, Menlo Park, CA, 1998.

Rahm, E. and P. A. Bernstein, "A Survey of Approaches to Automatic Schema Matching," *The VLDB Journal*, vol. 10, no. 4, 2001, pp. 334–350.

Ramakrishnan, R. and J. Gehrke, *Database Management Systems*, 3rd ed., McGraw-Hill, Boston, MA, 2003.

Rapoport, A., "Mathematical Models of Social Interaction," in R. D. Luce, R. R. Bush, and E. Galanter (eds.), *Handbook of Mathematical Psychology*, vol. 2, Wiley, New York, NY, 1963, pp. 493–579.

Roberts, J., *The Modern Firm: Organizational Design for Performance and Growth*, Oxford University Press, Oxford, UK, 2004.

Robins, G., P. Pattison, Y. Kalish, and D. Lusher, "An introduction to exponential random graph (p*) models for social networks," *Social Networks*, vol. 29, no. 2, 2007, pp. 173–191.

Rodríguez-Martínez, M. and N. Roussopoulos, "MOCHA: a Self-Extensible Database Middleware System for Distributed Data Sources," *ACM SIGMOD 2000 International Conference on Management of Data*, Dallas, Texas, 2000.

Rust, R., V. Zeithaml, and K. Lemon, *Driving Customer Equity: How Customer Lifetime Value is Reshaping Corporate Strategy*, Free Press, Glencoe, IL, 2000.

Sampson, S. E., *Understanding Service Businesses: Applying Principles of the Unified Services Theory*, 2nd ed., John Wiley and Sons, New York, NY, 2001.

Sandholm, T., "Making Markets and Democracy Work: A Story of Incentives and Computing," IJCAI-03 Computers and Thought Award Talk Abstract, 2003.

Sanz, J., V. Becker, J. Cappi, A. Chandra, J. Kramer, K. Lyman, N. Nayak, P. Pesce, I. Terrizzano, and J. Vergo, "Business Services and Business Componentization: New Gaps between Business and IT," *Proceedings of the IEEE International Conference on Service-Oriented Computing and Applications SOCA '07*, June 2007.

Schmidt, R. and J. Freeland, "Recent Progress in Modeling R&D Project Selection Processes," *IEEE Transactions on Engineering Management*, vol. 39, no. 2, 1992, pp. 189–201.

Schumpeter, J. A., *The Theory of Economic Development: An Inquiry into Profits, Capital, Credit, Interest, and the Business Cycle*, Harvard University Press, Cambridge, MA, 1934.

———, *Capitalism, Socialism, and Democracy*, Harvard University Press, Cambridge, MA, 1942.

SETI@Home, http://setiathome.berkeley.edu.

Sen, A., *Development As Freedom*, Anchor/Random House, New York, NY, 2000.

Setia, P., B. Rajagopalan, V. Sambamurthy, and R. Calantone, "How Peripheral Developers Contribute to Open-Source Software Development," *Information Systems Research*, published online before print November 18, 2010.

Shannon, C. E. and W. Weaver, *The Mathematical Theory of Communication*, University of Illinois Press, Urbana, IL, 1949.

Sheth, A. P. and J. A. Larson, "Federated Database Systems for Managing Distributed and Autonomous Databases," *ACM Computing Survey*, vol. 22, no. 3, 1990, pp. 183–236.

Shostack, G. L., "How to Design a Service," *European Journal of Marketing*, vol. 16, no. 1, 1982, pp. 49–63.

Shvaiko, P. and J. Euzenat, "A Survey of Schema-based Matching Approaches," *Journal on Data Semantics*, 2005.

Silberschatz, A., H. F. Korth, and S. Sudarshan, *Database System Concepts*, 4th ed., McGraw-Hill, Boston, MA, 2002.

Sim, K. M. and E. Wong, "Toward Market-Driven Agents for Electronic Auction," *IEEE Transactions on Systems, Man and Cybernetics, Part A*, vol. 31, no. 6, 2001, pp. 474–484.

Simon, H. A., *Administrative Behavior: A Study of Decision-Making Processes in Administrative Organizations*, 2nd ed., Free Press, New York, NY, 1997.

Solow, R., *Growth Theory: An Exposition*, 2nd ed., Oxford Press, New York, NY, 2000.

Sowa, J. F., *Conceptual Structures: Information Processing in Mind and Machine*, Addison Wesley, Reading, MA, 1984.

Spohrer, J., S. L. Vargo, P. Maglio, and N. Caswell, "The Service System is the Basic Abstraction of Service Science," *Proceedings Hawaiian International Conference on Systems Sciences (HICSS)*, Honolulu, Hawaii, January 7–10, 2008.

—— and S. K. Kwan, "Service Science, Management, Engineering, and Design (SSMED): Outline & References," *Proceedings of the IEEE*, 2007.

——, P. P. Maglio, J. Bailey, and D. Gruhl, "Towards a Science of Service Systems," *Computer*, vol. 40, no. 1, 2007, pp. 71–77.

—— and P. P. Maglio, "The Emergence of Service Science: Toward Systematic Service Innovations to Accelerate Co-creation of Value," *Production and Operations Management*, 2008.

—— and D. Riecken (eds.), *Special Issue on Service Science, Communications of the ACM*, vol. 49, no. 7, July, 2006, pp. 30–87.

——, P. M. Maglio, D. McDavid, and J. Cortada, "Convergence and Coevolution: Towards a Services Science," in M. C. Roco and W. S. Bainbridge (eds.), *Nanotechnology: Societal Implications: Maximising Benefits for Humanity and Nanotechnology and Society*, Springer, New York, NY, 2006.

Sterman, J. D., *Business Dynamics: Systems Thinking and Modeling for a Complex World*, Irwin McGraw-Hill, Boston, MA, 2008.

Stonebraker, M., P. Aoki, A. Pfeffer, A. Sah, J. Sidell, C. Staelin, and A. Yu, "Mariposa: A Wide Area Distributed Database System," *International Journal on Very Large Databases*, vol. 5, no. 1, 1996, pp. 48–63.

Susarla, A., J.-H. Oh, and Y. Tan, "Social Networks and the Diffusion of User-Generated Content: Evidence from YouTube," *Information Systems Research*, published online before print April 8, 2011.

Swaminathan, J., S. F. Smith, and N. Sadeh, "Modeling Supply Chain Dynamics: a Multi-Agent Approach," *Decision Sciences*, vol. 29, no. 3, 1998, pp. 607–632.

Sycara, K., M. Paolucci, M. van Velsen, and J. Giampapa, "The RETSINA MAS Infrastructure," *Autonomous Agents and Multi-Agent Systems*, vol. 7, no. 1–2, 2003, pp. 29–48.

Tao, L., "Shifting Paradigms with the Application Service Provider Model," *IEEE Computer*, vol. 34, no. 10, 2001, pp. 32–39.

Teboul, J., *Service Is Front Stage: Positioning Services for Value Advantage*, INSEAD Business Press, Palgrave MacMillan, New York, NY, 2006.

Tien, J. and D. Berg, "On Services Research and Education," *Journal of Systems Science and Systems Engineering*, vol. 15, no. 3, 2006, pp. 257–283.

——, "Services Innovation: Decision Attributes, Innovation Enablers, and Innovation Drivers," in C. Hsu (ed.), *Service Enterprise Integration: an Enterprise Engineering Perspective*, Springer Scientific Publishers, Lowell, MA, 2007, pp. 39–76.

——, A. Krishnamurthy, and A. Yasar, "Towards Real-Time Customized Management of Supply and Demand Chains," *Journal of Systems Science and Systems Engineering*, vol. 13, no. 3, 2004, pp. 129–151.

Turban, E., *Decision Support and Expert Systems*, 2nd ed., Macmillan Publishing Co., New York, NY, 1990.

——, D. King, J. McKay, P. Marshall, J. Lee, and D. Viehland, *Electronic Commerce 2008: a Managerial Perspective*, Pearson, Upper Saddle River, NJ, 2008.

——, and J. Lang, *Introduction to Electronic Commerce*, 3rd ed., Prentice Hall, Boston, MA, 2011.

Ullman, J. D., *Principles of Database Systems*, 2nd ed., Computer Science Press, Rockville, MD, 1982.

—— and J. Widom, *A First Course in Database Systems*, 3rd ed., Pearson, Upper Saddle River, NJ, 2008.

UN/CEFACT, United Nations Center for Trade Facilitation and Electronic Business, *Core Components Technical Specification*, version 2.01, November 15, 2003.

Valacich, J. S. and C. Schneider, *Information Systems Today*, 4th ed., Prentice Hall, Upper Saddle River, NJ, 2010.

von Mises, L., *Human Action: A Treatise on Economics (Scholars Edition)*, Ludwig Von Mises Institute, Auburn, Alabama, 1998.

von Neumann, J., "Probabilistic Logics and the Synthesis of Reliable Organisms from Unreliable Components," in C. E. Shannon and J. McCarthy (eds.), *Automata Studies*, Annals of Mathematics Studies No. 34, Princeton University Press, Princeton, NJ, 1956.

Watts, D. J., *Six Degrees: The Science of a Connected Age*, W. W. Norton and Company, New York, NY, 2003.

—— and S. H. Strogatz, "Collective dynamics of 'small-world' networks," *Nature*, vol. 393, no. 6684, 1998, pp. 440–442.

Weinberg, G. M., *An Introduction to General Systems Thinking*, Silver Anniversary Edition, Dorset House Publishing, New York, NY, 2001.

Wetherbe, J. C., *Systems Analysis and Design: Traditional, Structured, and Advanced Concepts and Techniques*, 2nd ed., West Publishing Co., St. Paul, MN, 1984.

Williamson, O. E., *The Economic Institutions of Capitalism*, The Free Press, New York, NY, 1985.

——, *The Mechanisms of Governance*, Oxford University Press, Oxford, UK, 1999.

Wisner, J. D. and K. C. Tan, "Supply Chain Management and Its Impact on Purchasing," *The Journal of Supply Chain Management*, vol. 36, no. 4, 2000, pp. 33–42.

Womack, J. P. and D. T. Jones, *Lean Solutions: How Companies and Customers Can Create Value and Wealth Together*, Free Press, New York, NY, 2005.

Wooldridge, M., *An Introduction to MultiAgent Systems*, Wiley, Chichester, UK, 2002.

Young, H. P., *Individual Strategy and Social Structure: An Evolutionary Theory of Institutions*, 2nd ed., Princeton University Press, Princeton, NJ, 2001.

Yourdon, E., *Modern Structured Analysis*, Yourdon Press, Englewood Cliffs, NJ, 1989.

Zeithaml, V. A., M. J. Bitner, and D. D. Gremler, *Services Marketing: Integrating Customer Focus Across the Firm*, 4th ed., McGraw-Hill Irwin, New York, NY, 2006.

Zhang, L.-J., *Modern Technologies in Web Services Research*, IGI Publishing, Hershey, PA, 2007.

Zhang, Z. Z., L. L. Rong, and S. G. Zhou, "Evolving Apollonian networks with small-world scale-free topologies," *Physical Review E*, vol. 74, no. 4, 2006, p. 9.

Zhao, J. L., C. Hsu, H. J. Jain, J. Spohrer, M. Taniru, and H. J. Wang, "ICIS 2007 Panel Report: Bridging Service Computing and Service Management: How MIS Contributes to Service Orientation?" *Communications of the Association for Information Systems*, vol. 22, March, 2008, pp. 413–428.

Index